The Sexual Side of Marriage

This is not just another book on sex in marriage. It seeks to give an insight into the factors that make for a successful marriage, with particular emphasis upon its sexual aspect, and the factors which contribute to maladjustments. In doing so it takes advantage of the pertinent and illuminating data provided by research studies.

This book is not meant to titillate, but to provide all the information one needs on the subject. It is positive in approach and helpful in explanation. The author M.J. Exner, M.D., is a doctor with long experience, who believes that nothing is to be gained by ignoring or hiding the facts of life. He has sought to point the way towards marriage at its best, which makes it the great, thrilling, creative adventure—which is the hope and dream of every normal human being.

Also in
Orient Paperbacks

THE
SEXUAL
SIDE OF
MARRIAGE

M J EXNER

Orient Paperbacks
DELHI | MUMBAI | HYDERABAD

Dedicated
to the memory of
Dr Thomas Walton Galloway
my beloved pioneer co-worker to whose
creative genius and devoted service to the cause
of family relations is deeply indebted

www.orientpaperbacks.com

ISBN 13: 81-222-0365-3
ISBN 10: 81-222-0365-5

The Sexual Side of Marriage

© M J Exner

Cover design by Vision Studio

Published in arrangement with
George Allen and Unwin Ltd., England

Published in 2005 by
Orient Paperbacks
(A division of Vision Books Pvt. Ltd.)
5A/8 Ansari Road, New Delhi-110 002

Printed in India at
Jay Kay Offset Printers, Delhi-110 041

Cover Printed at
Ravindra Printing Press, Delhi-110 006

CONTENTS

FOREWORD

*T*his is not intended to be just another book on marriage. A number of books dealing with the sex aspect of marriage have been published in the recent past and some of these we have welcomed because there had existed a distressing dearth of books on the subject which could be recommended to those who need them. However, to one who has specialized in this field for many years and has reason to be close to the public's need in this literature, most of these books have been disappointing. At one extreme are those the subject matter of which is sensible, but which over-simplify the problems involved and are not sufficiently informative. At the other extreme are books which are useful for the professional or special student but are too diffuse and technical for the lay reader.

In this book the writer has sought to strike a mean between these extremes. He has sought in brief compass, to give an insight into the factors that make for a successful marriage, with particular emphasis upon the sex relationship and the factors which so largely contribute to maladjustments and failures. He has endeavoured to bring an understanding of the essential differences in the sexual constitutions of the man and the woman, of the adjustment problems which arise out of these differences, and especially out of ignorance of them. He has also taken the opportunity to bring to the public in a popular book, some of the pertinent and illuminating data available in the important research studies made in recent years.

The author is keenly conscious of the danger of so frank a portrayal of the character and extent of the problems and maladjustments that prevail among the married—the danger of discouraging marriage, whereas the author's purpose is to make vivid the appeal of marriage at its best. He believes, however, that nothing is to be gained by ignoring, hiding or minimizing the facts. If we are to steer clear of shoals we need to know that they lie in our course and what their location and character is. Our emphasis throughout the book is intended to be not so much upon the formidable character of the adverse factors, but upon the fact that in the main they are preventable and remediable. The purpose of the book is to provide as clear as possible a sailing chart: to enable those who are contemplating marriage to avoid the shoals, and to help those who find themselves already among them, to discover a way out.

This is however, not our only objective. It is not enough to avoid the rocks. An 'adjusted' marriage may yet, and often does, move on low, mediocre levels and such marriage does not bring great fulfillment. The author has sought to point the way toward marriage at its best, which makes it the great, thrilling, creative adventure which is the hope and dream of every normal youth.

In order to forestall a pessimistic impression, it is well at the outset to take a glimpse at the favourable aspects of marriage, derived from the very research studies which portray so clearly the unfavourable situations that prevail.

Dr. Katharine B. Davis in her study *Factors in the Sex Life of Twenty-two Hundred Women* asked the question, 'Is your married life a happy one?' Of the 988 of 1,000 married women who answered the question, 872 answered unequivocally in the affirmative. 116 were either partially or totally unhappy. Since no standard of happiness had been defined it is obviously true that the answers embrace a wide range of individual standards. It is however, strikingly significant that in the face of the adverse conditions which are found in so large a proportion of these marriages, such an overwhelming majority of the women rated their marriage as happy.

Dr. G.V. Hamilton in *A Research in Marriage*, which is the record of a study of 100 married men and 100 married women, asked the question, 'Do you wish to go on living with your spouse because you love him (or her)?'

78 men and 75 women answered 'Yes' or 'That is the only reason.'

11 men and 16 women answered 'No.'

1 man and 16 women answered 'I don't know.'

10 men and 3 women answered inconclusively.

A second question was, 'If by some miracle you could press a button and find that you had never been married to your husband (or wife) would you press that button?' This question was answered as follows:

'No' 74 men (8 qualified) and 72 women (8 qualified).

'Yes' 18 men (3 qualified) and 14 women (2 qualified).

3 men and 2 women answered inconclusively.

A third question was, 'Knowing what you now know, would you wish to marry if you were unmarried?' The very significant answers are:

'Yes' 82 men (5 qualified) and 84 women (10 qualified).

'Uncertain' 4 men and 2 women.

'No' 11 men (4 qualified) and 8 women (2 qualified).

3 men and 6 women answered inconclusively.

These data are impressive testimony in favour of marriage. How significant they are can be fully appreciated only when the full story told in these researches has been studied. If, in spite of the factors and conditions which tend towards limitation and frustration of marital satisfaction and happiness, so strikingly favourable testimony for marriage can be given by those who have faced and battled with these disruptive elements, a great light of hope is shed upon the marriage scene when we consider that these adverse factors are not inherent in marriage, but their existence is for the most part unnecessary and inexcusable. They may be prevented and remedied. With the prevention and the remedy and with the encouragement of a more creative marriage ideal and achievement, this book is chiefly concerned.

The book is addressed primarily to the men and women who are approaching marriageable age and to those who are experiencing difficulties to happy adjustment in marriage. One of the chief incentives to the preparation of the book has been the extensive and persistent demand by physicians, clergymen and others placed in positions of responsibility for advising young married people, and those contemplating marriage, for a scientific, non-technical, straightforward statement which may be put into the hands of persons needing advice. It is hoped also that the book may be useful to teachers in schools and colleges who are concerned with education for marriage and family life, and with personal counsel of youth, as at least an introductory survey preparatory to approaching the more exhaustive and technical publications.

Appreciative acknowledgment is given of the illuminating and enriching material drawn from the studies of Dr. G. V. Hamilton, Dr. Katharine B. Davis, and Dr. Robert L. Dickinson and his co-author, Miss Lura Beam and also the valuable material derived from the writings of Havelock Ellis, Knight Dunlap, Frederick Harris and others who have been quoted. The author has drawn freely upon these studies without encumbering the text with excessive specific quotations and detailed text references.

It may be objected that the research studies referred to, deal with selected groups which do not fairly represent the rank and file of normal society. We do not, and the authors of these studies do not, claim that they do. Dr. Davis's 1000 married women who answered the questionnaire are a select group in the sense that they happen to represent mainly women of higher education and tradition. Dr. Hamilton's group of 200 is self-selected in the sense that they volunteered to co-operate in the study by way of giving sex histories and may be weighted with the maladjusted. It is to be noted however, that the group as a whole is remarkably content with marriage. Dr. Dickinson's data is derived from women who constitute a selected group in that they are women who at some time in married life came to the gynaecologist—most of them for medical reasons other than recognized sexual maladjustments. For the limited purpose of our reference, we believe the data are not invalidated. It has been our purpose merely to indicate in general, the character and prevalence of problems and difficulties found among such studies of the married; and particularly to point out the fact that these are largely preventable.

The excellent drawings of the sexual mechanisms were prepared under the supervision of Dr. Dickinson and his co-workers.

The Author

*Harmony and mutual satisfaction in the sexual sphere
is the sustaining vital breath of the marriage.*

INTRODUCTION

*I*n stressing sexual satisfaction and harmony as basic in an enduringly happy marriage, we are not to be understood to imply that the sexual life is all of marriage, or even the source of the largest satisfactions. There are unlimited areas in the mutual life of husband and wife that are non-sexual which, when shared, contribute in incalculable measure to their companionship and personal growth. So keen and absorbing at times are the interests and satisfactions of a well-mated pair in these non-sexual areas of their relationship, that frequently and perhaps for long periods, passionate sexual activity plays a subordinate role.

We must not however, minimize the fact that the basic marriage bond is sex attraction, the sex urge; and this being an inborn drive, its normal satisfaction becomes in most cases a *condition* for sustained harmony and mutual satisfaction in all the other areas of the marital relationship. Frustration or maladjustment in the sexual sphere seriously jeopardizes the attaining of a vital, creative companionship. Only in that sense is the sexual life basic in marriage. Harmony and mutual satisfaction in the sexual sphere is likely to be the sustaining vital breath of the marriage as a whole.

Dr. Robert L. Dickinson, in his analysis of *A Thousand Marriages*[1] says, 'Coitus is an index to marriage. If the data in this study reinforces any one concept it is that satisfactory sexual relations are necessary to a fully adjusted and successful union.' And again, 'The destruction of periods of sexual expression before they come to full development diverts the sexual cycle into solitude and opposition. In states of opposition, excitement exists but it is against the partner, not with him...erotic excitement withdrawn from the husband goes to frigidity, dyspareunia (painful coitus), maladjustment, separation and elsewhere.'

Dr. G.V. Hamilton in his summary of *A Research in Marriage* says, 'Unless the sex act ends in a fully releasing, fully terminating climax in at least 20 per cent of copulations there is likely to be trouble ahead. The serious consequence is a chronic sense of tense, restless unsatisfaction.'

A few references will suffice to emphasize the pervasive influence of the sex factor in marriage and to indicate the extent and seriousness of its frustration.

In the study of Katharine B. Davis, one hundred and eleven of the definitely unhappy group of married women gave 23 reasons for their unhappiness. The first three of these reasons, which embrace 77 per cent of the replies, are as follows:

	Women
Incompatibility of temperament or interests	40
Difficulties of adjustment of sexual life	23
Economic reasons	14

Of the group in this study which considered their marriage to be reasonably happy, 60 per cent found their marriage relations pleasurable throughout their entire married life. Of the unhappy group this was true of only 15 per cent.

In Hamilton's study, 39 of 100 men, and 45 of 100 women, name sexual maladjustment as the most unsatisfactory item in their

---

[1] *A Thousand Marriages,* Robert Latou Dickinson and Lura Beam (Williams & Norgate).

marriage. The meaning and force of these facts can be more fully appreciated when we note that while 54 of 100 women were rated as relatively normal as to orgasm capacity in the sex act, the other 46 women

    a. have never had the orgasm,
    b. are doubtful if they ever had it,
    c. have had it at most only two or three times in all their lives,
    d. have only the multiple, spurious, probably clitoral, minor climaxes.

In Dickinson's *One Thousand Marriages* two out of every five are sexually maladjusted. Three hundred twenty nine of the 415 cases of sexual maladjustment report the nature of the wife's attitude toward coitus as follows:

Positive (agreeable feeling and pleasant after results)	49
Indifferent	105
Verging toward distaste	29
Negative (dread, hatred, disgust, etc.)	146

Since 'indifference' really means going towards the negative, of these 329 maladjusted wives, 49 are positive in their reaction in coitus and 280 must be rated as negative or inclined towards the negative.

The belief has been, and still is, widespread among men that women do not have sexual needs and capacities at all comparable to those of men. This is a fundamental error. It is well known that while sexuality in women manifests itself differently than it does in men, women's sexual needs and capacities are wholly comparable to those of men. Indeed, full climactic experience for women in marriage is even more important to their happiness and their physical, mental and emotional health than it is for men, because sex is more intimately tied up with the whole emotional life of woman and irradiates more fully her whole personality.

The prevailing satisfaction inequalities in the sex experience of mates in marriage are not to be accounted for on the ground of inherent inadequacy of sexual capacity in women. While more extensive research is needed for an understanding of all the factors and their relations which enter into this complex problem, all trustworthy studies point to the fact that these marital inequalities arise mainly out of

a. cultural influences between infancy and maturity resulting in negation,
b. ignorance, and
c. crude, bungling lover's technique.

The hopeful thing is that the maladjustments which prevail are for the most part avoidable.

For a successfully adjusted and abidingly happy marriage a positive, objective, wholesome attitude toward sex in general, and the human sexual relationship in particular, is necessary. It is in this regard that our scheme of education and training fails the young most seriously; it is in this respect that it does youth the most serious damage. All too often the home and the parents unwittingly become the child's worst enemies. The mental and emotional patterns together with ingrained cultural taboos found in the prevailing atmosphere of many homes and in the general social environment, tend to condition childhood and youth to sex negation. A wide, yawning, often terrifying gulf has been fixed between love and sex. The one is pure, noble, thrilling; the other is low, animal, ugly. So in the act of life's rarest intimacy this same gulf often keeps lovers poles apart. Progressively this chasm comes to intervene in the other areas of life too and in time, and often soon, two strangers are living together in the same house with their children, while their longings and interests stray to more alluring fields.

Havelock Ellis voices the same truth when he says, 'The largest part of the troubles of marriage and of the perils of sex is due merely to ignorance and superstition.'

For a successful marriage, clear knowledge is needed: knowledge of the physiological and psychological factors involved; knowledge of the differences between the sexual constitutions of men and of women and the adjustment problems which arise out of these differences; knowledge of the art of loving which gives the most promise of accomplishing a happy adjustment. But all too often the best knowledge proves impotent in the face of an inhibiting, paralysing attitude toward the sexual aspect of the love-life. Having grown up in a social atmosphere which gives to sex an ugly mien, it is not to be wondered that the shocking incidents and experiences in relation to matters of sex, which come to most in childhood or youth, often leave psychic twists and inhibitions of a serious nature. We have only well begun to understand their import and consequences. In marriage, like ghostly hands reaching up out of a dead past, they choke and frustrate the normal capacities and powers of sexual love.

In some cases these inhibiting mental kinks are so deep-seated and stubborn, as to require the aid of the psychiatrist to resolve them. For many, fortunately, these barriers can be removed by way of a new, intelligent, objective view of the matter; one which sees, appreciates and accepts sex as a normal, wholesome life force which constitutes the dynamic factor in human love and which has potentialities for supreme happiness and creative power. Clear light needs to be shed upon human sex expression in order that it may be evaluated in true terms and its life-enriching powers appreciated and appropriated.

The sex motif runs like a golden thread
through the entire woof of the pattern of life.

CHAPTER 1

SEX IN HUMAN LIFE

$\mathcal{I}$n this chapter we shall attempt to sketch the nature and significance of sex, and the role it plays in human life, in the hope that it may aid some towards that scientific, liberating attitude which is necessary to successful adjustment in marriage.

Sex is an organic phenomenon apparently with a definite chemical base, discoverable in practically all organisms, plant and animal. Everything seems to point to the idea that it is, in spite of the variety of its manifestations, a consistent and homologous function throughout. Strictly speaking, it is as varied as, and no more definable than, life itself.

Nature seems to have experimented for untold ages with a method of perpetuating life which involved only the single organism. The single cell, which constituted this early form of life, merely divided into two new ones. There was but one parent. There was no sex. This method of reproduction did not seem suited to the progressive development of variety in forms of life. In time, nature arrived at a method of reproduction which required the union of two different cells which we have come to designate as male and female. Since this method provided for a wider combination of hereditary qualities, it offered greater evolutionary promise.

Sex is at its simplest in those essentially unicellular organisms in which there is no sharp distinction between parent and gamete, between germ plasma and soma (body). In many of these there exists a temporary or permanent attraction between two individuals of a given species. The attraction is primarily of a chemical nature, and arises ordinarily from a definite and often measurable difference in the individuals themselves. The attraction leads to a temporary or permanent union of the substances of these individuals.

Practically then, the biologic elements in sex, reduced to their lowest terms, are:

a. An adaptive difference between two types of individuals of a species, of such a nature as to result in,

b. a profound attraction between the individual, which in turn results in,

c. a union of these individuals.

The union (conjugation) is biologically the essence of the function. The unlikeness serves at least a main cause of the union, and the attraction furnishes the method by which it is brought about. The terms male and female are used to express the two types of uniting cells.

Sex seems more obscure, as it certainly is more complicated, in the multi-cellular plants and animals, in which there are two contrasted cycles of cellular history. In one group of these cells, the history is a relatively simple one. There are a series of divisions, resulting finally in two types of cells comparable in all essential appearance, capacities and behaviour to the single-celled organism already mentioned. These are the familiar dimorphic individuals, known as gametes (ova and sperm), possessing the power of union (fertilization or conjugation). These contain the germ-plasm, that fundamental substance which is potentially immortal and provides the continuing physical and chemical medium by means of which the characteristics and the very existence of the species are continued.

In the other group of cells a high degree of differentiation accompanies the cell division and complex bodies are developed, whose primary organic function seems to be to preserve and to make sure the functions of the gametes. In the evolution of organism, the germ cells must be looked upon as primary, and the soma or body (i.e., the parent) as derived, in all these essential adaptations, particularly in those related to the continuance of the species.

The Sexes: Differences, Attraction and Union

In spite of the fact that the bodily differences between males and females among humans and other complex animals are secondary to sexual differences in the germ cells, it remains true that these derived differences of parental bodies are what we usually have in mind when we use the term sex.

What then are the chief elements in the sex of 'parents' — i.e., in the bodies which carry the sexed germ cells? These vary greatly. In the least differentiated condition of 'maleness' and 'femaleness' in parents, the bodies are alike, each having two types of organs, from one of which male gametes (sperms) are freed, and from the other female gametes (eggs). Such parents are known as hermaphrodites. They are alike: but they have the essentials of sex nonetheless. These parents attract mutually and mate in such ways as to bring the sperm of one or both individuals into the neighbourhood of the eggs, and into a position where the differences and attractions of the gametes may result in their union.

In strictly dimorphic (two-formed) sexual parents, on the contrary, each carries and cares for only one type of gametes — male (sperms), or female (eggs). Here again the parental differences result in attractions between themselves and in some more or less intimate type of mating of parents by which the more fundamental union of the gametes is made probable. It is thus to be observed that sex in the multi-cellular bodies or parents involves essentially, as in the gametes, differences, attraction, and mating — the last a temporary contact which we call a union. Biologically the essential, permanent union is that of the gametes. The temporary union of the parents is but a means of assuring that end.

The differences of male and female parents in their extreme forms, comprise: the differences in the testes, ovaries and the internal secretions arising from them; in the organs of copulation by which the sperms are brought into the range of attraction of the eggs; in many items of bodily form and function — as size, shape, colour, odour, voice and numerous special organs for recognition, attack, attraction, clasping, etc; and finally in instincts, impulses, appetites and emotions, which help ensure mating, and in the satisfactions which accompany it.

The attractions between parents, which lead to union, initially involve largely chemical and physical senses analogous at least to the senses of touch and smell; but in the higher animals they involve the additional senses of sight and hearing — making use of the differences mentioned in the preceding paragraph.

In other words, there is a great augmentation and enrichment of the differences and the attractions between the somatic sexes (the parents) as compared with those of the male and female gametes. Similarly the satisfactions resulting from mating of parents are, without questions, more complex and keen than can be true in the union of the gametes. For these reasons somatic sex gives rise to much more in the way of emotional and aesthetic states, and to inner desires and urges which may exist independent of external stimulation. Increasingly the term 'sex' has come to be applied to these body differences, attractions, behaviour and satisfactions.

What has all this to do with the meaning of sex in human beings? In the persistence of a species, reproduction is a basic, organic necessity, as much as the development of individual life. Sex — whether of difference, attraction, union, or satisfaction is universally essential neither to individual conservation nor to reproduction. Sex is however, an aid to more effective reproduction and development. Its primary biological value is not that it is the basis of attraction between mates, nor that it furnished them incitements, satisfactions and ecstasies; but that it supplements and perfects the development of new individuals of a new generation among human beings.

Sex: Beyond Pleasure and Reproduction

We have seen now that in nature, the primary biologic function of sexual union is the continuance of the species. The keen pleasure premium associated with it arose as a by-product, as it were. But sometimes in nature, as in commerce, by-products become of equal or greater importance than the primary product. With the progress of psychic growth the elemental sex attractions have become increasingly elaborated and refined, until in the reasoning human being with his higher form of consciousness, gifted with memory and imagination, it has come to permeate and actuate the entire personality and to serve not only physical but also spiritual ends.

Without meaning to attribute personality and purpose to nature, we may say that she has never been merely a scientist, but has been a supreme artist as well, evolving spiritual gifts out of crude physical beginnings and exquisite beauty out of rough, raw materials. So out of this primitive physical attraction between male and female, serving primarily biologic ends, there has been woven strand by strand, the marvellous pattern of human sympathy, affection and love which so greatly enriches the life of man and which underlies the structure of our social life. The mating instinct in man and woman today serves not merely to assure the continuance of life but also to assure the healthy, harmonious functioning of the whole personality and to fulfill love. It may not be too much to say that while biologically procreation remains the primary function of sex in human life, psychologically its primary function has come to be to vivify, enrich and develop love.

Those who still insist upon animal analogy as a guide for human conduct, holding that sex union is justifiable only for the purpose of procreation, are in fundamental error. They fail to appreciate the great contributions sex has to make to the spiritual life of man. In human beings sex serves the ends of love independent of procreation. As the late Luther Gulick has said, 'Sex in human life can be rightly interpreted only in terms of the affections.'

The Physical Nature of Sex

A brief analysis of human sex nature, as it now exists, into its main constituent physical and psychic elements, may help us to a sound view of their functions and relations. We have first the biological sex base, the physical core, so to speak. This includes all those basic physical structures and their functions and the primitive psychic elements necessary for the perpetuation of the species; the physical sex mechanism and its functions and impulses; the hormones (internal secretions) produced by the sex glands; the states of mind which arouse and stimulate passion, such as thought, desire, imagination etc; and the primitive attractions between male and female which are essentially physical and self-centred. This biologic core of sex met nature's basic need for perpetuating the species. That physical base represents essentially the sex development of man in his primitive savage state, before his nature became elaborated into, and adorned by, the higher psychic and social elements found in human life today.

Let no one blind himself to the fact that this physical base of sex with its driving, self-centred impulses is as definite a reality in life today, both in men and in women, as it was in the most primitive savage. Every normal man and woman possesses it — and is possessed by it. It is ingrained in human nature and is a force to be reckoned with. It is as capable of direct crude, wholly selfish expression in men and women today, as at any time in evolutionary history. But let it not for this reason be despised. When, as the basic element in sexual love, it is controlled, humanized and socialized, it becomes the most powerful energizer of life on all levels, and the avenue towards supreme ecstasy and happy human fellowship. It is by way of, and out of, the physical sex base that man's social capacities — his most distinctly human qualities — have grown.

The Social Zone of Sex

Out of the self-centred physical base of sex there gradually developed the higher psychic, aesthetic and social elements which have so greatly enlarged and enriched human life and made an organized social world possible. Human sympathy in all its wide range of affectional and social expression undoubtedly had its starting point in the first peak of sexual sympathy which arose to assure the mating of parents. From its early beginnings this sympathetic response grew by natural selection. The most sympathetic types became the best parents and therefore, brought the larger proportion of young to maturity and hence survived, against the less sympathetic types. It is mainly so that love in the world has grown. It has had survival value. From the first appearance of sexual sympathy grew the two main strands of affections; conjugal sympathy and parental sympathy. These two strands united to form the basis of the family. The sympathetic and social qualities and relationships developed in the family gradually extended beyond the family in turn to the nearest of kin, the clan, the tribe, the state, the nation. They underlie our entire social structure.

In this social zone of sex are found the higher affectional attractions between male and female as contrasted to the self-centered physical attractions — including appreciation, companionship, sympathy, love, devotion, protection, service, sacrifice, chivalry, honour, etc. These qualities are psychic and social. They are the other-seeking, other-serving qualities which find their fullest satisfaction in the happiness and service of others.

In this emotional and social zone of sex we have also that group of elements which belong to parenthood, but which are closely connected with sex attraction — fatherhood, motherhood, brotherhood, sisterhood, the affectional relations between parents and child and the home with all its wealth of tender and social impulses. Galloway sketched tersely the social significance of sex when he said[1],

'Just to illustrate what a wonderful and vital influence sex has in life, one needs only to remember that all that is meant by the following words grows out of sex and its results:

---

[1] *The Biology of Sex,* Thomas W. Galloway.

manliness, womanliness, love, courtship, marriage, home, father, mother, family life, parental care and education, sons and daughters, brothers and sisters, filial devotion, brotherhood. These facts, ideas and relations — and the human adjustments and virtues that have grown up in connection with them — could not have existed but for that which we call sex. They are the normal and natural fruits of sex and reproduction... Undertake to remove from our lives and minds the ideas and facts for which these words stand, and nothing worthwhile would be left in human civilization, history, literature, poetry or happiness.'

Beyond this social zone of sex lies the large area of life which is not itself sexual, embracing a wide range of human interests and activities, but which is, nevertheless, profoundly influenced by the sexual sphere of life. The sex motif runs like a golden thread through the entire woof of the pattern of life.

Sex: Its Social Expression

In the measure that the sympathetic, social sex qualities have progressively developed in life, sex expression has increasingly been given psychic values and meaning. On the physical level, sex expression tends to be short circuited between desire and satisfaction. It takes the most direct route, on a physical plane, like an electric current between two poles. With the growth of the social elements, sex expression has become increasingly long circuited through the whole human range of psychic, aesthetic, affectional and social values and response. It has become increasingly refined, socialized, spiritualized. As Herbert says, 'Man has woven a beautiful pattern of love relationship where there was at first a mere rough outline; he has invented many finer shades of colour where there was previously one strong glaring red of lust.'

Let it not be thought that in this elaboration of the sex nature in the psychic and social areas, it has lost in keenness of satisfaction. On the contrary, its satisfactions have become vastly enhanced both in range and vividness. The psychic stimulations of love play, for example, awaken and release the physical responses to the full and these in turn vivify the psychic areas of the affectional life.

Intimacy, Sex and Passion

Many married couples, particularly the wives, have a vague feeling or conviction that in an ideal marriage relationship, passion must be excluded or at least rigidly minimized. The repressions and distortions of sexuality which grow out of such attitudes fill the graveyard of marital hopes and happiness. What has already been said should serve to dispel such erroneous conceptions.

Dickinson says, 'Passion is the critical stuff of which the fabric of marriage is made'; and Havelock Ellis[2] exclaims, 'it is passion, more passion and fuller that we need.' He says further, 'While it is perfectly true that sexual energy may be in large degree arrested and transformed into intellectual and moral forms, yet it is also true that pleasure itself, and above all sexual pleasure, wisely used and not abused, may prove the stimulus and liberator of our finest and most exalted activities. It is largely this remarkable function of sex pleasure which is decisive in settling the argument of those who claim that continence is the only alternative to the animal end of marriage. That argument ignores the liberating and harmonizing influences, giving wholesome balance and sanity to the whole organism, imparted by a sexual union which is the outcome of the psychic as well as physical needs.

'There is also the effect on the union itself. For through harmonious sex relationship a deeper spiritual unity is reached than can possibly be derived from continence in or out of marriage. Apart from any sexual craving, the complete spiritual contact of two persons who love each other can be attained only through some act of rare intimacy. No act can be quite so intimate as the sexual embrace. In its accomplishment, for all who have reached a reasonable human degree of development, the communion of

---

[2] *Little Essays of Love and Virtue.*

bodies becomes the communion of souls. The outward and visible sign has been the consummation of an inward spiritual grace.'

Frederick Harris[3] goes to the heart of the matter when he says,

'This sexual experience is a sensuous experience. Like all sensuous experiences, it will have for the married couple the meaning that they put into it. The physical expressions are gracious and inspiring according to the degree in which they express a worthy and unselfish love. But they are more than a mere expression; they become an actual part of love. Born of love, they in turn create love. The act of sexual intercourse, at the roots of which is physiological tension, is taken up by the partners and transmuted into a perfect experience of love. It becomes a precious possession. All this is profoundly true of the whole sexual experience from the touch of the hand to the climax of sexual intercourse.'

The measure of the spiritual values of the sex relationship is exactly the measure in which physical passion is given psychic meaning. In an ideal sex relationship we do not set apart the physical and psychic components as if they were antagonistic to one another. They become fused in the total experience of love. The physical and the emotional in sexual love at its best, all become spiritual together and irradiate and energize the total life of the partners. The loftiest peaks in the love relationships of mates are not to be reached by those who have minimum capacity for passion, or by those who most completely repress it. They are to be reached rather by those who possess great capacity for passion equally balanced by the psychic component of human sexuality. It is the psychic content that gives spiritual meaning to passion.

Let not those approaching marriage fear or shrink from the stirrings of erotic forces in themselves or their chosen mates. Let them rather hail these manifestations with pride and joy as the signs of normal being and a foundation upon which to build an ideal marriage. Let them understand that the achieving of that

---

[3] *Essays on Marriage.*

personal relationship and companionship which constitutes genuine marriage does not call for despising and repressing passionate powers but, to the contrary, for a full mutual release and harmonious adjustment of these powers in the service of their love and well being.

To be sure, marriages are not infrequently wrecked by excessive expression of passion on the part of one or the other of the mates. More often, however, the estrangement is caused by the failure of passion, a failure of passion to match passion in full and free experience of mutual affection.

The tragedy of the situation lies in the fact that in most such cases the failure springs not from the want of inherent sexual capacity, but comes rather as a result of negative cultural compulsions, ignorance and bungling methods. For abidingly happy companionship in marriage, mates, and especially women must rid themselves of any notion that any one of the elements which constitute love is ignoble. Only when its full capacities are released, developed and harmonized in the life of the married can love contribute most richly to personal development, abiding happiness and creative power. Like every human gift, sexual passion has capacity for good or for ill. On the purely physical level, it may carry man to the lowest levels of degradation. As an integral constituent of love, it makes for healthy personality; it yields supreme ecstasy; it feeds the soul; and it spurs life to creative endeavour. This realization is the task and the privilege of a lover in marriage. The harnessing of passion to the service of love and of life is fundamental. If this area of the marriage relationship can be fully and richly shared, a growing companionship and a glad, full sharing in all of its wide areas is reasonably assured. With failure of sexual harmony, the marriage structure rests on shifting sands.

Sexual pleasure, wisely used not abused, is the stimulus and liberator of our finest and most exalted activities.

CHAPTER 2

THE SEX MECHANISM

The Male Organs

The two testes or testicles hang side by side in a sac called the scrotum, behind the penis in its relaxed state. The testicle is oval or egg-shaped and is about 3 centimetres long and 2 centimetres or more wide. The testes have two different functions. The greater mass of each is made up of a series of lobes which are composed of minute tubules in which the sperm cells (spermatozoa) are formed and liberated. The tissues between the lobes (interstitial tissue) produce that marvellous chemical product, the internal secretion or sex hormone, which creates the sex impulse, causes the essential male characteristics in the individual and plays its part with the other internal secretion glands in the body in sustaining the normal functioning of the body. If this function of the testes is destroyed before puberty, the development of the individual becomes profoundly altered in form, temperament and impulses. The internal secretion is so-called because it is absorbed directly into the blood. It is wholly distinct from the products which go to make up the seminal discharge (semen). The internal secretion is never discharged from the body in ejaculation of semen.

The Sperm. The male sperms formed in the testes are the vital, active elements in the seminal discharge. The spermatozoon has the

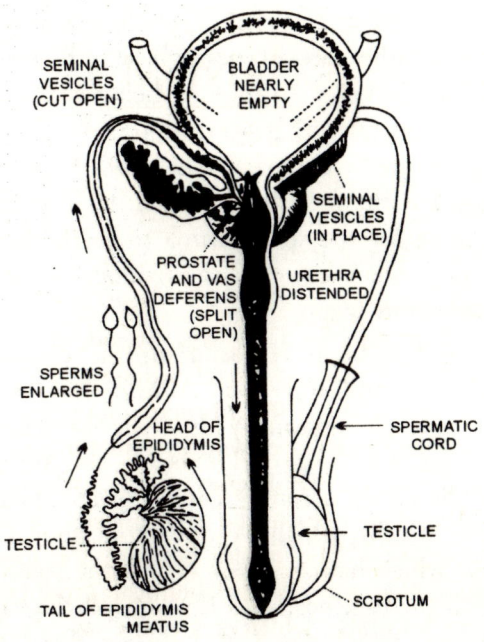

Fig. 1. Male Organs (front view)

power of fertilizing the egg of the woman and thus starting the development of a new human being. The spermatozoon is a highly vitalized cell consisting of a head, neck and long tail. The head contains the nucleus by which are transmitted the hereditary characteristics of the individual. The sperm cell has the power of independent motion, propelling itself in the liquid secretions in which it floats, by a sweeping, twisting motion of its tail approximately at the rate of its own length per second. The spermatozoon is, however, so minute, being visible only with the aid of the microscope, that its progress in relation to gross anatomical structure is comparatively slow. After the semen has been discharged at the mouth of the uterus, in coitus, it requires an hour or more for the spermatozoa to reach the cavity of the uterus and some hours to reach the oviduct or tube where they may meet the ovum (egg).

If an egg has been released and is encountered, one spermatozoon — and only one of the 200 to 500 million discharged in a single orgasm by the male — penetrates the cell wall of the egg, leaves its tail behind, and merges with the substance of the egg in a complex series of rearrangements of the elements of both cells, which we call fertilization. Of the myriad of sperm cells which have lost out against the victor in their race for union with the egg, nearly all flow out of the vagina with the liquid secretion in which they have been ejaculated; the remaining ones disintegrate and are cast out along with the other residues of physiological processes. The spermatozoa are being slowly formed and released in the testicle all the time. As they accumulate they are passed along the tube through fluid pressure and muscular action.

Each of the clusters of convoluted tubes in the lobes of the testes in which the sperm cells are formed merges into a single tube; the resulting mass of tubes in turn forms a complex network which constitutes a large annex to the body of the testicle. It is called the *epididymis.* The network of tubes of the epididymis unite in turn to form the seminal duct or *vas deferens.* (See Fig. 1, p. 31). From the epididymis each seminal duct passes

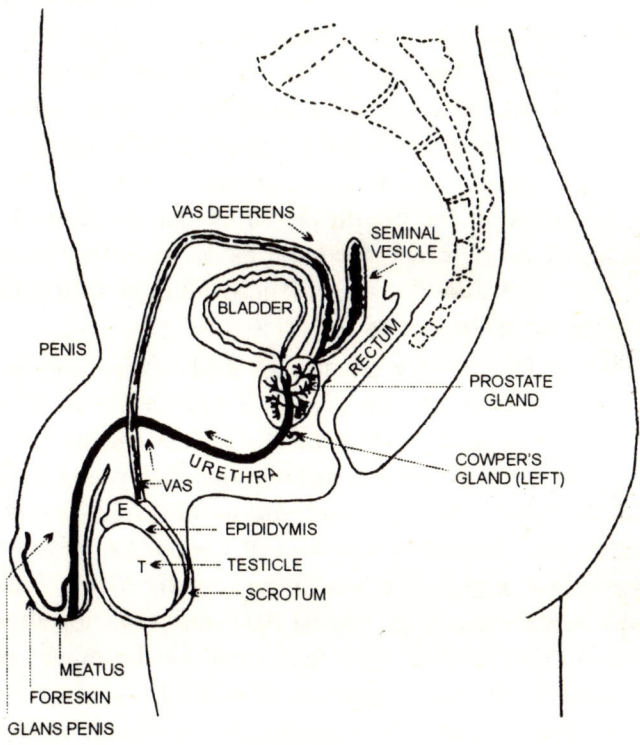

Fig. 2. Male Organs (side view)

upwards in the scrotal sac and enters the pelvis cavity where it continues its upward course, then curves forward and downward to enter the urethra which conducts the urine from the bladder.

Along the course of the channel from the testicle to the end of the penis, made up of the seminal duct and the urethra, a number of tributaries are received from the accessory sex glands. The first in order is the duct from the seminal vesicle (there are two vesicles, one on each side). Lower down, before the canal enters the penis, the two seminal ducts from the corresponding testicles join, and at this juncture the duct from the urinary bladder enters. At this point, at the neck of the bladder, is found also the prostate gland, the numerous ducts of which enter the urethra. The last contributory ducts to join the canal are those of Cowper's glands, two bodies about the size of small peas. Numerous glands which secrete mucus are found in the urethra.

The *seminal vesicles* are two oval glandular sacs which lie between the rectum and the bladder. They secrete an albuminous fluid which goes to form the largest portion of the fluid part of the semen. The salts which the secretion contains serve to stimulate the sperms to action, and its albuminous substances furnish them nourishment. The fluid constitutes the necessary commissary for the vast army of spermatozoa. Since the army may be called into action at any moment, the vesicles are slowly secreting all the time so that the commissary department may not be caught napping. The glandular activity is greatly accelerated by sexual stimulation and excitement. The vesicles seem also to serve as reservoirs for some temporary storage of spermatozoa.

Prostate Gland. The prostate gland, shaped like a horse chestnut, surrounds the neck of the bladder and the junction of the urinary and spermatic ducts, into which juncture the prostate empties its contents through some thirty outlets. The glandular structure is permeated by a muscular wall. This muscular mechanism squeezes the products of the gland into the urethra during the spasms of a sexual orgasm.

Nocturnal Emissions or Wet Dreams

Since the vesicles are slowly forming their secretions all the time, they become filled at varying intervals and distended with their contents. Nature has her own way of emptying full vessels. When the individual is asleep and hence conscious inhibitions and controls are eliminated, the distension sets off reflexes which bring about an orgasm in which not only the contents of the vesicles but all the seminal products are discharged, just as they are in an orgasm in coitus. The phenomenon is usually accompanied by a erotic dream and the pleasurable sex feelings of an orgasm.

It is important to understand that these nocturnal emissions or 'wet dreams' are a natural, harmless occurrence to be expected in most normal men, particularly between the ages of fourteen and thirty five. They are nothing to worry about.

Seminal emissions vary greatly in frequency of occurrence between different men and in the same man at different times. With the normal man the frequency may range between once a month to several times a week. A variety of factors — physical, mental and temperamental — enter in to cause the diversity. There is a small proportion of young men who rarely or never experience wet dreams. While the occurrence of emissions is to be regarded as normal, their absence does not necessarily denote abnormality. The 'overflow' may be in part or wholly taken care of in another way. Possibly some of the contents naturally ooze out into the ducts, aided perhaps by bowel movements, to be carried out with the urine in emptying the bladder.

Sleeping upon the back has a tendency to increase the frequency of emissions in most men, possibly for the reason that in this position the weight of the partly filled or full bladder resting upon the vesicles adds to the irritation which sets off the ejaculatory reflexes.

The secretion of the prostate gland, which forms a considerable portion of the seminal discharge, is a thin, milky, alkaline fluid the function of which is similar to the products of the vesicles. The alkalinity serves to protect the spermatozoa against acidity arising from the urine, which acidity is very inimical to the vitality and life of the sperm cells.

Cowper's Gland. Cowper's glands secrete, in response to sexual excitement, a thin, slippery, alkaline fluid which, passing into the urethra preceding ejaculation, aids perhaps in neutralizing any acidity that may have been left by the passage of urine. This secretion together with that of the urethral glands often emerges from the penis during sexual excitement preliminary to intercourse and thereby helps somewhat to lubricate the organ for vaginal penetration.

It will be seen now that the contents discharged (semen or seed) during the sexual orgasm represent the combined products of the testicles, seminal vesicles, prostate gland, Cowper's glands and urethral glands, each of these contributes to the semen having its peculiar functions. Through the convulsive action of a complex muscular and nervous mechanism, in response to powerful reflexes beyond control of the will, the various seminal products are mixed and shot out from the penis at the height of the sexual orgasm.

The active production of the male sex hormone (internal secretion) in the testes begins at about the age of fourteen and this is the principal factor in the striking physical, mental, temperamental and emotional developments in the early adolescent years. One result is the appearance of the external secretion of the testes, that is, the development and release of spermatozoa. Some time between the ages of fifteen and seventeen, the sperm cells attain capacity for fertilizing the egg.

The duration of sexual potency in men varies greatly. In many it continues into well-advanced old age. Physical and mental vigour are dependent in part upon the stimulus of the sex hormone, and with the gradual diminishing of that stimulus, senescence progresses. Many authorities are now agreed that in relation to the hygiene of advanced years, moderate continuance of sexual activity is advisable.

The Penis. The penis, through which the bladder is emptied and the sperms discharged during intercourse, is from 7 to 10 centimetres long and from 2 to 3 centimetres in diameter in its normal flaccid state. When erect, the organ measures about 2 to 4 centimetres in diameter and 12 to 15 centimetres in length along its upper side. The penis is composed in part of spongy tissue which becomes gorged with blood, rendering the organ hard and rigid and causing it to stand out at an angle from the body to conform in general to the normal vaginal angle of the woman in coitus. The erection, as this stiffening is called, is necessary in order to accomplish the penetration of the vagina. Erection is brought about through a nervous mechanism which, in response to mechanical or psychic stimulation, causes a rush of blood into the organ and at the same time greatly restricts its out-flow, thus causing rigid distension of the penis. The end of the penis (head or glans) presents a corona or rim which is the main area of sexual feeling. Sexual feeling in the man is much more localized than it is in the woman, as will be seen in the description of the female organs.

In the flaccid state of the penis, the head is partly or wholly covered by a loose layer of skin, in the uncircumcised state, called the prepuce or foreskin. This may be retracted for the purpose of cleansing and it becomes retracted naturally after entry in coitus. The mucous surface of the foreskin is supplied with glands which secrete a substance called smegma which, when it is not frequently removed by washing, becomes irritating and messy in appearance and fertile soil for the breeding of germs. In reference to sexual intercourse, scrupulous cleanliness in this respect is imperative. For her own protection the woman should insist upon cleanliness in this matter on the part of the man. Daily washing with soap should be the rule.

The Female Organs

The external sex parts of the woman included in the vulva are more hidden than those of the man, and their position makes it somewhat more difficult for the woman herself to become thoroughly familiar with their structure. Not a few adolescent girls actually do not know that they possess a vagina. As a basis for harmonious, mutually satisfying sex adjustment in marriage, it is of great importance that the essential anatomical structure and the functions of the woman's sex mechanism be understood both by the wife and the husband.

The two visible fleshy folds covered with hair, are the large or outer lips (*labia majora*). When the outer lips are separated, two lesser folds are revealed called the smaller or inner lips (*labia minora*), covered with mucous membrane on the inner surface. In some women the inner lips protrude somewhat. The inner lips meet at their upper ends and when separated, are approximately in the form of the wishbone of a hen (see Fig. 3, p. 39). The inner lips are one of the several areas of sex feeling.

The Clitoris. Just above the junction of the inner lips is the clitoris, the principal organ of sex feeling. This is roughly represented the knob of the wishbone, above the junction of the two wings. The clitoris is a miniature penis having erectile tissue, and a head and foreskin similar to the penis of the man. It is covered from above by a hood of skin. The clitoris is supplied with highly sensitive nerves which respond to sexual stimulation. From this, the centre of erotic response, sexual feeling radiates to the other areas in the vulva and vagina. When erect, the clitoris is about the size and shape of a pea or small bean.

The mucous membrane about the clitoris, like the penis of the man, is supplied with glands which secrete smegma. Because of the difference in structure, cleanliness in the woman is somewhat more difficult than it is in the man. Avoidance of offensive odours is important because they tend to inhibit sexual desire in the man.

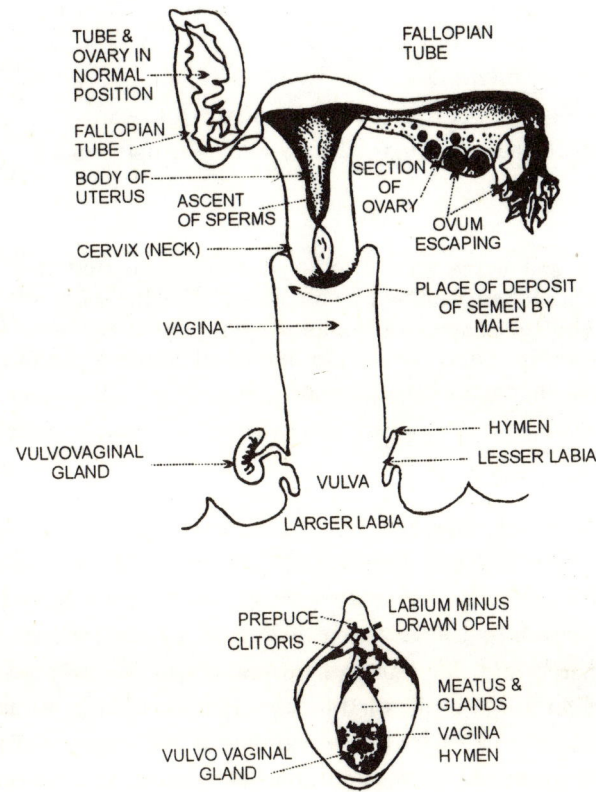

Fig. 3. Female Organs (front view)

About 3 centimetres below the clitoris is the small opening of the urethra, the duct which conducts the urine from the bladder. The urethra has only the urinary function and no sexual function.

The Hymen. Below the urinary passage is the entrance to the vagina. In the normal unmarried woman this opening is partly closed by a thin membrane, the hymen. It appears in various shapes but in most cases it is a crescent shaped forward extension of the back wall of the vagina. The hymen is usually nicked and

There are still those who adhere to the notion that the manifest presence of the hymen is an infallible sign of virginity, and its absence a contrary sign. This is not true. The hymen is often stretched by local washing and douches or in medical examination.

stretched at the first coitus, occasionally in many cases some slight bleeding and pain. The bleeding and discomfort, when they occur are not of sufficient consequence to warrant fear on the part of the woman in approaching this experience. Indeed it is important that fear be eliminated and that the woman enter into the first coitus with ready abandon, in pleasurable anticipation of the mutual satisfaction and joy to be achieved later, if not at once realized. This is important because fear powerfully inhibits her sexual responses, and the function of the lubricating glands, leaving the parts dry. This increases the probability of discomfort and bleeding and diminishes the possibility of experiencing any sex pleasure at the first coitus. Occasionally the hymen is so tough that it does not yield to the pressure of attempted intercourse. In such cases the aid of the surgeon to slit the membrane should be promptly sought. Ignorance and awkwardness are responsible for much unnecessary pain and unsuccessful coitus in the early efforts.

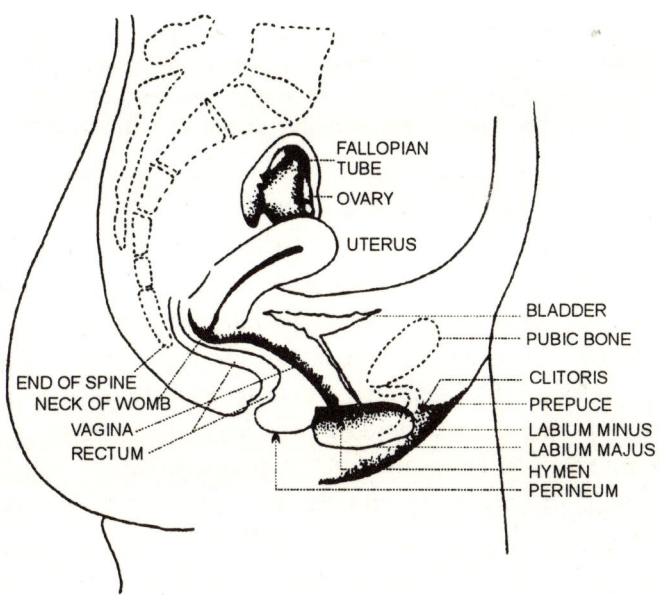

Fig. 4. Female Organs (side view)

The Vaginal Functions

During pregnancy the vagina and its outlet become capable of great expansion, permitting the passage of the child from the womb, without injury in many cases. In most instances, however, more or less laceration of the muscular structure controlling the opening of the vagina itself occurs. It should be understood that it is of great importance that such tears receive prompt surgical attention. The use and control of the muscles about the vaginal opening and of the entire pelvic floor are necessary to the woman's most effective participation in coitus. The relaxed condition and the loss of muscular control which results from the failure to repair perineal and vaginal tears may result in greatly diminishing sexual satisfaction in coitus for both partners, and may render it impossible for the woman to achieve orgasm at all.

The Vagina. The virgin vagina, the first in order of the internal sex organs, is a tube 9 to 11 centimetres in length along its back wall, in its normal relaxed state. It's remains collapsed until some object is introduced into it. Its walls are elastic and it lies in folds, hence it is capable of great expansion both in length and diameter. The inner end of the vagina is closed by the neck of the womb which extends into it. The function of the vagina is to receive the penis of the male in coitus, to receive the discharge of semen in preparation for the journey of the spermatozoa into the womb and tubes, and it is the canal through which the child at birth passes from its home in the womb to the outside world. Two masses of veins, the bulbs, situated just within the opening of the vagina which becomes erect under sexual excitement are the chief areas of sex feeling in the vagina.

The two vulvo-vaginal glands, the glands of Bartholin, are situated one on each side of the opening of the vagina. This pair of glands is of great importance in coitus. Their function is to pour out a very slippery mucous secretion which lubricates the vaginal orifice and its surrounding parts in preparation for coitus. These glands secrete freely only under sexual excitement. Hence inadequate preliminary stimulation of the woman in love-play leaves the parts dry and unprepared for coitus, a condition which is not only inimical to successful coitus but which may cause unnecessary pain. These facts need to be understood particularly in reference to the initial period of intercourse in early days of marriage, when inhibiting attitudes on the part of the wife may restrict the normal functioning of these glands. Where this is the case, artificial lubrication needs to be employed until a satisfactory adjustment of all the necessary factors has been brought about. These matters will be discussed later on.

The Uterus. The uterus (womb) is a pear-shaped organ of heavy muscular walls. The virgin uterus measures about 5 to 6 centimetres in length and 4 centimetres in width. The uterus of the woman who has had children is about 9 centimetres long and 6 to 7 centimetres wide. The organ is supported in the pelvis by strong ligaments. Its positions is at right angles to the vagina, the upper, heavy end being directed forward toward the front of the pelvis. The small end (cervix) opens into the vagina and closes its upper end. (See Fig. 3, p 39). During pregnancy the uterus increases in size enormously, expanding in conformity to the growth of the child, and rising high into the abdomen. After childbirth the organ gradually retracts to its former size.

In civilized life, through general lack of local muscular development and other factors, the uterus frequently becomes displaced or bent upon itself. Many cases of sterility (loss of power to conceive) result from these conditions. They also cause varying degree of indisposition and illness. Displacements or flexions are corrected by treatment or surgical measures. In about one third of these cases the correction restores fertility. Bends of the uterus are frequently permanently corrected by pregnancy.

Fallopian Tubes. From the upper end of the uterus the Fallopian tubes, each about 13 centimetres long, extend right and left to the ovaries. Their function is to conduct the ova (eggs) from the ovaries into the cavity of the uterus. This is accomplished through contractile action of the tubes, aided by very fine hair-like projections of the lining cells which keep up a sweeping motion in one direction, like a field of grain waving in the wind, thus keeping the current of the secretions and hence the egg, moving toward the uterus. In most cases of conception, the egg is fertilized during its passage through the tube and undergoes the first stages of its development during that passage.

The Ovaries. The ovaries are comparable to the testes of the male. They produce the female reproductive cells, the ova (eggs) and internal secretions. The ovaries are situated at the outer ends of the tubes, one on each side of the uterus. An ovary is about the size and shape of a large almond in the shell. The hormone function of the ovaries is apparently more complex than that of the testes of the male. In addition to the internal secretion which governs the development of the specific female characters and helps to sustain the normal functioning of the individual as an organism, the ovaries elaborate other chemical substances which control the reproductive functions. If the ovaries are removed before puberty, the development of the individual becomes profoundly altered, as was indicated in reference to male castrations.

An egg cell is about the size of the small dot of an *'i'* just visible to the eye. From the ovaries eggs are periodically expelled. A tiny pouch (follicle) is formed, containing a liquid substance and a single egg cell. When the follicle has ripened and reached the surface of the ovary, it bursts, the egg is liberated and finds its way into the oviduct or tube. If during its passage through the tube it becomes fertilized by a spermatozoon, it attaches itself to the wall of the uterus, the lining membrane of which has become specially prepared for its reception and nourishment and the development of the egg, already begun in the tube, continues until birth. If the egg is not fertilized, it is cast out of the body through the vagina.

Having expelled the egg cell, the follicle in the ovary becomes temporarily an internal secretion gland (*corpus luteum*), the function of which is to provide the best possible conditions for the protection and development of the egg. The secretions stimulate the physiological processes of the body generally and cause special growth of the lining of the uterus in preparation for the development of the egg. If the egg is fertilized the *corpus luteum* grows larger and exercises its influences during several months of pregnancy.

Menstruation

When the egg does not fertilize the *corpus luteum* diminishes and disappears; the special preparation of the lining of the uterus now being useless, the cells disintegrate, to be carried out with the mucous secretions mixed with blood, which constitute the menstrual flow. Menstruation means that an ovum released from the ovary has failed to become fertilized and that nature's preparations for the development of the egg having become useless, they are being demolished and the debris cast out. If the egg becomes fertilized the influence of the *corpus luteum* prevents the ripening of a new egg, for nature does not now need another. If the egg is not fertilized the growth of a new follicle at once begins.

Menstruation generally continues for three to five days but longer in not a few cases, while it is a normal physiological function, not to be regarded as 'sickness' or 'being unwell'. In severe cases the general let-down and the readjustments of the entire organism do involve nervous tensions and in many cases some aches and pains for which allowance needs to be made in the personal and social regime of the individual. In those cases in which the disturbances are considerable, a return to normalcy is greatly facilitated by spending the first day quietly, lying down much of the time, getting extra sleep and engaging in a congenial occupation such as reading.

Sexual desire in a woman is far more a matter of education through sexual stimulation and sexual experience, than is the case with a man.

CHAPTER 3

SEXUAL DESIRE IN MEN AND WOMEN

The psychological sex differences which so profoundly influence the functions and relations of men and women, are intimately intertwined with the anatomical and physiological differences and can be fairly discussed only in full recognition of this interdependence. For our purpose, however, the anatomical and physiological aspects have been sufficiently discussed in the chapter on the sex mechanism. We shall concern ourselves here chiefly with a consideration of the psychological differences, with due regard for their physiological setting.

The extreme importance of a clear understanding of the psychological differences and their bearings upon sound adjustment in marriage cannot easily be over emphasized. Knight Dunlap says,[1]

'Many cases of marriage failure come to the psychologist for adjustment; cases in which in spite of the real attachment of husband and wife, and the desires of both to realize a spiritual union, the union is not attained, and the family has begun to disintegrate. In these cases, the outstanding fact is ignorance of the psychology of sex; and the work of the

---

[1] *Social Psychology.*

psychologist in adjusting these families is largely the teaching of simple facts in regard to the mental sex life. Unless both the man and the woman understand the essential emotional differences between them, the chances of successful marriage are small. Very often, both mates learn with sufficient rapidity during marriage; but very often also a family is wrecked before the knowledge has been attained.'

Understanding Sexual Desire

In this discussion we shall draw fully, with acknowledgement and appreciation, upon Dunlap's clear analysis. It is first necessary to take a much more comprehensive view of what is included in the term sex desire than is commonly held. To most people it means desire for sexual intercourse. This is altogether too narrow a meaning. In Dunlap's use of the term it embraces all physiological and emotional urges that arise out of sex differences. He says;

'Just as we uniformly designate all characteristics which are peculiar to the female, or to the male, as sex characteristics, whether they are characteristics of the sex organs, or such differences as in stature, in form, and in bony development, so also and for the same reason, we designate desire which is determined as to its object by the differentiation of the sexes, as sex desire.'

In this sense sex desire ranges all the way from desire of a man or a woman for association with members of the other sex at the tea table, to passionate desire for coitus. Both these extremes represents desire for mutual stimulation in association with a member of the other sex in a way in which we do not desire stimulation in association with our own sex. The desire springs out of sex differences and hence is sex desire. For clarity in this matter we shall note Dunlap's further analysis. He distinguishes the following three forms of sexual desire.

Generalized personal desire. 'A man or woman may be "interested" in individuals of the other sex, without the selection of a particular individual who is desired above all others.' It is desire for the society of individuals of the other sex, for reciprocal stimulation in social intercourse with them; that is, the individual not only desires the stimulation that comes from social intercourse with members of the other sex, but desires that they also be stimulated by him and the consciousness that they are, enhances the stimulation he experiences. Desires of these types are satisfied in such social activities as conversation, walking, skating, dancing and playing games.

Particularized personal desire. This form of desire is focused upon a particular individual and yields a higher form of satisfaction. It is illustrated in the individual who is 'in love'. 'The personal desires of the lover are towards the loved one, and it is her or his society, her stimulation, and common stimuli and common activity with her, which are pre-eminently desired.' From desire thus particularized, generalized desire may be wholly excluded or it may tend to co-exist with it. Essentially, for the man really in love, it is no longer desire for *woman* but *the woman*.

Specific sex desire. This is desire primarily for sexual intercourse. The act itself and details connected with it are focal in consciousness. 'The stimulus desires and common activity desires are merely such as conduce most effectively to the completion of the act.'

In experience, these three types of sex desire do not, of course, remain so sharply defined, but they grade into one another through many stages. Between one extreme of generalized and the other extreme of particularized personal desire, we have the whole range: from desire which finds its satisfaction from general sociability with an individual of a type — which satisfaction could be furnished by any one of a number of individuals of the same general type — to the most exclusive particularization of the individual deeply in love. Again, 'the personal desire shades gradually into the specific and vice versa in a temporal way; and there is a gradation of blends of the two at definite times. Very often, the particularized desire begins in the personal form and grows in time into the specific; and frequently that which commences as relatively specific desire for a given individual grows in time into a comprehensive personal desire.'

The point which at the moment we wish our readers especially to note, is the inclusive range of sex desire. It embraces all the physical and emotional urges toward the other sex which arise out of the differences between men and women. All the emotions of friendship and of love between the sexes are included in sex desire.

Sex Differences in 'Desire'

The point of emphasis here is that the forms of sex desire manifest themselves differently in women and in men, and that these differences in manifestation are profoundly important in their bearing upon marital adjustments. We shall discuss the differences in some detail.

❏ *In men, the sex desire is more uniform in type, and in women, more diverse.*

While there are individual variations among men and while a few individuals may differ widely from the general type, the overwhelming majority of men differ only mildly in type of desire, however much they may differ in its gratification. In women the range of variation is much greater; the extremes are wider apart.

We may illustrate this point in reference to sexual capacity and responsiveness, by a diagram. In the diagram below, let the line A-B represent the range of differences in women — placing at point A the truly 'frigid' woman who is constitutionally anaesthetic sexually, and at point B, the nymphomaniac whose sex desires are

A   Women   B

          C   D
          | Men

so persistent as to be unremittingly pressing and beyond the possibility of satisfaction. Between these extremes, both of which are fortunately rare, we have shading up and down the scale a wide range of capacity and responsiveness. If the range of variation in men were to be represented on the same line, it would fall — very approximately, for we have no data adequate for accuracy in the matter — about between point C and D.

It is to be noted that not only is there a much greater range toward frigidity in women but also a greater range toward capacity for passion than there is in men. Dunlap says, 'It is not to be supposed that on the average the sexual desires of men are any stronger than those of women, although the conditions of arousal may be different. It is even possible that the reverse is true; and it is certainly true that in very many women the desires, when fully aroused, have a violence far surpassing that of the average man.'

It will be seen at once that the differences between men and women just indicated, create in themselves problems of sexual excitement. Suppose that a man whose sexuality would be represented at point D in the scale, married a woman half-way between points A and C. In such a case the problem of achieving a mutually satisfying and harmonious relationship is obvious.

However, with reasonably adequate knowledge of human sex nature, freedom from repressing inhibitions, skilful technique and a sympathetic, unselfish love-relationship, a mutually satisfying adjustment may be made. But ignorance, lack of skill and inconsideration are almost sure to stack the cards against such a marriage. A woman half-way between points D and B, marrying a man at point C, reverses the problems.

❑ *In men, sex desire is frequently present in a highly specific form without any particularization, and with a minimum of even generalized personal desire.*

In men sex excitement or physical passion often arises spontaneously without the stimulus that comes from women generally, or from association with a particular woman upon whom desire is centred. It may arise, for example, as a result of the internal secretion function of the testicles. These secretions gradually build up a physiological tension which at any moment may result in conscious passionate excitement without stimulation through association with the other sex.

Specific desire in women is less likely to appear except as it arises out of the particularized personal form; in many women it seldom or never arises in any other way. That is, desire for coitus arises in women much more generally through personal association with members of the other sex. While the internal secretion of the ovaries also produces a sex tension in women, it is on the whole, more diffused, less localized in the sex organs than it is in men, and hence does not, so frequently, result in specific desire and excitement.

❏ *Personal desire in men passes very easily and quickly into the specific form, without requiring intermediate activities, such as caresses.*

That is, the psychic stimulation derived from general social intercourse with women or a particular woman, may easily and quickly give rise to specific desire.

In women, 'personal desire does not pass so automatically into the specific but requires the intermediate stimulation of caresses. The woman, in many cases, must have personal desire for the man, involving finally the desire to be tactually and kinaesthetically stimulated by him; and these stimulations arouse the specific desire.

An understanding of, and adaptation to, this difference in arriving at specific sex desire in the marriage relationship is of extreme importance. It will be shown that upon this rock more than any other, marital ships that sail out of the harbour in high promise are wrecked.

❏ *On an average, men and women differ widely in the time required to achieve orgasm in coitus.*

Most women require a considerably greater prolongation of the act than most men. When the man reaches the orgasm instantly or within one or two minutes, and the woman requires from ten to fifteen minutes, the problem of adjustment may be formidable. But here also, understanding, skilful art in love and sympathetic consideration can in most cases bridge the chasm. The rock which marks this temporal difference between men and women, in sexuality, is akin to the rock mentioned in the preceding section (difference in arriving at specific desire) and lies in the same threatening shoal.

❑ *Men seldom lose the general desire for long periods of time, but are during most of their life, no matter how definitely they particularize, "susceptible" to women generally.*

When a woman's personal desire becomes particularized, although the general desire is seldom completely lost, it lessens or decreases more markedly than it does in man; to a degree so small usually that it precludes her particularization upon another man until she loses her particularization upon the first man.'

Dunlap, speaking of his description of woman's sex nature, which we in general adopt, says, 'The description applies to a certain range of types of women only, although that range probably includes the majority. There are others who in type are like the average man; and still others who go to the other extreme of never having any specific desire; an extreme which is seldom if ever approximated by man except he be mentally or physically defective, or seriously diseased. Between these two wide extremes all gradations in feminine types are represented.'

❑ *In the great majority of women sex desire varies with the menstrual cycle.*

At certain periods in the cycle she is more easily aroused sexually than at other times, or specific desire may arise spontaneously without external stimulation. There occurs a tidal ebb and flow in sex desire which in some women is so marked and so regular that they can definitely locate its peak by date, in relation to menstruation, while other women recognize a periodicity in desire but are not conscious that these periods come with regularity. Other women do not recognize any periodicity at all.

While the occurrence of the peak of periodic desire in those women who recognize a periodicity is scattered all through the menstrual month of twenty-eight days, in the overwhelming majority of women it falls in or about the menstrual period: a few days before; during; a few days after, before and during; during and after; or before, during and after.

In the Davis study, in the one thousand histories of unmarried women, all but 132 admit sex feelings, sex desires, or some form of sex expression. Of the 868 who make this admission, 272 have recognized regular periodicity of sex desire. Of these, 110 date it so closely that it was possible to chart the date of desire with reference to the menstrual period. A group of 298 reported experiencing desire periodically but not with regularity. A group of 238 women have observed no periodicity of desire. According to Dr Davis, of these women who could date their period of height end desire definitely, about half experienced a lesser wave of desire later in the month, following the greater period of desire.

The fact of significance in relation to happy adjustment in marriage is that most women experience a natural monthly periodicity of responsiveness to sex stimulation. A woman may be eagerly responsive and quickly aroused when at the crest of her desire, and indifferent or cold and slow to arouse at the ebb-tide of desire. This does not mean that full, mutually satisfying coitus may not be achieved during the period of ebb-tide, but it does mean that the whole approach and art of the husband and their mutual love play must be adapted to the physiological situation, and the corresponding psychological mood.

While the sexual capacities of the woman have not been altered, the conditions of arousal have been altered. It requires a different degree and kind of wooing. The direct and even crude approach that may be effective and welcome at the crest of woman's rhythm is likely to be ineffective at the ebb-tide and may be disastrous to marital harmony. Sex relations, for which a welcome by the woman has not been prepared, become to the woman, in most cases, not merely an indifferent experience; they tend to become an affront to and an outrange of her whole being. Lack of physical response tends to loss of spiritual intimacy and coitus without that intimacy wears a threatening mien. It threatens to give rise to a definitely negative attitude in the woman in which her emotional excitement is not with, but against the husband. In time such an attitude is likely to frustrate the woman's passionate responsiveness, even at the high tide and lead to complete separateness in sex life. It is ignorant or selfish bungling at this point that brings the expressions of shock, of disgust and of gnawing disappointment which run so extensively through the case histories of such studies as we have referred to. Happy adjustment in this regard requires mutual understanding, mutual, consideration and mutual acquiring of the art of loving.

Some have sought to discover in men a sexual periodicity somewhat analogous to the periodicity found in women, but there is as yet no evidences to support such a view.

❏ *A very important difference between men and women is that men, upon attaining sexual maturity in early adolescence, uniformly come into full possession of their sexual capacities and do not require sexual experience for the development of these powers.*

Says Dunlap, 'The development of sexual desire in the woman is far more a matter of education, through sexual stimulation and sexual experience, than is the case with the man. In many women the desire is very slight until developed by repeated stimulations and experiences and may thereafter be powerful and easily aroused. In many others, the desire is never developed to a very high level, even though they may be married for years, and to some of them, sexual intercourse eventually becomes intensely repugnant. In most of these cases, the conditions of intercourse have been abnormal through absence of the appropriate psychological details, frequently because of the ignorance of the husband.' This fact is abundantly borne out in Dickinson's and Hamilton's case histories and also those of Davis. They present a tragic array of cases in which the sexual capacities of the woman, although present, as the histories show, stood no chance of being released and developed in coitus with the husband, because of ignorance and blundering ways on the part of both, aggravated by deep seated inhibitions. The common sequence of experience shown is that the wife does not participate in the full sexual experience. Before long she drifts from passivity or partial response progressively toward indifference and definite negation. The husband concludes that 'she is not that way' and accepts the unequal experience philosophically, whereas the wife does so rebelliously. Her unsatisfied sexuality is driven in upon herself and while sexually cold to the husband, she has the problem of unsatisfied desire.

Of course, it requires a rare combination of personality and character traits to assimilate happily such a sexual relationship in the total relations of husband and wife. As we have intimated before, it is inevitable that in many cases this gulf should come to intervene in the other areas of their life also and the marriage should become 'unhappy' if not worse.

Havelock Ellis cites the case of a woman who failed ever to experience an orgasm in some years of life with one husband and subsequently with a second. A third husband quickly aroused her to full sexual experience and she developed a normal and vigorous sexual capacity. Other similar cases occur in case histories.

Women who are approaching marriage and young brides, should not fail to observe the hopefulness that lies in the fact that the sexual capacities of women are subject to education and development through experience. If the young bride finds disappointment in her sexual life in the early weeks or months of marriage, it is not necessarily of serious significance. In most cases it only requires a correct diagnosis of the adverse factors and an intelligent use of the appropriate remedy with persistence and mutually sympathetic co-operation.

In summary of the sex differences, we may say that in men sex desire is fairly uniform; it lies close to the surface and is easily aroused and quickly satisfied and man is always liable to sex desire in all its forms. In women sex desire is variable; it lies deeper and is more slowly aroused and more slowly satisfied; it is subject in most women to tidal rhythm; and it is subject to development to full power through experience. In the next chapter we shall discuss more fully the adjustment problems that arise out of these differences and out of ignorance of them.

The whole range of sexual acts must bring the same harmonious experience of love and joy to both partners.

CHAPTER 4

SEXUAL FACTORS IN MARRIAGE

W̶e will now consider the elements which most commonly contribute to sexual maladjustments in marriage, keeping in view the sex differences which have been discussed. This will prepare the way for a summary of the positive factors which make for an ideal marriage.

Sexual Needs of Women

The first among the many unfavourable factors is the commonly held attitude which denies the sexual needs and rights of a woman. While with the growing 'emancipation' of women there is a better understanding of a woman's sexual needs and a marked improvement in the attitude that treats sexual activity as an exclusive masculine function in which the woman's part remains a passive one, yet it does not easily give way. Throughout the research studies, male ignorance and disregard of woman's sexual capacities and needs is pointed out as an obvious prime factor in the apparent coldness of women, and the maladjustments that grow out of the unequal sexual relationships. We have already pointed out this fundamental flaw in relationship and have shown that a woman's sexual needs are, despite their different manifestations, fully comparable to those of a man. Persistent passivity and frustration of response in coitus are a violation of woman's biological nature, and like all violations of nature, are fraught with evil consequences. First of all, they are detrimental to the woman's physical and emotional health and balance. Hamilton says,

> 'It is, I think, one of the most suggestive findings of my research that, of the 46 women who are inadequate as to orgasm capacity, 20 had been diagnosed at one time or another in their lives as more or less seriously psychoneurotic. These diagnoses were made by psychiatrists other than myself. Only one of the 54 women who could have orgasm with reasonable frequency had ever been regarded as psychoneurotic.'

With the caution of a scientist Hamilton adds, 'Although inability to have orgasm and more or less serious nervous symptoms occur together with significant frequency, it is only in a qualified sense that we can regard one as the resultant of the other. Chronic sexual dissatisfaction may augment or even precipitate nervous symptoms, but the weight of evidence is strongly in favour of the view that when a psychoneurosis and an inadequate orgasm capacity occur together in a woman, they must be regarded as resultants of a common cause.'

Be that as it may, we cannot escape the conclusion that persistently frustrated sexuality in women is a powerful factor in precipitating, if not causing psychoneurotic disorders. We do not inherit insanity but only a predisposition toward mental imbalance.

The same principle holds true for other forms of psychoneurotic disturbances. Dickinson has shown that almost all of the women who were failing in orgasm experience possessed inherent erotic capacities, but that these powers of fulfillment were blocked by a combination of circumstances, which are for the most part, avoidable. In the light of the many case histories, one may fairly assume that if the conditions of coitus had been more favourable in Hamilton's group of women referred to, a large proportion would have achieved satisfaction and hence a better health record.

Failure to recognize the sexual needs and rights of woman cuts also at the roots of marital love and harmony. Coitus, under these conditions, instead of being an act of supreme mutual intimacy, vivifying, enriching and developing love, becomes an egocentric performance for the husband which in turn forces the wife's sexuality also to centre within herself. Harris says,[1]

'If either partner satisfies himself or herself at the expense of the other, the bond of affection may be strained beyond endurance.' Again, 'Men and women fail to realize that this phase of their common life is integrally a part of all the rest. The sexual relationship is not part of the partnership unless it is a genuinely shared experience. But what is meant by sharing the sexual experience? Precisely this, that the whole experience — from the first caress to the climax of sexual intercourse — shall mean essentially the same to both and shall bring the same enduring satisfaction to both. The whole range of sexual acts must bring the same harmonious experience of love and joy to both partners.'

A first requisite for a mutually satisfying and enriching love-life in marriage is a frank and full acceptance of mutual sexual capacities and needs. Ellis says,[2] 'Women whose instincts are not perverted at the roots do not desire to be cold. Far from it. But right atmosphere and the insight and skill of the right man is needed to dispel that coldness. In the erotic sphere, a woman asks nothing better of a man than to be lifted above her coldness, to the higher plane where there is reciprocal interest and mutual joy in the act of sex. Therein her silent demand is one with the Nature's. For the biological order of the world involves those claims which, in the human range, are the erotic rights of women.'

---

[1] *Essays on Marriage.*
[2] *Little Essays of Love and Virtue.*

Approaching your Partner: Prelude to Sex

A too direct, too exclusively physical, approach to coitus is one of the most common and most baneful factors in marital maladjustments. Every single act, if it is to be a truly shared experience, an act that has something of spiritual significance, calls for prelude, for courtship and wooing. It requires what Havelock Ellis has so aptly called 'the play-function of sex'. Truly human sex relationships mean not merely a union of bodies but a union of two personalities, hence there needs first to be a union in emotional mood, before there can be a physical union that is really vital to the marital partners. It is the greatest mistake to assume that courtship and wooing may cease at, or soon after, the wedding. If it ceases, marriage loses its romance and such a marriage tends to become commonplace, or an irritating imitation of life, or to go on the rocks.

Courtship needs to prevail in the total marital relationship as an atmosphere that exhilarates and renews the zest of life from day to day, through all the difficult as well as the pleasant vicissitudes of life. Such a relationship leaves a married couple at seventy, lovers more truly than they were at twenty-five. Whether or not such an ideal is realized in the total relationship, an approach to coitus by way of courtship intimacies in which both play their part is indispensable. Such prelude may be brief or prolonged depending on the mood and the needs of the partners, particularly the wife. The emotional quality of the prelude is the essential test of its efficacy. Here the skill of the lover comes to the test.

Woman's Erotic Nature and Foreplay

Some publications dealing with marriage have fallen into the error of implying that the activities of foreplay are a function and responsibility of the husband only, and of implying that it consists essentially of a sort of mechanical process of stimulating the woman by manipulating her erotic areas. This is a serious error. Such stimulation may enter in but only as a phase of mutual, reciprocal activity in play. The very term 'play' suggests shared activity.

Foreplay is not to be set off as separate from the supreme love-act of coitus. The complete relationship from the first touch or kiss to the postlude of repose is to be one of mutuality and sharing.

There are two important reasons for foreplay in coitus. The first grows out of the sex differences we have discussed. We have seen that in a man the personal desire passes easily and quickly into specific desire, or sexual excitement may arise spontaneously without any intermediate stimulation. A man is quickly ready, physically and emotionally, for coitus, at least up to the age of fifty-five or sixty. Most women, on the other hand, require more or less prolonged stimulation — emotional or physical or both — to awaken and develop specific desire. The point of readiness which the man may reach instantly or quickly, the woman in most cases must reach by way of a winding path through her psychophysical being, a path to be trodden not alone but in the subtle, delicate intimacies of love-play with her mate.

Another sex difference is the fact that most women, even after an adequate prelude, require considerably more time to achieve orgasm in coitus than men do. Hence without preparatory love-play the possibilities of satisfaction for the woman become extremely doubtful in a large number of cases. Even at best, there is always the problem of quickening for the woman and of slowing up for the man, with a view to reaching orgasm simultaneously if possible, or at least both partners achieving the culmination before the completion of the act.

What happens with such amazing frequency, as shown by researches of recent years, is the following experience:

The couple falls into a certain routine of sex relations, based in most cases upon the needs and desires of the husband. There are no preliminaries. The woman, even though she may be lovingly sympathetic, enters upon the experience emotionally and physically unprepared. The man must be prepared or the act is not possible. Not so for the woman. The man reaches his climax quickly and the act ceases. The woman has remained unresponsive or, what is worse, she has been partially aroused or even highly excited but 'left in the air'. The natural, desired and deeply needed consummation has not been reached by her. The natural reaction of the man is to become relaxed, drowsy and to go to sleep. This relaxation of body and soul should be for both. There are often no moments of greater spiritual meaning in the relationships of married lovers than those moments when love has had its way and they rest relaxed in body and spirit in each other's arms. Instead, the woman, if she has remained cold, will too perhaps, go to sleep, cold also in heart and spirit and with a dividing wall between. Or, if she has become stimulated and left unsatisfied, she may lie awake for hours, occasionally all night, tense and excited, unless she turns to auto-erotic relief. It requires but a moment of picturing the situation in imagination — the man satisfied, breathing deeply in sound sleep, while the woman lies at his side tensely awake with unsatisfied longing, or resorts to self relief — to realize how inevitable it is that sooner or later there should escape from her in the silence of the night such expressions, as 'selfish', 'brute', 'animal', 'stupid' and the like, and that this fundamental disappointment should bring disharmony into their whole relationship.

Developing Erotic Approaches

Speaking of the sexual life of an average man in our society, Ellis says of him,[3] 'The more one knows about him. ..the more one is convinced that... his conception of erotic personality, his ideas on the art of love, if they have any existence at all, are of a humble character. As to the notion of play in the sphere of sex, even if he makes blundering attempts to practise it, that is for him something quite low down, something to be ashamed of, and he would not dream of associating it with anything he has been taught to regard as belonging to the spiritual sphere. The conception of 'divine play' is meaningless to him.'

And as to the feminine side of the picture he says, 'Let us turn to an average woman. Here the picture must usually be still more

---

[3] *Little Essays of Love and Virtue.*

unsatisfactory. The man at least, crude as we may find his two fundamental notions to be, has at all events attained mental pride and physical satisfaction. The woman often attains neither, and since the man, by instinct or tradition, has maintained a self regarding attitude, that is not surprising. The husband — by primitive instinct partly, and certainly by ancient tradition — regards himself as the active partner in matters of love, and his own pleasure as legitimately the prime motive for activity. His wife consequently falls into the complementary position, and regards herself as the passive partner and her pleasure as negligible, if not as a thing to be ashamed of, should she by chance experience it. So that, while the husband is content with a mere simulacrum of pretence of the erotic life, the wife often had none at all... She has never once been profoundly aroused, and she has never once been utterly satisfied. The deep fountains of her nature have never been unsealed; she has never been fertilized throughout her whole nature by their liberating influence; her erotic personality has never been developed.'

And Ellis adds this warning, the force of which is dramatically emphasized by the tragic results of such inadequate and unequal relationships as are revealed in modern research studies. 'That alone is a great misfortune, all the more tragic since under favourable conditions, which it should have been natural to attain, it might so easily be avoided. But there is this further result, full of the possibilities of domestic tragedy, that the wife so situated, however innocent, however virtuous, may at any time find her virginally sensitive emotional nature fertilized by the touch of some other man than her husband.'

Another important reason for affectionate foreplay as a prelude to coitus is the fact that in most cases a direct physical approach not only fails to awaken the woman's erotic powers but is definitely inhibiting and repellent to most women, especially those of sensitive and refined nature. Let no man venture into the intimacy of coitus with any woman for whose personality he has sincere regard until he has learned that the avenue to the deep resources of passion in the woman's affectionate nature leads through the most sensitive, most idealistic areas of her emotional realm. The man who makes that approach on a physical plane does so at the peril of bitterness, estrangement and mutual defeat. The woman who related that on her bridal night, as soon as the couple had retired, the husband seized her in a passionate embrace and proceeded to intercourse, voiced the reaction of an endless number of women when she said, 'I felt raped and hated him from that moment on.'

The approach to the physical is by way of the spiritual.[4] When the woman has been wooed and won into spiritual harmony she will give herself to passionate expressions of love with free and full abandon. And only so can the man also experience real fulfillment of love.

Play and Foreplay: The Art of Love

It is in vivid consciousness of these realities that Ellis stresses in masterly fashion the 'play-function of sex.' He says,[5] 'There are, as we know, two main functions in the sexual relationship, or what in the biological sense we term 'marriage', among civilized human beings. The primary physiological function of begetting and bearing offspring and the secondary spiritual function of furthering the higher mental and emotional processes.'

By way of interpreting this secondary function he says, 'The play-function of sex is, in an inseparable way, both physical and psychic. It stimulates to wholesome activity all the complex and interrelated systems of the organism. At the same time it satisfies the most profound emotional impulses, controlling in harmonious poise the various mental instincts. Along these lines it necessarily tends in the end to go beyond its own sphere ...as we truly and wisely exercise the play-function of sex, we are at the same time training our personality on the erotic side and acquiring a mastery of the art of love.' Ellis continues; 'The longer I live, the more I

---

[4] The term 'spiritual' is not used in a mystic or theological sense but as denoting the whole psychic realm of the personality.
[5] *Little Essays of Love and Virtue.*

realize the immense importance of individual development through the play-function of erotic personality, and for human society of the acquirement of the art of love. At the same time I am ever more astonished at the rarity of erotic personality and the ignorance of the art of love even among those experienced in the exercise of procreation, in whom we might most confidently expect to find such development and such art. At times one feels hopeless at the thought that civilization in this extremely intimate field of life has yet achieved so little.'

Harris says, 'The development of sex relations until they are an art demands patience with each other, if not indeed a sense of humour at difficulties. Successful sex relationships have a definite technique and demand the development of skill as much as dancing, skating or other experiences of a man or a woman. At first, a couple will be awkward and clumsy. If instead of being hurt, they coach each other and have fun in their practice, their very inefficiencies may form the basis of their sharing...It is wise for a couple to approach their wedding with a full realization of this indubitable fact: it takes time to acquire skill in the art of love.'

The tragic course of the common factors in maladjustments which we have so far discussed — ignorance, bungling, denial of woman's erotic nature, physical approach, absence of foreplay — are portrayed with dramatic vividness in Dickinson's study of 50 young brides, among his case histories. These young women were seen by him chiefly or only in the beginning of their married life, usually not later than its ninth month. They were women in good health, contented and with excellent professional training, but who had difficulty in the sexual relationship. As a group, in these women, the anticipations of sexual engagement were not being realized. In the men there was hesitation, in the women there was fear, and these together with very limited knowledge resulted in a situation in which after less than a year of marriage more than half of these women were complaining of sexual difficulties. Eighteen of them had dyspareunia,[6] 4 were frigid, 5 had sexual maladjustment

---

[6] Painful coitus. It will be shown that in most cases this is due to psychic states.

of some sort. Of 41 reporting on the matter, 17 had not been able to achieve complete coitus and had not experienced orgasm. Of this group 27 were maladjusted, to 23 who were presumably adjusted.

That these difficulties are in the main preventable is strikingly indicated in Dickinsons's experience with this group. He states that there is a difference in immediate sexual adjustment between the fifteen women who had premarital examination and those who had not. The former were more easily able to get orgasm in coitus. In their reports to the physician after marriage, 12 of the 15 reported orgasm in their post-marital visits. On the other hand, of 35 not given pre-marital instruction 25 had had no orgasm.

Towards Simultaneous Orgasm

One of the most prevalent factors in marital maladjustments is too brief intromission (connection) in coitus. We have seen that even when there is intelligent and sympathetic adaptation in coitus, women require on the average more time in achieving orgasm than men do. The whole mutual technique must be adapted to the end of arriving at orgasm simultaneously or at least of enabling the woman to reach her climax also during the period between the entrance of the male organ and the subsiding of the man's erection, following his orgasm. Some men are able to control their reactions and to wait for the wife until she is ready to join him in the vigorous completion of the act with mutual climax. Some men although capable of such control, fail their partners in this regard because they are ignorant of their needs in this matter. However, a large proportion of men with the best of intentions have difficulty in successfully meeting this situation, and this fact is in large measure responsible for the appalling disparity in orgasm experience as shown in various studies.

All through the case histories runs the wistful or resentful complaint of women who are left cold—"he is too quick." Of those who blunder in ignorance, Dickinson observes, 'When he says "she is unresponsive," we nearly always find that she says he is "too quick". There is a correlation between frigidity and quick emission.'

In answer to Hamilton's questions, 'Do you believe that your orgasms occur too quickly for your wife's pleasure?' of the 100 husbands, 55 answered 'yes' (15 with reservations); only 28 answered with an unqualified 'no'.

In answer to the question, 'Do you believe that if your husband were slower in coming to his orgasm you would have orgasms more frequently?' 43 of the wives answered in the affirmative; and it is signifiant to note that exactly the same number of husbands also answered this question in the affirmative in reference to their wives.

Force is added to these revelations when, in answer to the question, 'Are there times when you feel unsatisfied after your husband has had his orgasm?', out of the 100 wives 74 answered 'yes' (19 with reservations) and only 8 answered with an unqualified 'no'.

In answer to the further question, 'Is your husband generally quicker or slower than you in coming to an orgasm?' 83 of the wives stated that the husband was naturally quicker; only 6 stated that the husband was slower than the wife; and only 6 affirmed that their orgasms were synchronous. Confirmation is furnished by the husbands, 84 of whom also stated that they were naturally quicker than their wives and only 3 affirmed that they were slower.

Obviously this natural disparity between men and women in the temporal range of their sexuality works hands in glove with the other adverse factors, especially the absence of emotional preparation for the women, to defeat mutuality in sexual experience. It is a problem which calls for intelligent study by the marital partners together, for patient, tolerant experimentation in a spirit of co-operative, companionable fellowship; and if need be, the counsel and aid of the wise physician or psychiatrist. It is a problem which must be solved if continued happiness is to be assured. Failing in an adjustment which will with reasonable frequency bring fully releasing satisfaction to the wife as well as to the husband in coitus, an adjustment in relationship and technique needs to be arrived at, such as will, through other means, bring to the wife climactic consummation. This is a compromise, to be sure, but life is full of compromises. Where there is sympathetic understanding and the will to adjust, many an otherwise impossible situation in the married relationship has been made to yield reasonably adequate sex experience for both, by such compromise measures.

Early Ejaculation Problems

Of Dickinson's cases 362 women furnished information as to the length of time between entry of the male and his ejaculation. 'It appears that the normal man holds an erection from five to ten minutes.' We would say then that the normal man is in a fairly adequate range provided all other conditions of coitus successful for both are observed. In the right atmosphere and with skilful prelude, one or two minutes may suffice when, ten or fifteen minutes may be inadequate under adverse conditions.

Dickinson finds that every eighth or ninth man discharges 'instantly', one in six does not exceed a two-minutes intromission. He states that 'up to three minutes' exhausts the staying power of 40 per cent. 'From five to fifteen minutes' accounts for 43 per cent more. The remaining 17 per cent can wait for more than fifteen minutes, some of them for any desired length of time.

Let us consider in detail some of the factors that contribute to unduly quick emission in men, omitting for the moment those who discharge 'instantly'.

1. **Nervousness:** A man requires self-confidence and poise to keep his ejaculatory reflexes within reasonable control. Nervousness, whether it springs from general awkwardness, undue haste, anticipation of failure or an unsympathetic attitude on the part of the spouse, lessens control of the ejaculatory mechanism.

2. **Fear:** This is really but another name for nervousness. Fear of failure, fear of pregnancy, fear of the wife's reaction tends to inhibit erection and incite early emission. By a sympathetic, reassuring, co-operative attitude, the wife can help greatly in

preventing nervousness and fear in the husband. A critical, adverse attitude tends to mess up the situation.

3. **Inadequate erection:** Penetration with only a partially erect penis is most likely to result in premature ejaculation. There is a surprising number of men who have difficulty in securing full, vigorous and sustained erection. An important contributory factor in many of these cases is unresponsiveness of the spouse. Coldness on the wife's part tends to inhibit the man's erection. The ineffectiveness of incomplete erection in turn fosters frigidity in the wife. Here you have the 'vicious circle'. In this matter, too, the sympathetic wife can be of great assistance. Few men who will not respond quickly with powerful reaction to the wife's deft fondling of the husband's genitals.

4. **Inadequate lubrication:** Anything which makes entrance difficult tends toward early emission. In cases in which the wife's lubricating glands do not sufficiently respond to provide sufficient natural lubrication, artificial lubricants need to be resorted to. The vegetable jellies are on the whole more suitable than the fatty lubricants such as vaseline.

5. **Wrong technique:** Haste is to be avoided not only in securing entrance but at any point in the act except from the moment when synchronous orgasm begins. Then, like athletes near the end of their course, both partners should rush to the finish. An amazingly large number of men seem to have no better idea of technique than to take the shortest route between desire and satisfaction, that is to finish as quickly as possible. Such a crude method limits very greatly the aesthetic, emotional, affectional embellishments which lie on the spiritual arm of the scale of coitus and which powerfully enhance the ecstasy of sexual communion. Coitus in which the whole of each personality participates, requires time and more leisurely course to the finish. An exhilarating stroll in brisk air and sunshine of two lovers during which there is fascinating, stimulating interplay of the spiritual responses of their

personalities will make it infinitely more thrilling and satisfying the final rush down the hill together, to end in relaxation and sweet repose on the bank of a smoothly flowing stream. From the point of view of quality and fullness of satisfaction there must not be undue haste.

We will consider the procedure by which many men are able to solve the problem of mutual orgasm.

Achieving Simultaneous Orgasm

Most men whose time range is short, find that the irritability which threatens emission is greatly upon entrance. It is advisable, therefore, not to pass on to motion at once but for the partners to rest passive when entrance has been made. It is found that the feeling of impending emission gradually lessens. For the man it may be necessary for the moment to let the mind rest upon non-sexual matters. When the man feels that it is safe, he begins motion gently and not deeply while the mate remains passive — as to action, not as to mood. As the man feels himself again approaching the brink, he stops and both rest. And all along the mates are practising the delicate and subtle interchanges of the art of love which will enhance the vividness and satisfaction of mutual climax manifold when it comes.

The man finds that gradually he secures increasing control and is able to extend each period of motion a little and to deepen the thrust. In a little time he will be ready to ask his partner to join him in gentle motion. He will keep her informed of his progress and both will rest again before the point of ejaculation is reached. And so they continue, their periods of mutual motion becoming steadily longer and more vigorous. Gradually the woman's responses become aroused and now she must keep him informed of her progress and when she is in position to tell him, 'I think I am ready,' then the climactic rush down the hill together begins by both participating in vigorous, synchronous movements. If at the end of his natural course, it is found that the wife has not been able to quite keep up with the husband, he will continue to run with her, so far as sustained erection permits, until she too reaches her destination. It is by such technique that some couples are enabled to prolong the act to a half hour or an hour. It is doubtful that this would be possible for any man with uninterrupted movement.

Probably the majority of women have the idea that motion in coitus belongs exclusively to the husband, except when in orgasm it becomes irresistible. This is a serious error. By participating in motion she not only elicits most powerfully the responses of the husband but facilitates her own orgasm manifold. Van Del Velde[7] says, 'The activity of the man and the passivity of the woman... in an ideal marriage should merge into a melodious mutuality of interaction and response.'

The cases of male inadequacy that are most distressing in their effects and often most difficult for the physician to deal with, are the men of premature ejaculation, who have emission either immediately upon entrance or before entrance has been effected. Of course, virtually all such men are incapable of bringing climactic satisfaction to their spouses in coitus. Fortunately, however, in many cases the factors involved are largely psychological and with friendly or professional assistance, the condition is remediable. The condition is found just as frequently among the most intelligent and educated of men — if not more so — than it is among men of ordinary gifts. No man who is suffering from this inadequacy should permit himself to accept it as one to be endured, because not only will it bar him from ever experiencing the full, energizing satisfactions of vigorously potent sexuality but it will surely frustrate the sex life of his wife, with all the baneful consequences that this holds out.

In many cases, as in newly married men, the condition is a passing one, due mainly to nervousness and inexperience, which adjusts itself when there is a spirit of mutual tolerance and co-operation between couples. But it is of the utmost importance that this condition be rectified early, for every delay operates to fix more deeply the habit of failure, to destroy self-confidence and

[7] *Ideal Marriage.*

lessen the possibility of rectification. Since with premature ejaculation men do have orgasm and hence some sort of satisfaction, there is too easy a tendency on their part to accept the situation and do nothing to remedy it. This is not only a short-sighted and unmanly attitude to take from the point of view of the man's own larger life, but it is utterly selfish in its lack of consideration for the woman. For her it means not merely a low grade of satisfaction, comparable to her husband's, but none at all, with probably the additional exasperation and strain of repeated partial arousal and frustration.

Case Studies of Premature Ejaculation

The extent of this problem is indicated by Dickinson's data already given, that every eighth or ninth man discharges 'instantly.' When we add to this number the men who do so within a minute or so, a condition almost as inadequate for most women, the number becomes greatly increased. Reference to four cases which have come to the writer's attention in recent months may help us to appreciate some of the bearings of this problem.

❑ Attendance by a young wife upon a lecture on marriage enabled her to get some insight into her own marital problem. She sent her husband for consultation. He was a man of good intelligence, holding a responsible business position in a highly competitive field. In sexual matters, however, he was as a very simple child. They had been married three years and in all that time had never achieved even the first stages of coitus. There was persistent premature ejaculation in the mere attempt at coitus. He was by now virtually in a state of psychological impotence. The first advice failed to help much. A medical examination revealed nothing organically wrong. The wife was found to be a normal sexually responsive woman. The couple were very congenial in all other respects but greatly distressed over this situation. They had agreed that if they could not succeed in working out this problem together in the near future, they would separate. Who shall say they should not?

When last seen, little progress had been made. In this case success in solving the problem is doubtful unless physical treatment should be found to provide a basis for a psychological adjustment.

☐ A second couple, also three years married, the husband having all this time experienced quick emission, became seriously estranged. The man had from the first accepted his handicap as inevitable and took no steps towards a satisfactory adjustment. The wife was by nature keenly responsive but the husband's capacity and method could not bring that responsiveness to fruition. The danger to which the wife called attention was realized here (see p. 62). She had found her slumbering responses awakened by another man and divorce impended.

☐ Another couple, exceptionally fine, intelligent and educated young people, unusually free from inhibitions, thoroughly modern in their outlook and attitudes, had been well instructed in sex matters before marriage. They had read together one of the most useful of the books on sex in marriage. They are great lovers — in the general sense — and exceptionally well adapted to one another in temperament and interests. Here seemed to be the possibilities of an ideal marriage.

Five months after the wedding it was found that the wife, though quite normally responsive, had not yet attained orgasm in coitus because of the husband's quick emission. With specific instruction they entered together upon experimentation. The technique suggested was virtually that which we have already explained — no haste, careful entry, rest upon entry, gradual approach to motion, gradual mutual participation in motion, etc. In many cases once full penetration without ejaculation resulting has been achieved, half the battle is won. Success in this case did not come at once but was achieved in a comparatively short time. Mutual orgasms were occurring in a sufficient proportion of copulations to assure ultimately a good adjustment.

❑ Another couple very similar in type and circumstances to the one just described, suffered from the same lack of harmony after six months of marriage, because of the quick emission of the husband. Considerable difficulty has been experienced in working out the problem but this modern young couple, appreciates its importance and the progress made points to ultimate success. Once the wife has achieved orgasm in normal intercourse, ultimate victory is in sight.

If success is not attained after experimenting for a period not exceeding two or three months — preferably sooner the man should consult a reputable genito-urinary specialist. Two promising means are employed; one, to instruct the man in the use of a local anesthetic to be applied beneath the foreskin shortly before coitus with a view to numbing sensibility enough to slow up without preventing ejaculation; the other, to treat the deep urethra to remove excessive irritability. Some specialists claim to get good results by this means. It is important to warn men against falling into the hands of the advertising quack. If he does he will be fleeced of money; he will not likely be helped and he may be injured by the treatment given.

The Rhythms of Desire: Variations in Sexual Response in Women

Failure on the part of a husband to respect and to adapt himself to the wife's natural rhythm of desire is another factor that frequently enters into marital maladjustments. We have seen that in most women desire comes in a more or less well-defined tidal variation which is related to the menstrual cycle. Men do not experience periodic variation in sex desire. Therefore, if they are ignorant of the existence of an ebb and flow rhythm in women, it is difficult for them to understand what seems to them merely variation in temperamental mood. Much friction and unhappiness arises out of this situation. A young couple marries. The young husband finds the wife at times eagerly responsive and participative. Then apparently suddenly there is a change. She is indifferent or cold and perhaps repels his approach. He may take this as an unexpected discovery that she is fickle, temperamental, or does not know her own mind. She, not understanding the differences in their sexual constitutions, may look upon him as inconsiderate and excessive in his demands. Here may be the beginning of misunderstanding and friction. Understanding is first of all necessary for happy adjustment. Each husband must study his wife in this regard. If for her and their mutual happiness it is found necessary to avoid certain periods entirely, in the matter of intercourse, he will respect her wishes. If he finds that it merely requires a diminished frequency and a more lover-like approach and more delicate and more prolonged wooing in prelude, he will gladly and skillfully adapt his art of loving to the needs of her happiness. It goes without saying that perfect frankness between husband and wife is needed in order that the adjustment may be a happy one for both. The wife must help him understand so that his adaptation to her needs and moods may be made with sympathetic appreciation.

It is readily seen that in marital relationships in which the rhythm of woman's desire becomes a factor of adjustment, anything like a set routine in the matter of coitus such as is so commonly followed by married couples, is wholly inappropriate. In the first place such regularity is usually based upon the husband's desires and this fact at once violates the principle of mutuality. In the second place it does not allow for the necessary adaptation to the wife's periodic variation in desire.

These are, however, not the only reasons against making sex relations a matter of satisfying a routine want like the taking of meals. This is living too close to the animal level. It is not the way of love. Love demands spontaneity, change with the changing moods of the sky and with all the influences and circumstances that play upon life. Such routine tends to become unaesthetic and love craves beauty. In love as an art, there will be periods when the passionate expression of love will hold the stage above all other interests, and periods in which the partners will concentrate their thought and energies together upon the serious demands of life to the exclusion of passionate relationship, and again, periods in which other congenial interests and other forms of play and recreation will dominate and when passionate relationships will take a subordinate place. Such a regime will yield mutual joy, development of personality and deepening and widening of relationship as no regularized routine of sex relationship can do. Routine tends towards the commonplace and the commonplace in love becomes deadening.

We have noted the fact that in women sexual responsiveness is largely subject to gradual awakening and development through repeated stimulation and experience. Cases have been cited to show that an adequate capacity may remain dormant during years of marriage for want of the needed appeal and stimulus to arouse and render it active. Ignorance of this characteristic of woman's sex nature leads to too ready an acceptance of the wife's defective responses as her real nature and hence the acceptance of unequal sexual experience as inevitable. In such ways the development of the woman's sexual powers becomes often permanently blocked. Young brides especially, and their husbands, need to be in full possession of this knowledge, so that when the bride, in the early weeks or months of marriage, finds that coitus has little or nothing of the same meaning to her that it has to her husband, she will not suffer shock and bitter disappointment but will apply her intelligence to the problem of her sexual education. The husband likewise will not rest content but will join the wife in the development of method and experiences which will gradually release the wife's natural powers.

Passion is the critical stuff of which the
fabric of marriage is made.

CHAPTER 5

SEXUAL PLEASURE
IN MARRIAGE

$\mathcal{I}$t is our purpose in this chapter to consider some factors in marital sex maladjustments that are less intimately related to sex differences than those discussed in the preceding chapter.

There's Nothing Wrong with Sexual Pleasure

Various references have already been made to influences of negative conditioning through our educational and cultural processes. This influence is so basic, so insidious and so widespread that it needs further consideration. We have two principal objects in view. The first, to aid those approaching marriage to see this menace of cultural refinements and have it out before they come to the altar. Young people need to be freed of every vestige of notion that sex, and passionate sex relations, are in any way ignoble. More than that, they need a positive appreciation of love in its wholeness — as the great dynamic of life and of the fact that with the sex factor eliminated from the love of mates — if that were possible — love loses its dynamic power, and becomes anaemic. The second, that parents, educators and leaders in all agencies that have to do with preparing the young for life may get some inkling of the extent of the damage which our social atmosphere and our cultural methods have done, and are doing, to marriage and the family and through them to society — done in the name of 'purity' and 'chastity' and 'marriage ideals'.

Conscious that in any attempt to estimate natural sexual endowment, the influence of education and religion must be taken into account, Dickinson selected from the 1,098 histories of sex life which he studied, 115 cases of women who were under more-than-average influence of cultural tradition with a view to comparing them with the whole group in reference to the effect of the cultural influences. Eighty-one of these were the wives of husbands engaged in religious occupations and 34 were college women.

In reference to the religious group, the doctor states that the drift of the data is towards a sexual aloofness in marriage for moral reasons. Of the 81 women, 54 were suffering from some form of sexual maladjustment. He says, 'It is intended to suggest, though not to assert, that these inhibitions which no doubt express the whole life code, run parallel to the patient's or the husband's interpretation of religious instruction.'

The point of view of the average woman in Dickinson's group is to the effect that sex is low, that it is concerned with the lowest part of herself; and this attitude is frequently shared by the husband. Such expressions as, 'There is something wrong in sex pleasure,' 'He will never dress or undress before me,' are examples of the many expressions used which reveal an apologetic attitude towards the sexual side of marriage. Dickinson remarks, in reference to the husbands, 'The wives of these... husbands are not free to take a spontaneous attitude toward sexual life; they have to fulfill the husband's ideal. To establish the other half of his theory, the really consistent wife must be somewhat cold.'

To approach the histories of the 34 college women with the expectation of finding a more favourable indication of cultural influence, as it would seem reasonable to expect, is to court serious disappointment. These women are a cross-section representative of the interaction of higher education and sexuality. They are of 'notably good health, and average fertility, but on every count hesitant when it comes to love.' This withdrawal from the sexual is largely on aesthetic grounds. The doctor says that an ordinary group of 34 patients selected at random would have come first for reasons of physical health, but 21 of these came first for consultation about sexual questions.

Here is the appalling record of the group: 'Of sexual adjustment in marriage, 11 had no complaint; of the others, 8 were frigid, 6 had dyspareunia; 3 were maladjusted; 2 were separated; 3 intended to divorce; and one had a divorce. This makes the ratio of maladjustment 23 out of 34, or 2 out of 3.'

Only 12 women gave data about coitus. Of these, 2 had had intercourse once in three months; 2 once in five months; one, monthly; one for procreation only; the others from one to three times a week. In 16 cases the wife had orgasm; in 15 cases she had it rarely or never; for 3 no data were given.

The doctor says of these women that their sexual reluctance was the most impressive single detail. He remarks, 'that only a third are adjusted in marriage and that 6 have come to separation or divorce may be a coincidence; but the sexual reluctance which winds through so many stories has distinct meaning.' The fact that while of the 1,098 histories of sex life 37.5 per cent have sexual maladjustment at some period, of the group of 115 women of religious and higher education tradition 67.5 per cent are sexually reluctant, is certainly noteworthy. Dickinson is careful to say, 'Nothing is proved by such small numbers as are here concerned, but it is significant that on assembling those who live under cultural taboo more arduous than the average, a higher degree of sexual maladjustment is present.'

It is no time to talk of the breakdown of monogamous marriage so long as the cultural traditions, the educational processes and the social atmosphere of our time tend so definitely and so powerfully to twist and distort and negatively condition the mating instinct, not only in those years in youth when it becomes a conscious impelling force, but even in the earliest years of childhood when attitudes and life-partners are taking form. It will be time enough to question the adaptability of the traditional marriage ideal to a modern world, when our boasted scheme of education and religious culture will function to speed the feet of youth toward love's high goal with the wings of a free spirit instead of forging shackles upon their limbs.

Sex Education

In the recent years a marked improvement in sex education has appeared. Parents everywhere are getting a new point of view; the younger parents particularly are manifesting earnest concern over these problems of sex education and are applying their intelligence to their solution. Some schools are gradually modifying their curricula so as to integrate sex education to aid in life adjustments and family life.

A recent study of the status of sex education in the colleges made by the writer showed that out of 111 institutions, only 105 were giving some measure of attention to teaching student to orient himself in life in respect to the sex factor. To be sure, the picture is not so rosy as these figures would indicate. Most of such teaching is as yet extremely fragmentary and haphazard. Only 30 of the 105 institutions giving some attention to sex education could be rated as doing a reasonably adequate task. It is regrettable that the large institutions and particularly the large state universities are as yet most neglectful of this aspect of successful living.

In the field of religious education too, there has appeared in recent years a rapid awakening to the need and responsibility for this aspect of the social education of the young. The emphasis in religious education circles upon specific education for marriage is particularly heartening. Altogether we seem to be well in the dawn of a better day, pointing towards the time when the social compulsions in matters of sexual love will be towards positive, not negative results.

To youth approaching marriageable age, it is pertinent to suggest that each individual put himself (or herself) through a rigid course of self-analysis, going back over the years of youth and

of childhood, with a view to gathering up the sex impressions, incidents and experiences and the whole general atmosphere that has been absorbed, and of bringing it all before the bar of reason. Attempt to diagnose and evaluate your real inner attitude towards sexual love and its passionate expression in marriage. If in a fair facing up to your inner feelings in these matters you become conscious of the restraining grip of cultural compulsions, set about at once upon a course of self-reeducation, and become thoroughly liberated from that grip before you join your chosen mate on the journey of life together — 'for better or for worse.' Starting with unfettered spirit it may be for the better, and even better.

Frigidity: Sexual hesitation, concealed desires.

Most of the major factors in sex frustration which we have so far discussed spring into prominence and merge when we discuss frigidity, and none more so than the factor we have considered in the preceding section, namely, cultural compulsives.

Frigidity in women is commonly thought of as a congenital absence of sex desire or incapacity for sexual response. Such absolute frigidity, in which all the factors are invariably negative and the woman is definitely anesthetic sexually, is rare. The condition we are discussing is one in which one or another factor or a complex of factors, operates to block sexuality against fulfillment somewhere along its course. Dickinson's study of 1(such cases is illuminating. The condition of frigidity was shown be mainly an affair of the marriage. The husband's function was question as well as the wife's. In 19 of these cases, original sexu capacity and interest in the husband at some time were shown a some had had full sexual experience, but somewhere along the li the woman's sexual capacity was diverted to coldness and negati

Twenty-four wives said their marriage was happy and 49 m indicated nothing contrary to happiness except the trouble w coitus. Eighteen stated they were unhappy, and 9 more w presumed to be so by certain complaints of the wife. One-fou of total were then to be classed as unhappy.

Of their sexual relations the doctor says,

'The characteristic coitus of these couples is brief and physiologically male, the female remaining passive and isolate. Once or twice a week there takes place, without preliminaries, an intromission lasting up to five minutes, at the end of which the husband has an orgasm and the wife does not. Both the man and the woman know that the woman has no animating desire. She submits without welcome to the embrace; it may occur without excitement and she expects it to terminate without orgasm. There is no other topic upon which a woman will talk with so much grief and bitterness.'

In half of the 53 cases reporting, the orgasm was not experienced; 24 women had never experienced the climax; 3 had had it formerly but not now; 21 had had it sometime and 5 rarely. Some had had orgasm in autoerotic practice, others had not known what it was.

Dickinson concludes that the term 'frigid woman' is poetical exaggeration; that frigidity is better understood as sexual hesitation, which takes some other than the expected course. He says, 'It trails passion as concealed desire and is a manifestation not of the absence of sexuality but of its direction away from the primitive satisfaction goal of the sexual embrace. In this series there is no case in which desire has not begun.'

We have presented these data not for the purpose of painting a gloomy picture of unhappy prospects in marital sex relations, but for the purpose of pointing out the possibility of solving these problems. There is nothing gained by dodging realities. If these conditions are to be prevented or corrected we need to be conscious of their existence, of their prevalence and of the factors and influence of which they are a consequence. If frigidity were an inborn state there would be nothing we could do about it with present knowledge. We have seen that the fault lies somewhere between the husband and the wife. They have lost the way somewhere in the course of their marital journey. A solution may

come through mutual co-operative application of intelligence, courage and effort to find the right way.

Whatever other factors may exist — and there may be many remote and obscure ones not yet understood — it is obvious that in these cases the common factors of marital sex maladjustments which we have already discussed are all at work. There is common ignorance; want of understanding of one another's sexual constitutions and even of their own; a social heritage of compulsion and attitudes which, in the woman, dispose toward negation and in the man towards a low, self-centred order of sexuality; there is crude, unintelligent method which utterly fails the woman; there is quick emission; there is no knowledge of and hence no regard for woman's periodicity of desire; and finally there is complete ignorance of the art of love. There is neither prelude nor postlude and the whole technique throughout is comparable to a person without the elements of music attempting to play sonata on a violin with a rasp. Dickinson remarks that none of these records contains evidence of a husband who was a great lover.

The way of prevention is to be sought first, in clearing the cobwebs and bars of inhibiting cultural traditions; second, in an adequate untrammelled knowledge of sex in life and how it may be made to contribute most richly to human happiness. The remedy demands a rigorous re-education to the same end, plus patient, tolerant learning together of the art of loving, practised in accord with the essential constitution of their respective natures. There is no royal road to the goal but a royal reward awaits those who reach the goal.

Dyspareunia: Painful Sexual Intercourse

Dyspareunia is the technical term for painful coitus. In general it is in effect but another form of frigidity. The frigid woman expresses her aversion or rebellion in coldness, the woman with dyspareunia, expresses them in pain. A difference between the two groups, is that the latter insists on physical cause. (Dyspareunia is to be distinguished from vaginismus, which is a condition of muscular spasm of the vagina which obstructs or prevents male entry.)

In the Dickinson Beam study, 175 cases of painful coitus were selected for special study. In the introductory summary of the chapter on the subject, it is said 'Pain to the wife in coitus appears as a form of frigidity among patients of the established social type, of ordinary health and marital condition. This condition may last for years and is characterized by low fertility and impoverished love life, yet it is impossible to establish physical cause in nearly half the cases. The remaining couples, including the married virgins, live on the emotional level of a psychic handicap accepted by both. Pain is endured for a long time before seeking relief. Cure of the pain is usual but not the return of enthusiasm. The cases illustrate both physical and psychic dyspareunia, with varying cause, circumstance and effect.'

It was found that these women brought to marriage the usual history of shocks and inhibitions. The sexual impulse in them was asserted in about the same proportion as in the entire thousand cases, as was also self-experimentation. Nearly half of the group admitted occasional auto-erotism and 30 more who denied it showed the characteristic signs. Of the 70 cases who claimed dyspareunia throughout the entire marriage period, 11 gave accounts of repulsion on the bridal night and as many more spoke of painful and distasteful beginnings.

The wife's attitude in coitus was recorded as positive pleasure in 21 cases, indifference in 48 cases, and various grades of distaste and fear in 36 cases. This means that only one woman in 5 was pleased in sexual intercourse.

After presenting the full data about this group of women, the doctor says of them, 'These data about sexuality have a familiar aspect. They are quite parallel with the data about frigidity and other forms of negative attitude. Except as pain for physical reason can be shown, we are dealing in these 175 cases only with a specialized form of frigidity.'

According to this group, the possibility of complete cure is not impressive. Twenty-three women were not cured of sensitiveness, 64 stopped having pain but remained without pleasure, 14 afterwards discovered an actual sexual life with climax and 74 were not followed up.

The writer wishes to observe that the lack of more favourable results as to sexuality in these cases raises the question how far, along with the treatment given by the physician, can there be brought about an improvement in the general situation which impelled these women toward sexual negation. It is clear that all of the factors which we noted in relation to frigidity have been at work in these cases also. Aside from sexual factors it is readily understood that so long as prudish attitudes, fears, shocks, ignorance, premature ejaculation, too brief intromission, want of emotional prelude and the rest continue to be operative, no better results can be expected. In addition to what the physician may do, the situation requires a rather radical reeducation and readjustment in the interactions of the mates in the sphere of their sexual life, a radical change in attitudes, personal relationship and techniques.

One woman gave the clue in the remark, 'The hurt of the first night disgusted me; he never tried to make me like it.' The real problem is to make her like it. The capacity is there but the total situation blocks it of fulfillment. Can it be released? The answer probably is that once this sort of situation has become set in an accepted mould, a radical improvement, in most cases, is difficult.

It is for this reason that the emphasis is to be placed upon prevention. The solution of these difficulties must come before marriage through a background of knowledge, understanding, insight, and appreciation, so as to develop more positive attitudes and equip men and women to adjust, develop and harmonize their sexual capacities and needs for happy fellowship and mutual satisfaction. In the last analysis the extent of frigidity and dyspareunia are a terrible reflection upon our education and social training.

Sex: Fear of the Unknown

While the problem of fear is of profound importance in a study of human sexuality, it is not our purpose to attempt a detailed analysis of the subject in this book.[1] It is a complex subject. Sexual fears cannot be isolated from life as a whole. They are usually an expression of a generally fearful attitude towards life. The women who list their sexual fears also have miscellaneous fears: of animals, the dark, burglars, noise, machinery, poison in food, sin, punishment, strange men, etc. It indicates that in those persons in whom fear is a factor in sex frustration the problem needs to be approached from a broader base than the sexual alone.

We have already shown that while in a certain proportion sexual fears in marriage have their origin in marital experience, in the main such fears trace back to cultural taboo and to earlier shocking experiences often reinforced by unpleasant experiences in marriage. The fundamental approach to the problem must come by way of a more sane education and social culture. For every man and woman approaching marriage, it becomes a task of self-analysis and re-education. From a practical point of view, this is where emphasis must be placed. Nothing paralyses sexual capacities and powers more completely and more quickly than fear. The fearful man cannot get or sustain erection; the fearful woman cannot respond. Success in these respects requires assurance, confidence, poise. As has been already shown, an attitude of fear means not merely frustration of the immediate act but a tendency to ultimate personality of sexual negation.

The Fear of Pregnancy

The particular fear to which we wish to give consideration here is the fear of pregnancy. This is a question which every couple must face intelligently and resolutely. If marital happiness and health are to be assured, the fear of pregnancy must not be allowed to hang as a sword suspended by a thread over the marital bed, at such

---

[1] An analysis of the subject as related to Dr Dickinson's case studies will be found in a chapter on Fear in his book, *A Thousand Marriages.*

times when pregnancy definitely does not fit into the life scheme of the couple. This naturally raises the questions of contraceptive measures.

It is not the purpose of the writer to persuade anyone for or against the use of contraceptives for the purpose of regulating or limiting procreation. We are insisting, however, that in the interest of marital success and happiness the question must be faced and settled. For reasoning human beings, every aspect of life that is not beyond volitional control should be brought under intelligent direction and control and not left to the play of haphazard influences. Certainly this applies to so fundamental and vital a human interest and function as the begetting of children. What we would stress, however, is intelligent regulation of procreation, not its avoidance. There is as much need for stressing both the personal and social importance and advantages of having children as there is of stressing the evils to the family and society of excessive and unregulated bearing of children. Those who deliberately avoid having any children at all need to be helped to understand and appreciate the fact that they are thereby blocking for themselves one of the highways of life toward self-realization and full, rich living. No compensation can wholly make up for this loss. Any movement for 'birth control' should be a movement for rational parenthood which works in both directions.

Contraceptives Make Sense

Common sense leads most couples sooner or later to resort to contraceptives in order to make child bearing fit into an ordered family scheme even while they may retain mental uncertainty or reservations about the propriety or ethics of doing so. Such mental uncertainty is unfortunate, for it necessarily partakes of the nature of fear and tends to inhibit sexual response and foster disharmony. While common sense dictates intelligent regulation, organized opposition of religious sanctions, serves to engender mental conflict. From the point of view of its bearing upon happily adjusted marriage, every couple needs to think the matter through to a conclusion, one way or the other, which will eliminate such conflict. Whatever the way out may be for any couple, it is of great importance that fear of pregnancy be reduced to the minimum, if not wholly excluded in marriage.

One point bearing on the use of contraceptives needs mention. The successful and most satisfying management of the act of coitus requires undivided attention from the beginning of love-play to the completion of the act. Any diversion is inhibiting, if not fatal, to a successful conclusion. We have already suggested that sexual intercourse should not be made too largely a matter of regularized routine but should follow upon mutual desire arising out of the general affectional relationship of the mates. When desire has arisen in such a way and both partners have become stimulated to the point of readiness for coitus, it often becomes exasperatingly distracting or completely inhibiting to have to go about making preparation for contraceptive measures. This is particularly true for men who have difficulty in securing or sustaining erection. This naturally leads to the suggestion that among the various methods considered effective, those be chosen which require the minimum of fussing, and that the means required be kept most conveniently at hand. Some women have solved the problem by making preparation as a part of their *toillete* for the night whether intercourse be anticipated or not.

In the choice of contraceptive means, it is important to be warned against hearsay. Advice as to choice of means and specific instruction, as to their use should be secured from reputable physicians, preferably specialists in the fields.

Premarital Sex Experience: Is it Desirable?

Young men have often contended that premarital sex experience is desirable in that it is of value in achieving successful sexual relationships in marriage. With the growing emancipation among women the same questions has been raised increasingly by them also. The question deserves to be scrutinized with care. We are not here concerned with the moral aspects of the matter but only with the possible bearing of such experience upon satisfactory marital adjustment. On the face of it, it would seem that logic favours those who assert this view. Does experience support logic on this point?

There is no question that in some cases experience in sex relations has been of service in working out a successful relationship after marriage. On the whole, however, the facts seem to be against it. This is easily appreciated when we consider how very different is the relationship, and the conditions of sexual intercourse, between a man and a promiscuous woman, from the relationship and the conditions that obtain in coitus with a wife. In marital sex relations, the act is the most intimate expression of the affections, of love passionately expressed. Aside from any procreative purpose it involves regard for personality, unselfish seeking of the highest satisfaction and happiness of the mate, or rather of finding the fullest personal satisfaction in the happiness and fullness of the love experience of the partner. It means the fullest and most harmonious physical and emotional interplay of the two personalities, all to the same end of mutual satisfaction and happiness. It means the study and exercise of the delicate and skilful art of loving. It involves an artful prelude of love.

In sexual intercourse of a man with a promiscuous woman the relationship and the conditions are almost completely reversed. Affection, regard for personality and unselfish consideration for the experience of the woman, except as consideration of her may enhance his own pleasure, are either wholly absent or reduced to the lowest terms. The experience is essentially self-centred, and mainly on a physical level. There is no need to study or to practise any skilful art of loving, no need for emotional prelude. Crude technique which serves the purpose of intercourse in such relations is all that is expected and practised. Excess, too, is the rule. The man who spends a night or an hour with a promiscuous woman purposes to get all he can out of it. To see 'how many times I can stay with the woman' is a common expression of such men. Having gained their conception and experience of sex relations in such connections and on such a plane, the tendency is to carry over into marriage the atmosphere, attitude, ideas, technique and habits thus acquired, with the result that they mess up the whole situation. Unquestionably the crudities, the selfishness and the excesses which so largely shock and freeze women into frigidity have a source in premarital experience of this type.

Premarital sex experience among acquaintances and friends who are not necessarily promiscuous is not to be considered in the same class with those just discussed. In the main, however, they differ from them in degree rather than in kind. For the most part such relations are self-seeking and self-regarding only in lesser degree. Statistics of such experiences indicate less favourable results from them than might be expected. A mutual understanding of one another's sexual make-up and of their own, on the part of lovers; a knowledge of the physiological and psychological elements; and a theoretical insight into the kind and quality of technique required, as a background and basis for mutual adaptation in marriage, seem to serve as a more reliable equipment for happy marriage than premarital sex experience. There is a wide range for mutual adaptation and adjustment in marriage provided there is understanding and the spirit and will to adjust.

Certain data in Hamilton's study are significant. He correlated premarital sex experience with degree of satisfaction in marriage. In both the men and the women it was found that a significantly higher percentage of those who were virgin at marriage had a 'fair to high degree of satisfaction' in marriage than did those who had had premarital sex experience. These data seem to point to the probability at least that premarital sex experiences weighted against rather than for advantage in promoting happy adjustment in marriage.

So far as women are concerned there is another important consideration. We have noted the difference between men and women in response to sex stimuli. On the whole women are protected by nature much more than men are against quick and easy arousal of specific desire and passion. The difference gives rise to much misunderstanding between engaged couples. Until sex arousal of the woman has gone beyond a certain point the man has a more difficult problem of control. What with him tends easily to become physical passions may long remain in her case a generalized glow of love. Each, however, is prone to assume that the experience of the partner is identical with his or her own. When, therefore, the passionate ardour of the man becomes manifest to the woman, she may hold him in disrespect as being 'animal'. He, assuming that the woman shares his experience, is prone, to act accordingly and thereby complicate the misunderstanding.

The point we are coming to, however, is the fact that once a woman has been fully aroused and has experienced the culmination of the sex relation, she can never be the same woman again. If her marriage does not follow, her problem now approaches that of the man. Dunlap says, 'After the psychological life of the woman has been once developed, she is a different person and her personal problems, previously rather simple, become much more like those of the man. The woman, therefore, who achieves her sex education without marriage is in a peculiarly unfortunate position, a prey not only to the enormous force which has been liberated in her life, but a prey also to the large group of males who constantly seek to play upon these forces. The attitude which men frequently take towards the inexperienced woman, namely, that the responsibility of her actions rests upon her alone, if she consents to sex relations, can therefore have no palliation except on the assumption that such are densely ignorant of the psychology of woman. The fact is that in few cases can she possibly know beforehand the consequences of the step which she may contemplate. It is not necessary to assume anything essentially wrong in sex experience, or even in promiscuity; the serious ethical problem grows out of the psychological facts, together with the fixed definite conventions of the social system from which no individual can escape.

'On the other hand, the more fully the woman or girl understands this situation, the more capable she is of protecting herself. Knowing that once having entered upon a new realm of experience, no return to the former security is possible, and that the complexities of the new life are such that she cannot evaluate them in advance; and that society is so organized that woman is put at every possible disadvantage in dealing with these complexities; she is not apt to entertain lightly an experimental attitude. Further, the young woman should know the awakening of her sex desire is a smoothly progressive process, beginning in details that may seem to her not in the least dangerous, but grading by small steps to a culmination in which she has no further control; and that she cannot foresee the point at which control will be lost.'

The whole range of sexual acts must bring the same harmonious experience of love and joy to both partners.

CHAPTER 6

IDEAL MARRIAGE

*H*aving considered the sexual factors we shall now look at other factors which contribute to a successful, happily adjusted marriage.

It is our purpose to ground the discussion as solidly as possible, upon the facts of human nature and upon experience. For a number of years the writer has focused observation upon the successful marriages, rather than the failures, for two reasons: he found an increasing number of modern young people, especially young women, say something like this, 'I am afraid of marriage. I look about among my acquaintances and friends and I do not find any of them making a go of it, not the kind that would suit me. If that is what marriage means, none of it for me!' This was disturbing if true. The writer sat down with a pencil and paper and let his mind roam over his rather large circle of acquaintances and friends, jotting down those marriages, which from intimate knowledge, he could rate high in degree of success. He sought out mainly couples who had reached at least middle life and hence had demonstrated the wearing qualities of their marital relationships.

The exercise proved to be most heartening. While the highly successful marriages were proportionately all too few among those that could be termed 'adjusted', there was nevertheless a fair proportion which had justified the high hopes with which every normal couple makes the venture. Quite a few among these represented marriage at its best — couples in their sixties and seventies who were lovers more genuinely and firmly than they could have been in the days of glowing youth — a love that had never lost its romance; a companionship which had not ceased its growth, which had become sweeter, broader, deeper and more serene with the passing years; a person's relationship which furnished the conditions for the fullest development of the self; a fellowship which forced the very hardships of life to contribute to a deeper harmony and a firmer spiritual bond. The writer felt that so long as there were so many of such wonderful examples of what marriage may become, there is no need to be unduly pessimistic about marriage. The tragedy of the situation is that many who did not reach these levels might well have done so, had society, which impels them to marriage, either blindfold or with distorted visions, guided their steps — and their heads and hearts — in the path where success may best be achieved.

A higher rate of dissatisfaction among young married couples today is not altogether an unmitigated evil. Certainly one factor is that they expect and demand more of marriage than their parents and grandparents expected and demanded. Upon the whole they enter upon marriage with a higher ideal. On the other hand, they are not much better equipped to attain that higher satisfaction and ideal than their predecessors were. We are going through a period of tremendous and rapid transition in all human relationships and in none so great as in the relationships of the sexes.

A second reason for searching out the highly successful marriages was the fact that they need searching out. The smoothly going, happily adjusted, highly satisfactory marriages do not obtrude themselves upon public attention. They are not news. They have no sensational or dramatic quality. They are not food for tabloids. It is not about them that the stage, the screen and the novelist build their plots. No, it is the marriage in which there is conflict, maladjustment, clash, cruelty, suffering, unfaithfulness, desertion and the like that hold the stage and come to the public eye. These facts tend to give a distorted perspective of the marriage life.

The positive factors which we shall discuss are essentially those which are found to have played their part in highly successful and happy marriages.

The Marriage Ideal

What in reality is marriage? Is it a legal bond, a contract? A social institution? A business partnership, or an association for legalized cohabitation? All of these may enter in but they represent marriage only in a legal or conventional sense. They represent the social sanctions of marriage, and social sanctions are needed, for society has a tremendous stake in marriage. But essentially, marriage is a personal relationship, a mutual psychological state, a spiritual bond. The stamp of legal and social approval alone cannot really marry two people. They can become truly married only as a result of a psychological process which unites them in a personal relationship which makes possible a growing companionship in which each may progressively find life's richest fulfillment.

Marriages have come about by various procedures and from a variety of motives. Many have been arranged by parents without choice on the part of the couple, and many of these have proved successful. Many have taken place from motives of economic security, to escape the stigma of old maid or old bachelor or what not, and many of such have turned out successfully. But whenever a marriage has come to have spiritual significance, it has been because the parties arrived at a psychological union of the two personalities, at a personal relationship which essentially is marriage. Harris says, 'At its best, marriage is a personal partnership of love and esteem.'

It is the lack of this creative companionship in many marriages, more than any other thing, that makes young people question marriage. The adolescent youth senses instinctively that the deepest yearnings of life are to find complete satisfaction and fulfillment in union and companionship with a mate. But youth today is disposed to view this ideal against a background of reality. They learn that in the United States there now occurs one[1] divorce to about every six marriages; it is obvious that a much larger proportion continue to live together in the same maladjustments which lead others to separation; they observe particularly that a still larger proportion of marriages which society views as successful achieves no more than a commonplace, bread-and-butter relationship, bereft of spiritual significance and beauty. Unfortunately they tend to stop here and fail to note and to study that upper level of marriages in which lovers have become genuinely married psychologically and spiritually; in which an intimate companionship makes life richer because of the sharing; which has made marriage truly 'the great adventure, and fulfilled the adolescent ideal and dream.

Sex in Happy Marriage

Harris says[2], 'The future of monogamous marriage depends upon the degree to which we can bring ourselves to appreciate it as a personal relationship and to address ourselves to the genuine personal problems involved. The state, the church, and even the home seemingly have been content as long as the external decencies have been observed; the splendid possibilities of creative companionship have been shamelessly neglected. The present-day demands for more freedom, for easier divorce, for trial marriage are not necessarily symptoms of depravity. A sympathetic view discerns in them the protest against a conventional conception of marriage which persists in regarding it simply as a social institution and studiously disregards or minimizes the human interests involved.

The whole possibility of a deeper experience in the futures lies within the area of the personal relationship and that relationship will never be explored adequately until there is achieved a reasonable adjustment between the persons concerned.' The issue

---

[1] This must not be taken to mean that one out of every six marriages will fail.
[2] *Essays on Marriage.*

is stated in the words of Harris, 'Circumstances are remorseless. They have forced us to face the plain truth that an ill-adjusted personal relationship in marriage falls apart no matter what legal, social or religious support is brought to its aid, whilst a satisfactory partnership seems so easily to resist all assaults made upon it that sometimes death itself is powerless to dissolve it.'

It will be readily seen that psychologic marriage, marriage as a creative personal relationship, is an achievement between mates and is not necessarily entered into at the wedding; indeed it seldom is. In most cases the wedding is but the point of departure towards marriage, a beginning of that vital relationship which essentially is marriage. Some arrive quickly at this first goal which joins them in unity of spirit, preparing them to set out further upon the adventurous quest. Others must travel for varying periods of time before they reach that marriage milestone, and how many there are who tramp that road together for years and have their children, but never arrive at marriage in any true sense!

Marriage is not only an achievement; it is a difficult achievement. It means nothing less than a harmonious adjustment of two different personalities — the most complex creations in the universe. It requires intelligent study, devoted application and rigid self-discipline. No couple can safely expect to drift into an ideal marriage relationship. The currents are apt to smash their ship upon the rocks.

We have in this book dwelt upon the fundamental character of the sex factor in happily adjusted marriage. While an ill adjusted sex relationship will certainly prove the greatest of hindrances to the achieving or sustaining of a creative, personal companionship, a permanently satisfying sex relationship is not likely to be attained or sustained without the spiritual unity which is the essence of that personal relationship.

Choosing your Spouse
No subject discussed in this book deserves greater emphasis than the subject of mate choice. The unintelligent, impulsive, emotional

basis upon which so many marriages are entered into render maladjustment and failure a foregone conclusion. Whatever else may enter into an abidingly happy marriage, there must be first of all a reasonable harmony of character qualities, such as a degree of compatibility that will make possible the mutual adjustment necessary for a satisfying companionship.

During courtship and engagement lovers are prone to keep the best foot forward; to display the more agreeable side of their natures. In marriage they must meet life together, not alone on the mountain top of inspiration and in its shady dells of peace, but in the hard, wearing grind of a work-a-day world. They must meet life under conditions that bring out the angles and unlovely sides of their natures. Then will come the test as to whether their natures are compatible to a degree that love may build a supporting and inspiring companionship upon these very irritations and hardships of life, and lift their marriage relationship above them, or whether their natures will clash to turn love anaemic and eventually cause its death. Lichtenberger remarks, 'The glamorous halo which surrounds courtship makes it difficult for lovers to discover or to disclose their true selves, or to appraise qualities in each other which under the greater intimacies of married life would possess enduring charm or which would tend to mar endearing companionship. Hence the disillusionment which often follows marriage.'

A fine example of frankly facing up to this situation on the part of a pair of lovers came to attention not long ago. They were deeply and genuinely in love. They had many interests in common — literary, artistic, musical and the love of nature. Their tastes harmonized well. 'An ideal combination for a happy, enduring marriage', most observers would have said. Yet these lovers found their companionship marred by a fundamental antagonism they found difficult to pin down. They found they did not naturally entrust their confidences to one another. There was an ill-defined but effective wall between them at points where love requires freedom and mutuality.

These young people were intelligent and courageous. They talked the matter through frankly and sympathetically and agreed that it was best for them not to marry. The ordeal cost heart wrenching and tears, but their ultimate happiness was at stake and the price was not too great to pay.

Genuine, mutual love as a first requirement for successful marriage is generally taken for granted. Where young people need help is in discriminating between what is genuine and what is spurious in love. Physical attraction and harmony between mates is indispensable. Marriage rests upon that biological base. But physical attraction alone, however thrilling and breathtaking it may be, is not enough. Such attraction, unsupported by the finer spiritual elements of love, can in a year, a month, turn to satiety, indifference, disgust. Genuine love is an affectionate response to the whole personality of the loved one, a response infused with utmost respect and abiding confidence. Love requires the test of time in the midst of the varied exigencies of life.

But even love of the more genuine kind does not necessarily assure happiness. There must be at bottom such a degree of compatibility of the two personalities as will not foredoom marriage to failure but make possible a harmonious adjustment. We must guard against expecting perfection here. Human nature at best has many weaknesses. Fortunately, when supported by a genuine unselfish affection and an appreciation of what is involved, and a will to adjust, it has also great capacities for adjustment. We are not arguing for perfection, but for an intelligent discrimination which will rightly evaluate the possibilities. It needs to be urged that such intellectual evaluation needs to come before the emotions have become so deeply involved that judgment becomes hopelessly unreliable. The choice of a mate requires at best a judicious mixture of discriminating intelligence and emotion.

Sound Health. All of life is limited by the functioning of the physical mechanism, the marriage relationship not excepted. From every point of view it calls for a reasonable degree of constitutional vigour. Occasional serious illness is to be expected. Where there is a harmonious affectionate relationship such time will serve only to deepen that affection and call out the reserves of unselfish devotion and sacrifice. But a persistently ailing or constitutionally neurotic husband or wife is almost certain to prove a formidable obstacle to a permanently happy and adjusted marriage. General lack of health and vigour is prone to affect sexual harmony adversely, to limit the marriage relationship in all other respects, and to render sustained tempermental harmony unusually difficult.

We have in literature and in experience, those rare examples of building an exquisite structure of life-long affectionate devotion upon the physical frailties of one of the mates. We do them honour and hold them in highest respect, but the significant thing is that they are so rare. Successful marriage, as all of life, requires a sound physical base. It is important to face this question not only as a matter of the apparent health of the individual but in the light of the inherited constitutional vigours of the family for at least two generations.

Compatibility of Temperament. The unhappy group of wives in Dr. Davis's study listed 23 reasons for marital unhappiness. Incompatibility of temperament or interests stands at the head of the list as the most frequently mentioned, being about 30 per cent of the total. Lichtenberger says, 'There are temperaments or dispositions which are organically incompatible and which under the strain of domesticity become morbidly antagonistic.' Temperaments need to be tested out before marriage, not only at dates when lovers are on their best behaviour, but under trying situations such as will be met together in married life.

Harmony of temperaments need not be perfect. It rarely is. But there must be compatibility to a degree that, coupled with intelligence, sympathy and the will to adjust, will make possible a harmonious relationship. Serious clashing of temperaments before marriage is a warning to be earnestly heeded. The test in marriage comes not usually over big issues but in life's nagging daily routine. As Harris puts it, 'The strain of married life is serious; it is no picnic. After all it is not perhaps the 'great difficulties' that cause most of the trouble; it is the constant rub of what we have foolishly called little things occurring every day that stir up the pre-eminent irritations.'

A Community of Interests. The heart of personal relationships is the sharing of interests common to both partners. For a sustained and growing companionship it is imperative that the mates have enough interests they can share, enough things they enjoy doing together, to furnish material for companionship. A lack of common interests will tend to drift lovers apart or sink their relationship to commonplace, drab levels.

This does not mean, as is often supposed, that in the marital partnership all of life is to be shared. Actually the proportion of their daily interests and activities which most husbands and wives share is quite limited. Harris says, 'Even under the best of circumstances there are ranges of experience which are not shared between husband and wife and some few perhaps which never can be shared.' He suggests that the partnership as such comprises those interests which are shared by husband and wife, and its success generally depends upon the degree to which those shared interests can satisfy both. On this point Walter Lippman says,[3] 'Lovers who have nothing to do but love each other are not really to be envied; love and nothing else very soon is nothing else.'

An all too common experience is for couples to drift apart because the one grows while the other stagnates. Such a calamity is forestalled in a relationship in which the mates have congenial interests to share, in which the habit of sharing is mutual and in which from time to time the partners extend their interests and their sharing into new fields.

Harmony of Tastes and Desires. What we want and what pleases us is much more important than what we know, for we are governed more by our desires and our tastes than we are by our knowledge. Clashes in tastes are more serious and threatening than intellectual differences. They tend to limit companionship and

---

[3] *A Preface to Morals,* George Allen & Unwin Ltd.

become a serious strain in the marriage relationship. A wide range of common interests coupled with agreement in tastes presents a large and fascinating world for married lovers to explore together and in which to grow together.

Harmony in Habits. Human beings are creatures of habit. By the time we are 25 years of age our habits of life are pretty well rooted. Let not lovers be deceived into believing that they can radically change one another in their habits. Let them rather make sure before marriage that they and their respective habits have the capacity to adjust to one another. There is probably no area of the marital relationship in which friction is more likely to arise than the areas of their habits. For example, a neat housewife who is annoyed by disorder and a careless, slovenly husband, are certain to try one another's patience severely. Many divorces trace back to such sources.

Harmony of Character Qualities. We need not attempt to define specifically, but we have in mind such qualities as honesty, integrity, dependability, initiative, courage, loyalty, unselfishness, mutual consideration and others that go to make up the composite of a worthy, attractive character. Neither of the partners must expect perfection. Rather each must let a wholesome consciousness of his or her own human weaknesses develop a growing sympathy and tolerance toward the weaknesses of the partner.

We have discussed sketchily the bases for harmony in respect to certain important qualities of personality and character which must be weighed with care in mate choice. They represent a series of fundamental adjustments to be made in marriage. Studies of marital experience increasingly show that when the sex relationship is soundly adjusted there is good prospect of making the other adjustments also, provided, of course, there exists a personal relationship of genuine affection and equality; but that with serious maladjustment in the sexual area, there is slim chance of making a satisfying adjustment in other aspects.

Courtship and Engagement

Courtship leading up to engagement is the chief period of exploring, discovering and testing the other party. This is the period in which there needs to be not only a judicious mixture of intelligence and emotion but a dominance of the intellectual critical faculty, exercised particularly at those times when the emotions are most fully in abeyance. All the elements which enter into mate choice need to be fairly weighed in the full consciousness. It is important that the companionship of the courting period embrace a wide range of interests, activities and situations best calculated to reveal the personality and character. It is a time for testing not only the reactions and responses of the other party, but of one's own reactions to one's companion. One's discoveries need constantly to be projected against the background of the marriage situation with the questions, how will we wear in the daily grind?

The lovers should not allow themselves to regard the relationship as an irrevocable commitment. It is best that it continue to remain one of exploration and testing so that in case either one should conclude that marriage would be unwise, no breach of good faith would be involved; engagement usually and quite properly opens up new areas of intimacy and comradeship which render the exploration more searching and revealing.

The question as to whether engagements should be long or short cannot be settled categorically. It depends upon the situation in each case, and much depends upon what has gone before. From the point of view of sound choice, the engagement period should be long enough to evaluate the resources of the two personalities and their compatibilities. If the courting period has furnished such a basis then engagement may well be brief. From the point of view of the sex factor, long engagements are on the whole not desirable. Biologically engagement is an abnormal state. The relationship is one which tends to stimulate and arouse the sexual urges, while it does not appropriately permit their normal, fulfilling release. In many cases the situation becomes one of severe strain. The reasons for and against a long engagement may come into conflict and both need to enter into the consideration.

Sex During Engagement. The question as to how far physical intimacies are appropriate in engagement is always a burning one. While to this question too, no categorical answer can be given, nevertheless the imperious forces in human nature suggest caution. Without reference to morals or ethics, expediency counsels limitations. The physical urges tend so easily to dominate the whole situation to the exclusion of the interplay of all the other areas of the personalities. From apparently innocent beginnings they often easily and quickly pass beyond the limits of control.

While in engagement a degree of intimacy may be expected, it is desirable, both from the point of view of physical and emotional health, and that of conserving the finest values of the relationship, to keep well within such bounds as will forestall a dominance of sexual passion. Engagement is likely to contribute more richly to the marriage companionship when it is devoted to appreciation and understanding of each other's personalities so as to make their married life a passionate as well as a spiritual experience. Restraint at this time may prove richly rewarding in marriage.

It is sometimes argued that the deeper intimacies in engagement are needed to test the physical responses and compatibilities of the lovers. For this purpose it is not at all necessary to fully arouse the passionate powers. Assurance of physical responses comes along before the deeper areas are reached. The stirring of a sleeper is assurance that he is alive and that he may be fully aroused.

It is to be strongly recommended that engaged couples frankly talk over the sexual side of the marriage, to compare and to share their understanding, their attitudes and points of view. These need to be included in a final estimating of the harmonizing possibilities. The great value of talking of things over is its effect upon their respective attitudes. No other thing is likely to be more effective in smoothing away restraints, tensions, fears and embarassments, and in creating an atmosphere of confidence between the couple. The very fact that in conversation they have brought this relationship out into the light, together with all their other interests and problems, tends to put their companionship upon a new plane of security and assurance. It proves in most cases of incalculable value in minimizing the adjustment problems of the first months of marriage and in realizing early a satisfying relationship.

The attitudes with reference to sex at which the engaged couple should arrive together before marriage should embrace at least the following concepts:

1. An appreciation of sex as a natural, normal life force, the urges of which are not ignoble any more than the craving for food or music or any other desire that arises out of natural life functions. That, indeed, the sex urge when wisely used and harmonized with the interests of life as a whole has creative contributions to make in the life of the individual.

2. An acceptance of the fact that in human life sex serves not only the purposes of procreation, but also, and particularly, the purposes of affection; that normally the human sex act is first of all the supreme form of the passionate expression of love.

3. An understanding that sex intercourse in marriage not only promotes physical, mental and emotional health and well-being, but when rightly conceived and used, it serves to vivify, sustain and develop love.

4. An appreciation of the normal human body as a noble creation in its entirety, and that the segregation of any of its parts as ignoble or shameful is abnormal and unworthy; that in the mutual exercise of 'the play-function of sex' in the prelude to coitus no area of the body of the lovers need be excluded from the service of love. None is to be regarded as 'untouchable'.

5. The conscious possession of passionate power and its spontaneous manifestation is not only normal but serves as a natural foundation upon which to build an enduring marital companionship of love. In coitus a full and free release of the passionate powers on the part of both mates is not only desirable but necessary to the full fruition of sexual love.

6. Married lovers need not put undue restraint upon their sex desires. Barring excessive artificial stimulation, their mutual desires may serve as their guide. (It is to be observed that we are not advocating no restraint but no *undue* restraint. For wholesome living there must be restraint in every area of life and the sexual sphere is no exception.)

7. The acceptance that in the best interests of all who are concerned in procreation, including the offspring, and in the interest of mutually satisfying sex relations unhampered by inhibiting fears, the bearing of children is to be intelligently regulated and controlled.

The above outline of attitude has been stated with care. It represents the essential minimum against which those approaching marriage need to evaluate their feelings and convictions.

Premarital Examination

A thorough physical and medical examination preliminary to marriage is to be strongly recommended. It is indeed desirable that some general examination precede announcement of engagement, for if any condition were to be revealed which should preclude marriage, the shock and the complications would be less.

Premarital examination is important for the following reasons: to discover lurking disease or physical conditions or hereditary tendencies that would render marriage precarious; to discover any conditions needing remedy before marriage; to secure the assurance and help of professional advice and instruction needed for adjustment in marriage. The woman is likely to receive the greatest aid from the gynaecologist and the man, from the genito-urinary specialist.

The examination should of course include scrutiny of the entire sex mechanism from the point of view of successful coitus. In the man there may occur adhesions of the foreskin which require correction, or excessively long or constricted foreskin which may make circumcision or other corrective measures advisable. In the woman there may appear adhesions about the clitoris, displacements of the reproductive organs and other conditions such as a too rigid a hymen. Small women are often worried for fear they are 'too small' to bear children, or for coitus. This can be easily ascertained by means of measurements made by the gynaecologist.

As a matter of assurance to one another, the medical examination of both parties should include thorough examination for venereal disease.

As a matter of security it has already become an accepted principle among a small proportion of young people to secure a medical certificate of health and fitness for maternity, as assurance to themselves and the partner. A movement has also been gaining ground for legal requirement of premarital medical examination for the issuing of marriage licences. Some states have established such laws. As a matter of precaution and of fairness, in addition to the personal advantage of professional advice, couples contemplating marriage should not wait upon legal requirements but should avail of premarital examination as the sensible thing to do.

Sexual Knowledge and Information

We have repeatedly stressed the importance of specific knowledge of the sexual life and have shown the lamentable consequences of ignorance and misinformation. The facts that have been presented should make it clear that, granting a favourable choice of mate, successful marriage, especially in its sex aspects, awaits first of all upon a certain background of attitude and understanding. Understanding will of itself go a long way towards correcting unwholesome attitudes.

In the Davis study it is found that of a group of 116 women who considered their marriage happy, 57.5 per cent had received specific preparation for the sex side of marriage, whereas of a corresponding group of 116 women who were unhappy in marriage only 38.2 per cent had received such preparation. This becomes more significant when we observe that in most cases such instruction was very fragmentary, such as would be considered quite inadequate from a modern point of view. Instruction 'would have saved years of difficult adjustment.' 'It would have kept me from misjudging my husband and avoided years of unhappiness for us both,' are samples of the convictions expressed.

Dickinson has set down a list of items in which he has found accurate significant information lacking:

1. Woman's anatomy and physiology, especially as to menstrual and ovarian function and the rest of the reproductive cycle; its possible mental and emotional meaning.

2. The theory of psycho-sexual relationships.

3. Methods of effecting painless entry of the virgin hymen at early coitus — its preludes, rhythm, mechanics, stages, completion; the physiological interpretation, emotional, and social implications.

4. Comprehension of the roots of sexual life in childhood experience, imagination, and previous practice.

5. Difference between men and women and possible drift of each in the psychology of sexual love.

It is obvious that Dickinson is speaking from the point of view of the woman. It is important that each partner have an understanding of the sex anatomy and physiology of both the man and the woman. We would add to the list a knowledge of the character, prevalence and consequences of the venereal diseases.

Physical Preparation

Physical preparation for marriage relates primarily to the woman. With the exception of occasional structural abnormalities in the male, such as we have mentioned in discussing premarital examination and which may require correction, the male is fully prepared physically for the full accomplishment and enjoyment of coitus. The woman is not quite so fortunate. She possesses in the hymen an anatomical structure which, with few exceptions, requires alteration before sex union can be accomplished. With the exception of a few, this alteration takes place in the first and a number of subsequent acts of coitus. In the first complete penetration the edges of the hymen, which partially obstructs the vaginal orifice, are nicked or slit and the membrane pushed aside, entailing often some pain and frequently a little bleeding. The pain is likely to be increased by unskilful penetration.

While the hymen itself presents a physical handicap to mutual participation in the early acts of coitus, the greatest handicap usually lies in the inhibiting anticipation of the 'rupture of the hymen'. The hesitant and fearful expectation on the part of the man is often quite as great as it is on the part of the woman. The result usually is that the woman has no pleasurable experience in the first act — and often not in subsequent acts — but meets instead with disappointment and not infrequently shock, which may play its part in a permanent negative conditioning of her sexual life. For the inexperienced man this situation naturally increases his initial awkwardness, and this contributes to their mutual spoiling of a situation which they desired to be a beautiful act of love.

The importance of this handicap and of dealing with it intelligently is much greater than is commonly realized. The way sex comes into experience in marriage tends to have a profound influence upon the whole marital adjustment and relationship ahead, especially so far as the woman is concerned. When an experience which has been anticipated as one profoundly thrilling and deeply satisfying turns out to be a rather crude, physical, and painful performance, the anticipation of love easily and often quickly swings to the extreme of aversion and disgust, and frequently the wife becomes permanently conditioned against the realization of her sexual capacities.

The facts which have been revealed by various studies point to the importance of removing every possible obstacle to making the initiation of sex relations a mutually agreeable, if not a deeply satisfying love experience. The obstacles of ignorance and attitudes have been discussed. We are now concerned with the physical handicap presented by the hymen.

The problem is really comparatively simple. It is merely a matter of stretching the hymen *before* marriage instead of leaving it to be accomplished awkwardly and with mutual confusion, if no worse, in the first act of coitus, an episode which at best is likely to be somewhat trying. The expansion may easily be made by the gynæcologist a few weeks before marriage, or the doctor may instruct the woman in a method of stretching it by herself in advance of marriage. Such service or advice may well be made a feature of the premarital examination. This preparatory measure is a simple matter but one that is likely to be enormously rewarding. Intelligent management of the initiation and gentleness on the part of the hushand are of course imperative, especially when the hymen remains intact. If natural lubrication fails to appear, artifical lubrication becomes necessary.

The Initiation of Sex in Marriage

We have shown how important and often cruical is the initiation of sex experience in marriage. The wearing tensions and strains of preparations for the wedding and the ordeal itself are usually exhausting, especially for the bride. To have to initiate their sex relationship under such conditions is unfortunate.

The question is frequently asked how soon after the wedding sex intercourse may properly begin. The question is important but no categorical answer can be given. It depends upon a number of factors and the temperamental makeup of the wife. The initiation may be appropriate upon the wedding night and it may not be, in extreme cases, for weeks. The general principle is, when it is agreeable to or desired by both the partners and not before. This means, of course, that the wife must be the critereon in the matter. Nearly all husbands are ready and glad to have it begin upon the wedding night or very soon after. Not only that; for most men a postponement for any considerable number of days may involve tension and a struggle for control. But whatever the strain and the struggle on the part of the man, the initiation must wait the wife's glad — not merely willing — acceptance. The way must be won not by persuasion or urging but by the delicate wooing of courtship. From great numbers of happy marriages comes the testimony that there has been no one thing in their marriage relationship which the wife has appreciated and treasured more than the husband's delicate consideratness in the first few days of marriage. Let the husband not forget that what matters is not how soon the joys of sexual love may be realized but rather what it may mean to their whole future relationship.

This point is well illustrated in the case of a couple well known to us, now in the late years of life. Upon the wedding night, after retiring, the husband merely placed his hand lovingly about the wife's shoulder and so they talked of their love and their future. Some years along in their happy marriage the husband one day asked the wife, 'what would you have done if I had made any approach to intercourse upon the wedding night?' The reply was, 'I would have made no protest but I would have always hated you for it.'

We have said that the time of initiation depends mainly upon the wife's attitude and what has gone before. If both mates have freed themselves reasonably well of constraining inhibitions; if both are well informed in sexual matters; if they have talked these matters over freely and frankly and hence are ready to incorporate the sexual relationship happily in their love-life; if the couple has arrived at a relationship of mutual confidence, the initial nuptials may very appropriately and to advantage take place on the wedding night. Under these conditions it may make the wedding night a richly memorable occasion. However, with the lack of such preparation, which is so common, we are disposed to advise against it and to favour a more gradual approach.

The strain of the wedding and preparing for it usually leaves the couple fatigued. Such a condition is unfavourable to successful coitus. We wish to repeat that if the wife does not quickly achieve full satisfaction with terminating orgasm, there is no occasion for immediate concern or disappointment. Let the wife remember that it is the nature of woman to develop her sexual capacity gradually. Only let not any couple permit themselves to drift into an acceptance of an unsatisfactory situation. Harris's suggestion is pertinent, that the couple should enter upon experimentation in the spirit of play and with a saving sense of humour. If, however, mutual satisfaction has not been achieved within a reasonable time, a few weeks or three months at most, professional advice and help should be sought.

As to the matter of frequency of coitus, whatever, the regime may be that will ultimately prove to be the best adapted to the needs and desires of both the partners, moderation is advisable in the early weeks or until the wife's capacities and inclinations have become developed and revealed. A frequency that may later prove to be quite acceptable and desired on the part of the wife may be objectionable to her during the awakening, developing period. Frank, open confidence between the lovers on these matters, and mutual considerateness is the key. But let the husband never forget that in nearly all cases the problem of satisfaction is the wife's, if the couple has decided that it is not desirable that the wife should become pregnant early and that contraceptives are to be used, it is in many cases desirable that during the early days of marriage a measure be chosen which is applicable to the man and does not require fussing on the part of the wife. After the wife has become more adjusted to the sexual regime, measures which she will take care of may be found more suitable.

Husbands who have become informed on sexual matters before marriage, and appreciate the women's need for orgasm, understand the propriety of producing her orgasm by clitoris friction or other artificial means may feel impelled to do so on the wedding night or the early days of marriage in the absence of orgasm in coitus. This is not advisable, unless the couple are so closely in accord with these matters that this may be decided upon between them. What later may be welcomed as an emergency measure may prove shocking during the initial days.

The Sexual Regime

Granting now that the sexual relationship has been soundly and successfully initiated and adjusted in the early weeks or months of marriage, there remains the task of perfecting the relationship and of gradually arriving at a regime that will be most satisfying and creatively meet the desires and needs of both husbands and wife. The lovers need to remain aware that anything like perfection in this strategic area of their marriage requires time, continued patience, tolerance and sympathetic co-operation. If the initiation has been mutually successful the rest of the journey may be viewed with courage and confidence.

The pair need to keep their sexual goal clearly before them, namely, mutual satisfaction with fully releasing, completely terminating orgasm in normal intercourse, all richly enhanced by a skilful art of love. Though a given couple may never attain the ideal, let them never cease their efforts to approximate the ideal. In cases in which the ideal as to regularly mutual orgasm seems for good reasons to be beyond reach, it is all the more important that the loss be compensated for by a peculiarly rich lover relationship and art.

'Unity' in the Bed

Let us be reminded that the essential marriage bond is a psychic and a spiritual bond, else it is not really marriage. Our goal is to make the sensuous sexual experiences serve spiritual ends. Harris's words are to the point,

'True spirituality is a sense of partnership and unity. This sense is achieved through all ranges of life. But, as far as sexual intercourse is concerned, the first step towards this unity is to perform the act properly in a sense of unity... spirituality in marriage goes aglimmering with astounding rapidity if the partners are kept in a state of unsatisfied desires.'

His words in another place adds emphasis here.

'Husbands report a complete satisfaction which is not shared by the wives when the truth is told. The really serious aspect is not the cases of disastrous maladjustment but the large number of limited satisfaction, of continued struggle for adjustment, of the continuance in married life of a 'sex problem' — something still unsolved.'

It is for these reasons that we have urged that no couple entering marriage permit themselves to drift into an acceptance of an unequal, unsatisfactory sex relationship but that they grapple with the problem together with the intelligence and persistence that may be expected from men and women who appreciate that they are playing for life's high stakes.

Granting that a spirit of harmony rules in the relationship of a newly married couple, their task is to develop a lover's technique that will serve to sustain and develop that harmony. Skill in this art is required in every phase of the act of sex communion. And what are its phases? For the sake of clarity in description the total ideal sex act may be divided into three successive stages; the prelude of love play, the copulative stage, and the postlude of repose which Van Del Velde has so aptly called 'the afterglow.' In ideal coitus none of these stages can be omitted or slighted.

Foreplay and the Erotic Zones

A good deal has already been said upon the first stage, that of love play. Our study of the difference in arousability between men and women has shown us the importance of this first phase particularly from the point of view of the woman. It serves to develop a common emotional mood; to arouse the passionate responses of the wife so that she may enter the second stage as nearly as possible on equal terms with the husband; to lift the entire act to the plane of the asthetic and to bring the sexual organs of the woman as well as the man's into the physiological state required for normal intercourse. It may include the whole range of pleasing lover-like contacts and caresses which their imagination, skill and practice may devise; tender words of love, kisses wherever most pleasing, deftly, gentle caresses seeking out particularly those areas which experience shows to be the most responsive. This includes the definitely erotic areas — the breasts, the external sex organs, and

Contents

Contents

Prologue

S tephen Fry – entertainer, wit and self-professed geek – was explaining on the radio the other day that blog is short for 'web log', which is just like an on-line diary. You cried: *No, Stephen, it is not!*

In a fundamental way a diary is the very opposite of a blog. A handwritten diary is something private and personal, a secret friend in whom you may confide. Some may lock it, some hide it away. Samuel Pepys wrote his in code.

There are of course some diaries that were intended for posthumous publication, but the diaries of ordinary people are for their eyes only, a record, a therapy, a way of enjoying the moment – or enjoying it again, as they write it up.

A blog, on the other hand, is public the instant it is written. It is intended to be read by strangers as well as fans. It may well have its uses: publicity, information, sales, the logging of a voyage or a project... More often than not it is an expression of pure exhibitionism by the writer, though perhaps not so obviously egotistical and self-delusional as some of the social networking sites – and Twitter is that affliction taken to extremes. Anyone who wrote in a blog or on Facebook, say, what they would write in a diary, their intimate thoughts and observations perhaps on loved ones, even a record of their more shameful actions, must at the very least be an attention seeker, at worst very sick indeed.

The pleasure in writing a diary, however, is that you can be entirely free; you have no image to project, be it true, false or imaginary. You can be honest. You can be yourself. This does not exclude description, narrative, record, but you can also give vent to your emotions; you can confess your weaknesses, explore your doubts, investigate your failings and give yourself a pat on the back for a deed or job well done. You can say what you like as long as it is true.

If you were intending these same words for the blogging public or for posterity you might lie, omit or embellish. In a diary the incident is stripped bare, as is your soul. Your diary is the shell without which you would be utterly vulnerable.

You had your first diary when you were quite small, and you were determined to fill every page. Many days have one word, 'school', written across them. Others: 'play with Mice', which is how you spelled Mike, your friend's name. Often in those days of post-war rationing you recorded the meals you ate.

Then, when you were nine, a family friend who passed as an aunt gave you a five year diary with the challenge that she "bet you cannot keep this going for five years". Five years seemed a life time then, though now it rushes by as quickly as five weeks. You kept the diary going though, and when you had finished the aunt had disappeared or died. She never knew she had lost her bet.

You still have all your diaries in a chest. You will never re-read them and you suppose you will destroy them before you die. You do not want to experience again, let alone have anyone else read those pages of adolescent introspection, of fumbling encounters with the opposite sex, of moral and ethical dilemmas which would now seem laughable in our more enlightened times.

You squirm even to think what you wrote as a student, night after night, though no doubt your views would throw light on the social attitudes of the time towards race, religion and behaviour, politics and the arts. You have long ceased to believe that we are individually capable of original thought, so probably just as much could be gleaned from contemporary newspapers. You are but the product of your times.

As a writer it is tempting, however, to mine the diaries of a particular year for such local or period colour, but you never want to discover what kind of person you were. It is bad enough living with the person you have become.

There is one constant. You always have kept, and always will keep, a diary.

1
On Keeping a Holiday Diary

Your parents used a box brownie to take black and white photographs of their two weeks a year at the seaside. Your own first camera was a Bakelite development of this, the Kodak Brownie 127. A roll of film stretched at most to a dozen photos. Later you took up 35mm photography and built a cumbersome library of transparencies, but this was expensive. A film took only 36 pictures. Prints were more expensive still and so early holiday photos are limited and precious, stored in bulky photo albums. Then came digital photography, and mobile phones that functioned as cameras. The value of the permanent image was devalued, if not lost for good, among such a promiscuous abundance of photos – if that is still the correct term for disposable e-snaps.

But you also have better pictures, better than any taken by traditional or digital cameras; pictures that cannot fade or get deleted – for you have always kept a holiday diary.

Looking at an old-fashioned, two-dimensional snapshot you might laugh at the clothes and the hair styles, wonder at how young your parents looked, admire the old cars or struggle to remember the time and place of a pose. Names of beaches, villages, whole cities are lost to your memory. Years later you do not easily recall the names of other people either, hosts, friends or lovers, who occupy the frame.

In your diaries you may not often have described appearances, fashion per se has never been important to you, but occasionally you did try to capture the likeness of a person or describe a scene particularly significant in that moment. These sketches you now treasure. Your diary evokes, better than a physical picture, the feel of a place: the sound of the sheep's bells in the Norwegian mountains; the scent of a French bakery with that mix of distinctive disinfectant from the floor and the chocolaty aroma coming from the jar of *Caram'bars* when the heavy glass lid is lifted; the oppressive humidity you first encounter in the tropics as you step out of the dehydration of the aircraft and swim across the tarmac like a fish in a tank – an almost liquid envelope in which you will live and work until you reboard the plane, but an ambiance that appears in none of the photos except perhaps for a dampening darkness of clothes around the waist, across the chest and beneath the armpits. Still in the tropics, in the remotest depths of an African forest that looks pristine in the photo, your diary records the awful, tearing scream of the illegal chainsaw felling another distant tree.

Your diary will also have captured other sounds, perhaps in that same forest at night, or perhaps the total lack of sound: the silence of the Norwegian *vidda* broken only by the regular sliding of your cross-country skis uphill, or the uninterrupted scraping on the downhill slopes. Occasionally you have recorded meals, or attempted to capture the taste of a particular mango after a thirsty drive; the pleasure of that first swig of cold beer on returning from a trek.

But a diary is not simply a record of the five senses. It records also the hundred moods of the traveller, the dejection and the elation, the occasional boredom, the irritation with a spouse or a child. Anticipation, excitement; the misery of four days of migraine or an incapacitating bout of Delhi belly.

These diaries are certainly not literary works. They tell no story, merely note down scenes that take your fancy – mostly fleeting moments or incidents, the occasional anecdote perhaps. Sometimes you are as elaborate as a painter trying to fix a particularly striking scene, sometimes you simply list the places visited that day, that month, that year; or the things you might have bought on Tuesday, the cost of a meal on Wednesday night, or a tank of petrol on the way home.

Sometimes this is useful as a reference tool months or years later, to settle an argument about whether you saw minke or finn whales, or – wasn't it humpback that you watched blowing bubbles and breaching through a shoal of fish?

Sometimes, as a writer, you refer to your dairies for conversations recorded to capture the speech habits of East Coast waitresses, Australian farmers or African politicians. Some incidents you might take as written, fresh in their emotion and immediacy, and incorporate them into a story.

On the other hand, you still have a vivid three page account of a near shipwreck of the coast of Lanzarote written the same day, and for which years later you still have to invent a tale that would do it justice. Like so many other episodes, this one has remained buried. Only by browsing through the diary years later do you chance upon it with pleasure, having forgotten, if not the event, certainly the details.

The fundamental difference, however, between the holiday photos and the diary is that the albums show how much you have changed, and the diaries how little. Re-reading them is a pleasure tinged perhaps with shame and guilt; and very, very secret.

2

The Morning Post

A striking feature of Wilkie Collins' 1860 novel *The Woman in White* is the absolute reliability of the Royal Mail, depending as it did on a fast and regular rail service. Overnight letters fly back and forth between Cumberland and London without anyone doubting they would arrive by first post the next day. On one occasion Laura is at Blackwater Park in the north and requires an immediate response from her London solicitor. She writes to him on Day One beseeching him to send his reply on the 11 o'clock train the next morning. By 2 pm on Day Two she has received her reply, delivered to her home. The Victorians hardly needed email.

Today few of us still write letters by hand. Email is

cheaper, easier and informal. Even so, however immediate, there is no guarantee anyone will open your message, or if they do they may not look at it the same day. For domestic purposes within these shores a First Class letter, though an expensive luxury, will probably be just as quickly read and, being more personal, better appreciated.

Although less and less correspondence arrives by 'snail mail', you still await the sound of the red Post van in the lane, the click of the latch on your garden gate and the thump of letters on the mat. Much of the delivery comprises junk mail: catalogues, holiday brochures, and whole forests of offers from the ever optimistic *Readers' Digest*, but there is enough of a personal nature most mornings to give you a pleasurable sense of anticipation that your less charismatic electronic mail box fails to rouse.

It may be the memories of letters past, letters from the days of first post, second post – and in the village where you lived there was also an afternoon post that came at tea time. Now that there is only one daily delivery it seems unpredictably to fill all or any of these time slots, carrying with it past associations.

One quality of real mail is that it is more individual and therefore more personal. For a start, the envelopes come in all shapes and sizes and are easy to sort at a glance. Not all are welcome, but even some of the business ones are informative: utilities bills, credit and bank accounts, invoices... some of these formal envelopes might even contain a pleasant surprise: a £50 win on the premium bonds, a rebate from the Inland Revenue, or a windfall from an insurance company.

Most welcome of all are those written and addressed by hand. In some cases this is handwriting you have known all your life. Like a voice, the writing of a relative, a lover or a friend is instantly recognisable. Like a voice, too, the handwriting may become quivery and shaky with age, but the character is not lost. You have sometimes noticed that children and grandchildren inherit the handwriting of their parents as they do their looks, their voices and other mannerisms.

Seasoning the pleasurable anticipation of the morning post is a certain clinging dread. Bad news usually travels fast and will have arrived by telephone or by a policeman at the door. Sometimes, though, you tear open a daughter's or a parent's letter to be sure that everything is all right.

Your real dread stems from the vestiges of a fifteen year barrage of threats and admonitions from a neurotic ex-wife. Her letters have long stopped, but the poison hangs in the otherwise pleasantly scented miasma wafted in on the post. In your mind's eye you still see your address on the envelope, big and brazen, written in whatever the demented woman had to hand: pen, biro, pencil, crayon, felt tip, lipstick. And on the reverse, every second word underlined three times, her afterthoughts or second thoughts or third thoughts scrawled across the paper for all to see.

Inside it was always worse, saccharine sweet but sprinkled with accusation, menace and demands. The woman who stole your children continued for twenty years to steal what little peace of mind she had left you.

But the bitter increases the sweet, and over the years you have received many more pleasant than unpleasant letters, and still expect to do so: your Godmother, who for half a century has never forgotten you on your birthday or at Christmas; birthdays and Christmases themselves, when old friends and far flung family still send cards written and addressed in their own hand, often with unintentionally hilarious accounts of their doings over the year. Then there is the daughter who is predictably early, and the son who is always a week late. The joy is that they remember you at all.

Fairly often it is your own handwriting you recognise on the A5 envelopes that drop onto the mat. Though most of your literary correspondence takes place now by email, there are still those small journals and publishers, those competitions, that require one or more printed copies of your manuscripts. Ninety percent of these are returned; your working life is one long and regular rejection, but it is just this that adds spice, because once in a while a contract, a cheque or an acknowledgement arrives. Three lines of appreciation, one or more noughts on a cheque or a letter forwarded from someone who has enjoyed something you have written; any of these communications wipes out a score of rejections, if not the cost of your initial postage.

The clatter of the flap, the tumble of falling mail, carry resonances also of other acceptances and rejections – of exam results and university acceptance, of job interviews and ensuing results, of hospital admissions and of medical reports condemning you to life.

Despite technological change, the volume of mail and with it the promise of some life-changing decision, event or visit still fills your morning with a familiar *frisson*. You cannot go out until the morning post has arrived, with all of life's disappointments... and sometimes with a few of its rewards.

3

Hello, It's Me...

A nd you know it is. You know *who* it is. Probably the 'hello' alone, whether spoken in the next street or from the furthest continent, clear or down a crackling phone line, is enough to reveal the identity of the caller.

Hello, it's me. Wherein lies the clue?

We all have an accent, particularly in England; an accent that betrays our social class or aspirations, our regional origins, even sometimes the countries or counties we have resided in for long periods – a different mother tongue even... but in the landscape of the voice these traces form only the background scenery; we all, too, have an idiolect, our individual manner of speaking. After all other features have been taken into account, this is the recipe that makes our speech our own, gives it a special flavour.

Yes, it contains accent, vocabulary, syntax, our unique way of expressing ourselves; but when you hear *Hello, it's me*, it is the tone and timbre of the voice that you recognise. Your voice is your oral fingerprint, your iris, your spectrum of sound. It is just as possible to be turned off by a voice as it is to fall in love with one.

Hello, it's me offers the briefest of pleasures. The rest of the call is far less important. What matters is that your lover, your child, your friend or your colleague has called and that you have immediately recognised him or her.

Hello, it's me. What follows may not be a pleasure. It may

8

be a call for help, a distress signal; it may be disappointing news or simply a time-wasting chat. On the other hand it may be a huge relief. The missing child that has finally made contact; your mother to say that everything is all right now; a colleague to say your project has been accepted.

Hello, it's me may be practical information. *I'm on the train and am arriving at Etchingham at 19:11.*

It may be good news. *I've passed my exams, I'm getting married, Julia has had twins and mother and babies are all doing well.*

It may be a welcome inquiry. *Are you free to come to the theatre next Thursday? Stay for the weekend? Would you like to come on holiday with us?*

Hello, it's me may be something more intimate. *Hello it's me. I just wanted to tell you I love you.*

Except sadly nowadays, more often than not, such messages are texted; and a printed or digital text is devoid of just those qualities that make the spoken voice so special.

4

On Not Having A Headache

You wake up knowing immediately something extraordinary has happened. You are relaxed, but no longer sleepy. There is a lightness about your body, about your head. As you swing your legs out of bed and stand up you are aware that the cape of pain has been lifted from your shoulders, the heavy hood thrown back from your temples and skull. You are as light-hearted as you are light-headed. For the first time in weeks your mouth explores a smile and you realise it is going to be one of those rare days of remission: you have no headache.

A gentle euphoria as you brush your teeth and take your shower; a sense of amazement that this is how most people must feel most of the time – pain free. Free, too, of the dreary muzziness of a clogged brain.

The clear-headedness is the best of it, and this clarity of thought leads to all kinds of possibilities. You feel hungry again, a hunger for food and a hunger for life. Your whole mood has risen, borne on albatross spirits and a soufflé heart.

At first you catch up on the backlog of little jobs, still not quite believing your luck. You tidy your desk, sort your more pressing bills and business, but your body, trapped for days in tension, demands a job to do too. So you clear up in the kitchen or in the garage, you turn the compost, mow the lawn. And while you relish this life-affirming activity your mind, like a sheepdog, chases after plans that have long gone astray.

Now is the time to see that play, film or concert, visit those friends you keep letting down, even to risk a glass of wine. Perhaps there will be time to throw a party, to plan a long weekend away, to take a holiday. You dare to contemplate the future.

Sometimes in this early stage of recovery you are truly inspired. Lines of verse or story, like flies that have been caught in the web of pain, now float free and drop into your imagination. You snatch at them, examine them and sink into such concentration of composition that a whole morning has gone by, lunch time too, and the sun is going down – before you resurface and wonder whether you are not squandering this gift, this precious space between migraines.

For always you are aware, deep down, that your parole is short. Nonetheless this pain-free mind is quite separate from the one usually thrashing about in torment and mist. You understand only too well that you are inhabiting this healthy body only temporarily... or perhaps that this happy being is only visiting you, and that the tyrant will sooner or later make his return, as unwelcome as a cancer. Those thoughts of long term plans, of holidays and of commitment are merely pipe dreams. All the more reason now, then, to get on with the present, to regain a life.

Depending on season and circumstance you may just luxuriate in the sheer comfort of not having a headache, of being able to think and dream and to write letters and poems; or you may pack your rucksack and go for a day's hike. You may rush up to town and take in an exhibition or a theatre, or you may even chance a long weekend away.

What adds piquancy to any of these options is the knowledge that at best you are only out on bail, that there will be no escaping another spell inside the throbbing, nauseous cage of your next migraine. But that, at the moment, is a distant threat. For now, it is only *this* very moment that matters. *Carpe diem.* The pure, unadulterated happiness of not having a headache offers up a day to be snatched, run with, and treasured.

5

Simplicity

You were once stranded for three days in a small town in the rocky wastes of Andhra Pradesh, Southern India. An old man winkled you out of the small hotel where you had taken refuge from the heat, with an invitation to his home. You no longer remember how you travelled from the hotel to his house. You might have walked; or perhaps this upright old man in a white dhoti and sandals drove you there in an old Ambassador car.

You do remember, as you entered his house, that you were hot and thirsty and that he took you into a room that you have never forgotten.

On the way there he told you he was a retired judge and currently president of the town's Shaw Society. As a young man, he had been privileged to meet George Bernard Shaw off the boat in Bombay. The writer was to make a triumphal tour of the subcontinent, presumably spawning Shaw societies along the way.

The judge's house was a small bungalow: two or three rooms at most. The room he led you into welcomed you like a blessing. To this day you recall the whiteness, the coolness and the simplicity. The four walls and the floor were bare; there was an unpolished wooden table in the centre of the room, and two plain wooden chairs.

You sat opposite one another and drank tea, brought to you by a silent woman from the other side of a beaded curtain. There was nothing else in the room and the old man's mind was similarly uncluttered, if a little one-tracked.

"I had an ulterior motive," he confessed with great charm, "in inviting you here."

"It's nice to be here all the same," you replied guardedly but sincerely, enjoying the respite from the glare of the sun.

"Good. Now I have mentioned the Shaw Society to you. Always we are looking for fresh speakers, and today the gods have thrown an Englishman into our laps."

Pity you were not an Irishman, you thought, and protested that apart from having studied Pygmalion for 'O' Level, you knew next to nothing about the great man.

"That I find hard to believe. You are too modest."

"No, really," you said, "and I certainly know less about him than do the members of your Shaw Society."

The judge saw that you were in earnest and said, "It does not matter. You may choose any literary topic."

You had taken with you a pirated copy of *The French Lieutenant's Woman,* by John Fowles, on your trek into the *mofussil.* You suggested a talk on that, and once he was reassured that it contained no bad language he accepted your offer.

When you both rose to leave you peeped into the other room. The walls were just as bare and white, the stone floor uncarpeted, and the only furniture was a bed and a chair. There were no clothes, no bookshelves. It was as simple as the sitting room – minus the slow turning ceiling fan.

You had a day to re-read Fowles' clever novel and to prepare your talk. You no longer remember what you said or how it went down. Looking back on those lost days you see an upright old man in his home-spun *dhoti* and *jibba* and the two rooms, beautiful in their simplicity inside the white bungalow kissed by dark green bougainvillea fronds, and bloodied with deep red flowers.

Ever since, you have attempted to clear your desk before and after getting down to work so that the surface at least is free of distraction. One day perhaps you will go a step further and build a cabin in the garden with only a chair and a table in it. Come to think of it, didn't the great GBS do something similar himself?

6

A Private Reading

The best poetry readings are small and intimate and enjoyed among friends. Then it is like a conspiracy. The one reading you will always remember was given by Nissim Ezekiel at the home of R. Parthasarathy, then editor of the Oxford University Press in Madras, as Chennai was still called.

The sound of your leather *chappals* on the concrete steps leading to Partha's first floor flat announced your arrival during a power cut to the quiet group within. When your eyes had grown accustomed to the darkness you recognised that those present were mainly your friends. They were reclining on low seats and cushions around a long coffee table on which two candles wrestled listlessly with the evening breeze. While you all waited for the power to return you chatted pleasantly, oblivious of the occasion for which you had all come and so savouring the informality all the more.

Eventually it was decided not to wait for the capricious electricity, and the poet/professor agreed that he would be able to see quite well enough by the candlelight. He sat sideways on the floor at the end of the table and Partha moved both candles up for him. Their halos encircled the poet's face and the untidy sheaf of hand-written papers which he held in his right hand. His thin rimmed, gold spectacles leaning slightly out and away from his bony nose seemed to balance on it like a pair of fragile scales.

He began quietly to speak.

He said that magicians usually kept up a patter during their performance, but he intended reading his poems as they came to hand. At the mention of magic the lights silently and swiftly flooded the room, making everyone and everything less attractive. The room, stripped of its shadows, took on an austere appearance. The straight edges of the few pieces of furniture redefined the symmetrical, pink-walled space in which we sat; the white refrigerator and hand basin at the far end glittered beneath the bare bulb. A slow ceiling fan began to stir the air.

Nissim took no notice of the change.

All these poems, he continued, had been written during the previous two years. He had been trying to write poems in themes, such as family, love, his 'unreality' set and the poems in Indian English, some of which had already appeared in *The London Magazine*.

He read at random in a clear, conversational tone. It was rather as if he were speaking about himself in an unostentatious way. The confessions of a gentle man. His audience liked the poems because they liked the voice that read them and they liked the man who had experienced them. But they listened mainly in silence, and no-one spoke while he fingered through the papers, mischievous under the fan, for the next poem.

Some were narrative, some descriptive, some were a little bitter, some a little sad. Several were ironically amusing, and then you softly laughed. He timed these readings like a professional and his eyes twinkled when he announced the occasional love poem which, he said, could not possibly be read in public. You were all flattered, of course, at the inference that you were his friends and not his public.

Before anyone had time to fidget, or wonder when dinner was to be served, he stopped reading and returned to his original place on the settee, leaving his papers to dance lightly on the table top. The empty space this bird-like figure had occupied seemed absurdly exaggerated by the two heavy ladies who flanked it, each spilling out of her chair and bright pink sari. Because it was an intimate circle the poet was not particularly on show, and you talked almost privately. He must have been asked the same questions a hundred times before, but he gave the impression he was answering them for the first time. He wrote in English because he did not know Marathi, his mother tongue, well enough to be able to write in it.

When he wanted to write he shut himself away for four or five hours at a spell. He rarely managed a poem at one effort but constantly wrote and rewrote, although strangely enough the latest Indian English offering, the poignant and delightful portrayal of a simple old professor, had come quickly at the end of a day's hard and fruitless work at a more serious one.

Ambition? He had often thought of writing an Indian *Inferno*, "but I am not good enough, not 'great' enough." Despite the growing assurance of his verse and the objectivity with which he was able to discuss it, this modest statement was like a stone thrown into a pool, whose ripples spread throughout his poetry. He recognised that he was only a minor poet, a poet who wrote detached but accessible verse. And yet in so many of the experiences he was describing – his loves, both family and sexual; encounters, friendships – there was already an anxiety that the fire would burn out. As his technique and assurance increased, his preoccupation was to keep the spark alive.

Nissim Ezekiel was to remain prolific for many years. In his poem *The Professor* he wrote:

How is your health keeping?
Nicely? I am happy for that.
This year I am sixty-nine
And hope to score a century.

As it turned out, Nissim's fears were realised when he fell victim to Alzheimer's disease. He lived only another ten years, and you miss his gentle voice. In the same poem quoted above he finished:

If you are coming again this side by chance,
Visit please my humble residence also.
I am living just opposite house's backside.

7

On Being Carefree

Y ou cannot consciously be carefree: it would be too much to worry about. No, carefree moments in adulthood (in this troubled world) catch you by surprise, and are fleeting. Like happiness, being carefree cannot be sought after; only enjoyed incidentally.

It was not always so. An infant's demands are basic and urgent. A baby bawls for milk, enjoys warmth and love – not free of but instead completely dependent upon care of another kind.

The years from two or three to eleven, though, as far as your memory goes, were carefree in the sense of being free from anxiety. School was an adventure, a place of exploration. Your mind was limpid and receptive, your friendships spontaneous.

Then came secondary school, a bigger society in which some boys were bad and some masters worse. There were other pressures: exams, competitive activities, building a CV, setting out the starting blocks for the rat race. In your studies you learned about the problems your world faced, and you felt you had to do something about them. You might have been challenged at times, stimulated, but in those turbulent days of youth and innocence lost you could not have been carefree. What adolescent is not troubled?

There followed university, a career, a family, all with their rewards but also bearing a heavy weight of responsibility. You despised material wealth, and wealth creators, and consequently always were (and still are) laid low by money worries. And all the while the world was getting more violent, weapons "improved", society fragmented. Your own values were regarded as quaint and old-fashioned.

You became care *worn,* rather than care *free.*

This was the norm, you thought, for most responsible, thinking people. In your naivité you assumed you should and would continue to shoulder the burden, whether by composting your waste, signing petitions, going on marches or joining *Médecins sans Frontières*. You still cared. Action, however despairing, was better than no action, was a positive force. You could no longer be carefree but life could still be enjoyed. It was not all doom and gloom – but how could it be carefree?

Nevertheless there do remain routes to reaching a carefree state of mind, without becoming an out-and-out Buddhist. They can be various, and variously effective. Some choose drugs and alcohol, others attain it through study or meditation, sex, religion or mountaineering.

But the simple moment of *being carefree* is not ecstasy, nirvana, engrossment, or any sense of elation. Neither is it a conscious escape from the realities of life. It is neither a physical nor a deep psychological state. It is more a soufflé of emotion, a short lived breeze of contentment. For a few brief minutes you are free of care; that's all.

You might capture this in a waking mood, in a dream, coming round from an anaesthetic just before full consciousness sets in; it might appear after a busy day when you come in, make yourself a drink and settle down for a few minutes to relax and enjoy it at leisure before turning in for the night; or conversely you may experience it when you set off on a short break. You feel the weight of responsibility slip from your neck and shoulders, you feel light-headed, you have for a weekend out-paced your cares.

Provided, that is, you have not left your passport behind or forgotten to make arrangements for the cat.

8

The Fleeting Moment

The idea comes to you in a waking moment, in the shower or during a walk. Sometimes it comes in the shape of a poem, sometimes a story or a situation, sometimes it is just a line, one line full of promise. For a second or two you brim with bliss. If you turn over and go back to sleep, if you carry on washing your hair or you stride on to the next landmark, the idea will slip away, never to be recalled. If you were better organised you might have a notebook beside the bed or in your pocket (though probably not in the shower). It is sometimes possible, if you are so prepared, to jot down a phrase, a sentence or some memory of the fleeting idea. And perhaps later you will work something up from it. This is better than nothing, but it will not be the same. You will never quite recapture that original thought, any more than an enchanted toddler can catch hold of a soap bubble.

What is this *coup de foudre,* this rare moment when some apparently original and brilliant idea strikes you like lightening, burns through your imagination and sends out sizzling sparks? When it is a whole poem, a drama or a story that has never been told, it appears as a distillation of all that you have ever wished to write. It is the purest and simplest truth. It may be as short as a sonnet or as long as a saga. No matter, it is perfect and you have glimpsed it all. It is there for the taking.

When this happens to you, you will spring from your bed, you will emerge from your shower, you will pause in your rambling, and try to pin this vision down. You are radiant, excited. You are the medium. Your pen is poised over the paper, or your fingers hover over the keyboard...

And you can write nothing. To write it down would not do it justice, would damage it; to capture this elusive angel of inspiration would mean clipping its wings. It would no longer fly, no longer soar. On the other hand you do not want to let it go, you cannot bear to watch your vision dissolve.

You try again. Your mind's eye still holds the complete, the perfect picture, but the thinking brain, the hand, the fingers cannot find the words that will capture it. If ever proof were needed that thought preceded language, this is it. Yet how else other than with language can a writer convey his thoughts, his vision? A composer has music, an artist paint, but perhaps even to them at times sound and colour seem as inadequate as words so often do for the writer.

You go on trying nevertheless, and the more you try the more the concept shrivels up. You try a word, one word, just to pin a corner of it down, but the word diminishes it. You rush out a whole sentence, sometimes quite a good sentence; but dull as dirt compared with the shimmering purity of the original concentrate. Whatever you try, a summary, a description, a few keywords, a critique – all complicate the awful simplicity of the insight that jolted you from sleep, in the shower, in a rambler's reverie. All your interpretation does is to drip water onto whisky. A dilution, a pollution.

All the same, you cannot give up now. You may even write for hours. Possessed. Your efforts may result in the rough draft of something useful, good even. But you know that it is only the shadow of a shadow of the inspiration that touched you. You will continue your search for a personal holy grail, for it is in these fleeting moments you find inspiration and a certain cruel satisfaction.

This, after all, is what keeps you going.

9

BBC World Service

You are in Southern India: your only personal communication with the outside world is by weekly aerogramme, a flimsy letter folded in on itself and sent by airmail. Your work correspondence similarly you write in longhand, and give to an Anglo-Indian stenographer to copytype and despatch. There is a telex machine that occasionally rattles into life, but no-one has ever thought of telephoning London and you have never rung friends or family in the UK. Fax, which also will depend on a good phone line, is twenty years into the future; email and the internet await the turn of a new century.

Your news, then, comes from All India Radio, the local press, and from visitors. The British papers are usually a week out of date by the time they reach the British Council Library. This does not matter much. The centre of your world has shifted. You go on leave only every eighteen months. Between times, none of that exists. Your life, and a rich and varied life it is, is very much centred in South India. Your work is a mere distraction, a means of earning a living.

Then suddenly there is war in the north. East Pakistan, formerly East Bengal, breaks away from Pakistan. The Pakistani army invades. India intervenes to protect her fellow Bengalis, ten million of whom flee across the border. There are blackouts in the northern cities – New Delhi, Calcutta and Bombay. You are assured that Madras, where you are, is beyond the reach of Pakistani missiles and bombers.

Nevertheless the papers are full of scare stories about Pakistani atrocities, of soldiers biting through the cheeks of the women they have raped; of prisoners being hung by the ankles from ceiling fans and spun around until the blood bursts from their ears; of children slaughtered.

You realise much of this is propaganda. But how much? You want the truth. You want to know what is really going on. You want to keep up to date. So do millions of Indians.

The solution is to turn to the BBC World Service.

Reception on your Yachtsman Short Wave Radio is poor. The BBC obligingly sends you a length of thin, white aerial and a complicated diagram on how to rig it to suit local conditions. You and your gardener climb onto your flat roof and rig up posts to the water tank and the coping. Run the first length east/west, you read. The one thing you do not have is a compass, but you imagine your *mali* with his local knowledge would know.

"Moses, which way is north?"

Moses eyes you in astonishment, takes the diagram from your hands, studies it and points with his finger at the illustration of the points of the compass.

"N means north, other way south, I am thinking, Master," he says.

You know that, but cannot get him to relate the diagram to the location. He climbs down the ladder, shaking his head at your stupidity, you make a guess based on the position of the sun and rig up your aerial on your own. It works. You get a signal.

You are now able to listen not only to news of the war, but to news about Britain, to quiz shows, comedy, drama and even to *Match of the Day*. The signal rises and falls in volume rather like the noise from a football stadium heard from a distance, it pipes and whistles and crackles. But somehow you feel you are in touch again, the BBC is your umbilical cord pumping a pulse from the Mother Country into your increasingly foreign body.

Fifteen or so years later the reception has not improved. You are now in an even more remote area, where there is not even the luxury of electricity or of fans. And you are listening to another war. Argentina has invaded the Malvinas, Britain recaptures the Falkland Islands. From the centre of Africa, where your watchman guards your compound with a bow and arrows, the progress of this modern war is as exciting as any drama.

Now, back in Britain with the entire world's media in your lap, you still tune in to the BBC World Service. Not the fatuous, time-filling TV offspring, but the radio version. When you are tired of being talked down to by local radio and bored with the parochialism of national radio, you can still get a more or less objective account of what is happening elsewhere in the world (or in those parts where there are still correspondents).

There is no longer any problem with reception. Sometimes you wish the technicians would enhance the even digital signal with a few squeaks and whistles and sudden fades. There is, after all, still a time warp. Is Nicholas Parsons really still alive? Sadly, Alistair Cook is not. But the very act of listening to the BBC World Service is another link in the chain of circumstances and events that has been your life.

10

On Finishing A Swim

Once a week you go for a swim. You do not enjoy it. Sometimes you have to force yourself to make the effort. You will feel better for it, you tell yourself, and you know this is true. It is for this psychological – and the physical – afterglow that you go.

Of course you pretend the whole exercise is to keep fit. But where else but the swimming pool do you ever catch athlete's foot, ear ache, colds, coughs and sore throats? Despite the ritual removal of footwear at the entrance, padding through the damp in dirty socks or bare feet, despite the compulsory shower before you enter, the heavy chlorination of the tepid (31°) water, you are fully aware of everyone else's spittle and expectoration (not to mention likely seepage from other orifices), shed skin and dislodged hairs. Worse than the human contamination of the water is the infection of the air that hangs over it, heavy with chlorine fumes and often further polluted by booming muzak.

Nevertheless the pool is better than most: modern, functional and popular. Its popularity is the main problem. You do not go there to play, to splash about, to chat or to do aerobic exercises. You go to swim. You therefore choose the hours for lane swimming. During this time swimmers plough up and down in a straight line along clearly marked channels. There are two slow lanes, two medium, and two fast, each with its Up or Down direction. There is no room to overtake or to be overtaken.

The slow lanes are occupied by beginners, or those recovering from illness or accident. The fast lanes are for serious swimmers, sleek as seals, who effortlessly cleave the water, length after relentless length, clearly in training.

You are too quick and impatient for the slow lanes and nothing like fit or proficient enough for the fast lanes. You slot into the medium lanes, sandwiched between the incompetent and the achievers. The story of your life. The story of most people's lives, for these are the most crowded lanes.

Sometimes you find a large enough gap to do your thirty lengths unhindered, counting them down as if each were a day until the end of a prison sentence. Usually there is someone in front of you who is that bit too slow, or worse, someone behind you who keeps catching up, swimming that bit faster than you find comfortable. You could of course pause at the shallow end and let him pass, but then invariably someone else will jump in to fill the space you have created; rather like trying to maintain six clear car lengths between you and the next car on a motorway.

On a slack day you can forget everybody else and fall into a rhythm. The counting becomes hypnotic, until with relief you realise that there is only one more length to do. You like to finish with a fast crawl, imagining you are winning a gold medal. As a result you are sometimes too breathless, your muscles too weak, to haul yourself out of the pool and up onto your feet. When you do, you sway and pant. For a minute or two becoming vertical again is a challenge: distant ancestral memories of life emerging from the sea, perhaps.

Now the pleasurable part of the exercise begins. First the hot shower and a shampoo; the warm water eases your shoulders, and by the time you are dressed and back in the car your body radiates relaxation. It is as though you are centrally heated. This effect will last for the rest of the day; all aches and pains and many worries have been sluiced away. A drowsy lethargy comes over you. You could doze off but a sharp appetite needs satisfying. You prepare a lunch that contains twice as many calories as you have just burned off, but each calorie tastes better after a swim than on other days.

To add to your sense of wellbeing is the knowledge that you have not got to go for a swim again for another week. You have done it.

11

Smile Of A Baby

Hastings, England

L ate summer, and wife and daughter, grandson and you sit at a pavement table on the Stade in Hastings Old Town. You are waiting to be served 'traditional' fish and chips.

Although the Old Town itself is attractive the beach front this end is kitsch, vulgar and loud. The clientèle of the pubs and cafés are mainly fat, poor, shapeless women who have never given up smoking cigarettes, and men with beer bellies and oaths for their dogs and children.

Charlie, your grandson sitting in a high chair, has no social prejudice or preconception. The stream of day trippers along the pavements, the constant passage of plates and people, the screech of gulls, all hold his attention, as mother and grandparents simply enjoy the sunshine.

At the next table a particularly hardened group of middle-aged women sit smoking and drinking, their gravelly voices making Marge Simpson and her sisters sound sweet and sophisticated. They complain about the cost of living, the government, the schools, the traffic. Their jaws are set, their mouths grim straight lines, their eyes narrow behind the cigarette smoke.

Charlie watches these old witches in fascination. Only fourteen months old, he already knows a trick or two. Studying each woman in turn, he tries to catch an eye, a look. When the first woman does notice him he smiles. She turns away in disgust as though the infant were something dumped by a dog.undismayed, Charlie tries his charm on the second woman, catches her attention for a second, smiles – and she cannot help herself: she smiles back, and Charlie chuckles in delight. You, noticing the interplay, smile too and inadvertently catch the woman's eye as well. For two or three seconds you all hold the moment.

Southern Sudan

Y
ou had driven out onto the plains with your two year old daughter for an evening walk: an exercise and concept impossible to explain to anyone not European in that poor African town, and especially difficult to the Arab soldiers who kept the curfew and manned the checkpoints.

You had lifted Emily into the front passenger seat of your Land Rover and fastened her into the child seat; when you slammed the door shut she was invisible from outside. You climbed into the driving seat and set off back for Juba, confident of arriving well before the six o'clock curfew and the darkness that half an hour later would fall like a shutter.

At the bridge you were stopped by two young soldiers who normally would have waved you through. However one of them, eyes red from drink and dust and boredom, pointed his rifle and ordered you to accompany him to the little hut twenty metres from the road, where the militia logged the coming and going of vehicles and tried to extract favours and bribes.

You did not object in principle to accompanying him to his cabin, but not knowing how long it would take, you had no intention of leaving a baby alone in the heat of the stationary vehicle. The only way to reach and release her was to walk around to the offside and open the passenger door.

You tried to explain this to the soldier, but as soon as you stepped around to the front of the Land Rover he stopped you and called for reinforcements. Now three soldiers were prodding you with their weapons, angry that a white man should refuse to obey their orders.

You talked, you gesticulated, you pointed. One of them at last understood that you had something urgent to impart.

"Come," you pleaded.

You led him to the door, climbed up and, turning, stepped back down into their midst holding your drowsy daughter. The movement woke her and, seeing all these new faces, she smiled. The soldiers laughed and smiled back. One of them pinched her cheek. She cried and her animation made them laugh again. All the surliness and the threat evaporated. The men signalled you to carry on, one even waving goodbye.

You realised you were smiling, too, at the power of a baby's smile.

12

On Meeting Yourself

A mail order catalogue advertises a radio for use in the shower. Your first reaction is one of disbelief. How long, then, do other people spend in the shower? Longer than an average pop song, an aria, surely not a symphony? *Thought for Today* perhaps, but not an episode of *The Archers*. The only reason you might spend longer than a few minutes, surely, is to wash your hair, and if washing your hair it would be difficult to hear the radio, shower proof or not.

No, having a shower radio is a symptom of something else. You have noticed how people cannot go jogging without an iPod, make a journey without a car radio or go to bed without TV. Many younger people are unable to sit in a room, even when there is a TV turned on, without texting or consulting the internet. Why? Perhaps because they are frightened of meeting themselves, of confronting the person they really are.

And yet it is a pleasure to be free of noise, of distraction. It is a pleasure to be alone with yourself and to get to know what you are really like. You might meet yourself briefly even in the shower, as you stand and let the water massage the tension out of your neck and shoulders. On a run, on a hike... it is an opportunity to spend several hours in your own company, to sift through your concerns, explore ideas together.

Je ne suis jamais seul avec ma solitude, sang Georges Moustaki *(I am never alone with my solitude).* Certainly the best way to start the day is on your own, by and with yourself. The only disadvantage of having visitors to stay is that you have to talk to them at breakfast, a meal that should be taken in silence. You want to concentrate on the flavour and texture of the grapefruit, the cereal, the coffee – whatever it may be. After all, you must surface slowly from the depths of unconsciousness, or you will get the psychological bends – a condition most injurious to your wellbeing. The radio, the TV, even a newspaper detract from this slow and peaceful acclimatisation to a new day. Guests are a bigger threat, hard work that encroaches too soon on your ascent.

A car journey for many is a chore. If it is routine this is understandable, and you see why many drivers lend half an ear to their radios. For you, however, the drivel so often spewed out by illiterate local radio presenters is more of an irritant than a pleasant distraction. If you resorted to the banality of local radio you would miss the opportunity to spend valuable time with yourself.

You may daydream together, you and your self, yet you remain more alert to the traffic and its inherent risks than does the driver with a mind drugged by the dross of, for example, a phone-in programme. Covering the ground towards your destination in silence you filter out the inessential. You can have a heart to heart with yourself in the privacy of the cell that is your car. And you will both emerge from that metal retreat refreshed and invigorated.

Often the self you encounter is not a person you would like to spend much time with, but occasionally the melding of minds into one can be helpful, even a pleasure. Many people like the sound of their own voice. How many, you wonder, listen to their own inner voice?

13

When Letters Mattered

Before email and GPS the world was a bigger place. It was easier to get lost in it, and time stretched like elastic. In the wonderful solitude of the traveller a letter could be a lifeline.

To be in a strange place then was to be ahead of habit, was to have to invent the pattern of each day, was to have to force momentum on it. There could be no falling back on the familiar, no riding along on routine. Such a life required a constant effort of will, of forcing that will on others and on circumstances.

It meant repeated exposure of, and sometimes damage to, whatever 'self' it was that had to be asserted. This could be quite enervating. One pause for mental breath and despondency or depression could soak in to stain the day. So a letter from a loved one, from a friend, carried special significance.

In more remote places the arrival of the mail bag was infrequent. In the heightened state of mind in which the true traveller lived, the absence of an expected letter could be a serious blow. For, lacking conversation, you lived largely in your own mind. Problems 'back home' (if you still had some point in geography and the past that you still called home), if they did not seem entirely distant, loomed larger; worries that should at most only have gnawed began to bite deep. No letter from A. Has she had an accident? No news from B. What can have happened to him? C has not sent a letter for a long time. Is anyone looking after her?

The truth probably was that they all had written or intended writing; that in their full and clockwork lives it had not seemed to them time to write to you again so soon. Or, unaware of how precious their words were, they were unmindful too of the intricacies of the route the letter must take and the weeks it would need to reach its destination. And so, in time, the letters would arrive, never singly, never spaced, nor even in the order in which they were written. But usually they would arrive in a batch, later rather than sooner. Like Number 9 buses across a wilderness.

And what mattered of course, was the letter that did come. A letter that, received at home from a friend and read hurriedly over breakfast with a quick nod and a smile and tossed aside among the toast crumbs, possibly never to get another reading – that same letter read at a poste restante in a lonely place, or inside a baking Land Rover outside some agent's office in a bush town – that letter carried an altogether different load.

A word of encouragement, a bit of news, a simple, "we thought of you the other night when...", could charge you with great strength, renew your spirits. And the charge was repeatable on re-reading in whatever shelter you found that night, on waking from your makeshift bed in the first light of a yet-to-be-imagined day.

A word of love that spoken in a restaurant or on a train might be acknowledged by a squeeze of the hand or a decent kiss, when sung across continents from a letter lit up the savannah, coloured a whole day of your travelling life.

Some friends boast that they "never write letters" or today never bother with email; some relatives are "always too busy" but expect some mystic family tie to bind and to excuse them.

To the traveller, that is not friendship, that is not love, for it is lacking in imagination. Travelling, you learned the difference between love and duty, between friendship and simply liking. Real loved ones, real friends knew this instinctively. Their letters came into existence as a means of communication across the gap, but they were created, they were called to life as a result of their love. Theirs were the letters you waited for; they were your emotional food and drink.

They were, perhaps, why you travelled.

14

Escaping English

Y ou stayed in a budget hotel in Oslo. Exploring the TV channels on offer in your room you found it refreshing that there was no Sky or BBC news. Not that you have anything against these programmes, but they do tend to be very Anglo-Saxon centred. Unlike the huge choice of programmes in British hotels almost entirely in English, in your Norwegian hotel you could for once escape the dominance of your native tongue. This is a rare pleasure for an English speaker. An Arab, an Asian, a Russian visitor can readily plunge back into his own culture. So could you if you travelled to those countries, but in much of the world escape from the English language media is not easy.

So channel-hopping in your Norwegian hotel was a joy. First you tuned in to the various Norwegian stations and got re-acquainted with various dialects. For one hour on one of the channels you were even able to enjoy an excellent German documentary on Richard Strauss with Norwegian subtitles. There were also Swedish channels and if you craved 24-hour news there was the French world service – quite a different world from that of the BBC. Instead of wars and weather in anglophone Africa you heard about Chad, the Congo, The Central African Republic and Senegal. Admittedly, if you had to have your fix in English there was CNN, but that meant taking a tablespoon of adverts with every teaspoon of information.

After a spell of delighting in different languages rarely accessible at home, except on-line and then usually limited, you realise the world is a little bit bigger than the social media and the dominance of the English language would lead you to believe.

How fortunate are the many Europeans who take it for granted that they will use several different languages in their daily life, and are also proficient in English when they need a lingua franca. How pleased you were to get away for a week from your blinkered, monolingual little island where only immigrants are lucky enough to speak and share their various languages in addition to English, and therefore to have another perspective on their world and their lives.

15

Solitude

While loneliness is a misfortune, solitude is a blessed state of mind and being. It is a truism that you can be lonely in a crowd, in a city, even in a village. But if you have your own space in any of these places you may achieve *solitude* in each of them.

Even so, it is preferable to get right away. A few hours alone is not enough, however refreshing a brief respite from partner, family, friends or colleagues might be. The seed of solitude requires time to grow and bloom. Solitude is more than a 'bit of peace and quiet'. Solitude has to be sought and cultivated.

Certainly to grow your solitude you need that peace and quiet, as well as tranquillity of mind. You need to remove yourself from interruption and external distraction: a telephone interrupts, a computer brings emails, both offer interaction with the world outside your solitude. It is impossible to be alone with a mobile phone. Radio, and (worse) television, suspend thought. You must leave all these devices behind.

A book is perhaps an exception. True, it opens windows onto that same world, but you can take it up and put it down at will, study or read at your own leisure. In fact a book is probably best read in solitude. If you accept a book, however, you might then want to admit music, and your mental space becomes too cluttered for real solitude; too many competing voices.

Once possessed of solitude, what can you do with it? The mystic might pray or meditate, the more practical might garden or sail the oceans, the driven might get on with a piece of work – intellectual, artistic or manual – that requires undivided attention.

Whatever your temperament and inclination, the plant of solitude puts out tendrils of creativity. Solitude nourishes the writer, the thinker and the inventor. Solitude pollinates the imagination. For better or for worse, solitude leads you to look inwards, to embrace the *self,* or at least to shake hands with it, rather than to flee from it in daily distraction and the drug of work.

There are situations where loneliness and solitude meet: the condemned prisoner, the defeated politician, the disgraced official, the bereaved spouse. The solitude of the widow is not to be envied, but her loneliness is the greater trial.

Solitude however is more than being alone. We cannot share our solitude. My solitude is not your solitude. By definition it is closed to others, to enemies as well as to loved ones. Solitude is not for the faint-hearted. Even so it perhaps should be taken only in small doses. An overdose might lead to madness or, worse, to thoughts of God.

16

On Not Belonging

I f I had to choose between betraying my country and betraying my friend I hope I should have the guts to betray my country." So wrote E.M. Forster.

Today you might add, "If I had to choose between my religion and my God, I hope I should choose my God." Only you have neither.

You have worked in a university and you have worked in bureaucratic organisations. Your most successful colleagues, you have noticed, regardless of ability, are those with the social skills of joining, of networking, of belonging; of conforming in fact.

A colleague once astonished you when he said, "I always dread my leave. After three days I am dying of boredom. I just don't know what to do with myself." Yet he was a married man with children. You on the contrary enjoyed some of your job some of the time, but the highlight of your eighteen month or your two year postings was the three months leave you had accumulated by the end. Three months in which to live. To be free. Not to belong.

You met the same now ex-colleague recently and asked him how he was coping with retirement. He had less time than ever, he cheerfully told you. He was a councillor, active in the Rotary Club, a churchgoer. He was happy. Joiners do not necessarily join because they are essentially lonely or unhappy. But when they do join it makes them a lot happier.

You on the other hand are happier on your own. Even in your own small village you could join in, and sometimes out of a sense of civic duty, you have participated in Neighbourhood Watch, the Footpath Society, you have read for the blind and volunteered in the local shop and on stalls in fetes. You are content to help these worthy causes but you do not like to join them. Likewise you support, and may be a member in name only of, several charities such as the Woodland Trust. You value their work but not particularly your membership per se.

It was always thus. As a rural child you were happier walking your dog on your own or playing with a solitary friend, than joining anything. There were brownies and scouts and there must have been Sunday schools, but luckily your parents had no desire to institutionalise or indoctrinate you. When you were bigger there were cricket and football teams and bell-ringing. None of these appealed, either.

You did once out of desperation for a girlfriend go along to a meeting of the Young Conservatives. There was nothing political about them. Living in rural Kent you had no idea there were other political parties anyway. Indeed, you thought the Young Conservatives was a party in the festive sense. Not terribly festive, you discovered. You only went once, put off by the sherry drinking men and beehive-haired girls.

At primary school you had been divided into tribes: Ojibwa, Chippeway, Mohican and Deerfoot. In your next school there were 'houses'. You performed for, played for and ran for your tribe or house and felt comfortable with the solidarity it conferred. You resented, however, when standing on the touchline during a 1st XV rugby match, being punished for not cheering on the school heartily enough.

You have never returned to your school or joined any old boy network. The same goes for your first university, though you enjoyed your undergraduate years. You have kept in touch with friends, not with the institutions. No alumni association for you!

Anyone reading this might judge you churlish and anti-social. In the sense that you dislike parties, celebrations, weddings and other gatherings, perhaps you are, but you also get on with people when you have to. You like most of them and for some reason a few seem to like you. You have run offices and projects, lectured, taught and given seminars; you have directed workshops and plays. Though in the latter case you do remember running out of the theatre and away down the road when the foot stamping audience called for the director.

No, you do not normally turn your back on groups, on society, and you have a large and friendly extended family you like to be with (albeit in small doses!). It is just that you prefer to go it alone. To do your own thing. Be your own man.

Writing, that loneliest of occupations, may not be what you do best, but it is what you do most. Perhaps that is why you moved from writing plays to the more individual pursuit of pure fiction. It would be nice, though, you must confess, if you could share your work with someone, with the public, that is, for you could of course never even consider joining a writing group.

17

On Visiting The Barber

M ost men visit their barber for a haircut. Here in this small town a good many go for the entertainment. True, those patient enough might emerge shorn, but several who crowd into the little room have no intention of taking a seat in the barber's chair. Rather, they come to pass the time of day, to buy and sell second hand tools, to exchange banter with Graham and with one another.

The barber's shop is a side room in the oldest house, leased by the council at a peppercorn rent because they believe a local barber performs a useful service. Just how useful, they are probably unaware. Graham has installed his own porcelain sink saved from a demolition job. Its large brass taps come from another site. Most of the fittings are features Graham has 'rescued' from here and there, DIY being one of his many hobbies. Any actual haircut risks interruption from some character or other 'just dropping by' with a bag of nails or an electric tool which he will leave on the window sill 'in case it is worth something.'

If you want a haircut it is best to choose a chilly day. When the weather is fine you are likely to find the door closed and the notice *Gone Fishing* stuck in the window. If it is cold a coal fire burns in the grate and Graham, whether he has a customer in the chair or not, holds court.

His store of jokes is endless and shameless. Country people have no truck with political correctness. A few days after the September 11 outrage in New York he told the following story:

It's the year 2051. An American farmer brings his son to town. They pass by the former site of the Twin Towers, now a memorial park.

"Just think, son, fifty years ago thousands of people were working in two huge blocks that rose from this place."

"What happened to them, Pa?"

"Well, son, I guess a coupla Arabs hi-jacked some planes and flew them into the buildings. Knocked them down and killed most everyone inside."

"Dad?"

"Yes, son?"

"What's an Arab?"

Whether his stories are political, scabrous, or merely zany, Graham has the perfect timing of a practised performer. If you are unfortunate enough to be sitting in the chair while he has an audience you may well wonder when he is going to take the next snip. The scissors are flourished more as an aid to storytelling than to cutting hair.

Even when he is alone with a customer he will break off the tedious business of hair-dressing to sip a cup of cold tea – indeed, to brew a fresh pot of hot tea. He will pause to talk and since he does a lot of talking the pauses joined together take longer than the business of cutting hair.

One particularly cold day you found him on his own warming his hands at the fire. You settled in the snug chair, but no sooner had he set to work than the door opened and an old man stamped in. When he removed his cap and revealed only three strands of hair, you assumed he had come in merely to survey the bric-a-brac on the window-sill and to get warm. "Morning, Joe. Missus locked you out again, has she?" asked Graham.

The man did not answer. He had spotted a photo album on an empty seat. Photography was another of Graham's hobbies and he did produce some striking landscapes. There were one or two local spots he loved with feeling, a particular field and a bend in the river. Like Monet with his water lilies, Graham would return again and again to photograph them in different lights, in different seasons. But this album was different. "That won't interest you, Joe. I brought it in to show old Jack my home improvements."

"I can have a look, can't I?"

Graham shrugged his assent. For a while there was quiet. The scissors snipped, the fire crackled, the pages turned. Then Joe piped up, "This your wife, then?"

This was Graham's cue. He stepped up to Joe, looked over his shoulder and said, "Oh yes, the clock is on the other wall."

"She don't look like no home improvement to me."

"I'll tell her you said that, an' all."

As well as being a bit of a joker, though, Graham has hidden depths. These were revealed in one of the first serious conversations you had with him. Unusually, you and he were alone. The haircut was progressing between sips of tea and the heaping of coals on the fire. Conversation turned to car boot sales. Graham had just spent £60 on a painting.

"£60!" You were impressed.

"It's a lot, I know, but it took my fancy. I do know what I like."

Trying not to sound patronising, you asked him what it was a painting of.

"It was a portrait, oil, quite old. I don't know if it's worth £60. Could be a lot more. I bought it for its subject matter and what they call its 'execution'. It really got to me. I'm a sucker for paintings. Do you like painting?"

You told him you did not paint but admitted to going to exhibitions.

"Do you?" exclaimed the barber as though you were his soul mate. "Turner's my man. I love Turner."

Imagining that he did not travel much, you told him somewhat tentatively that you had recently visited a Turner exhibition at Tate Britain. His reply set you straight.

"Oh yes? I go there once a month."

"To London?"

"To the Tate, yes. Just to see one painting. The old man in the armchair. By Turner. Do you know it?" Now, you think of Turner as a landscape painter and could not remember the portrait. Graham was forgiving. "Not a lot of people notice it. But I love it. I really love that picture."

He then went on to describe the painting. In plain vernacular he conjured up the portrait of an old man sitting alone in the corner of a dark cottage, his face lit by the firelight. He described the quality of the light, the expression of the man, the composition of the whole better than any academic catalogue. More than that, he conveyed his own deep passion for the painting.

When he was finished you were speechless. In his mind's eye Graham was still contemplating the portrait, but after a brief pause he caught your eye in the mirror, raised his scissors and said, "And do you know what?"

You shook your long untouched head.

"Turner's father was a barber, too."

18

Freedom Of Movement

You have been lucky living in the spaces and time allotted to you. In time especially. Your rural childhood was unthreatened by vehicles or menacing adults. When later you lived in Indian and African cities it was still safe to walk around most of them freely and unmolested; your offices and libraries not yet targets for terrorists. For much of your working life you have been in a minority as a white man, but viewed at worst as a curiosity rather than an enemy.

Growing up in the UK your freedom was remarkable. Never again will you capture the sheer joy of the school holidays. Always, even as a teenager, you rose early bursting with energy and things to do. You would begin your day taking your dog for a walk. And what walks! What a dog! You were never out for less than two hours. There was the farm to reconnoitre, there were streams and rivers to investigate, there were woods to penetrate. Meena, your dachshund, was as bright-eyed and enthusiastic as you, eager for rabbits, torpedoing fresh molehills and happy to splash up the Kent Ditch while you turned stones in search of eels.

You were always outdoors, in winter or in summer, and your parents never worried where you went, nor even asked. Provided you were back for lunch at one and supper in the evening they were content. Besides it was inconceivable that you or your friends should be indoors during daylight hours.

When your closest friend and his family moved to another

farm eight miles away you would cycle over to play, as it was called. You had no special clothes, cycle helmets were unheard of, though your bicycle did have a dynamo that powered a feeble front light and a dull red rear light. Up hill these lights almost petered out if you slowed down too much. But traffic was no worry. Nowadays on those same, twisty and narrow roads you would not contemplate riding a bike in broad daylight. The traffic is unceasing, placing the cyclist at huge risk from the impatient and inattentive motorist.

Once a year you left the countryside and stayed with your grandparents in Broadstairs, a busy seaside town with seven bays beneath chalk cliffs. You followed the same routine with the same dog. You would go out after breakfast, and depending on the state of the tide, patrol all the bays. At low tide you would linger over the rock pools, Meena catching and fiercely shaking crabs that you uncovered by removing rocks and stones. Sometimes you hired a pedalo and headed out to sea, Meena standing in the bows like a figurehead and looking down into the water.

Your grandmother was always pleased to see you again when you returned safe for lunch but she never questioned or limited your movements. No one imagined a young boy would be prey to paedophiles or to any other predator, let alone be stupid enough to drown or injure himself. There was one pleasant and innocent old man, a friend of your grandmother, who had a flat on the cliffs above Viking Bay. You sometimes called in for a chat and he would let you look through his telescope trained out to sea and the Goodwin Sands. He had a soft spot for your grandmother and would give you little gifts, usually of food, to take back to her.

When you were older, probably in your mid-teens, you kept a Heron sailing dinghy in Broadstairs harbour that you had built yourself at school. You took it out single handed, relishing the high winds and rough seas of the North Foreland. Your little dinghy heeled over almost to the horizontal but you were always in control and with the insufferable arrogance of youth, you revelled in showing off to the holidaymakers watching from the jetty. Once the harbour master told you off for entering the harbour under sail. Since the dinghy was gaff rigged and had no engine you wondered how else you could have got back in.

Nevertheless he must have spoken to your grandparents for they gently advised you to be more careful. They rarely went down to the beach themselves, even though their little house was only ten minutes walk up the hill.

At university, too, your freedom of movement was absolute. The campus was three miles out of town. If you went to a film in town it was easy to miss the last bus, but on the three mile walk back to your Hall of Residence you never met a mugger. Not surprising since no one in those days carried anything of value, no mobiles, certainly no money, and credit cards had not been invented. As far as you knew no one carried knives or used drugs either. It was an innocent era. The only excess for some was beer and, for you, too many books to read. You all studied hard.

When you emigrated to Australia as a 'ten pound Pom' the White Australia Policy prevailed, the pubs closed at 6 p.m. and in that uniform, Anglo-Saxon society your movements were safe and unchallenged, except when you opened your mouth to speak. No Australian could bring himself to call you William. Always it was Bill. When you spent four months crossing from Melbourne to Perth with a VW Beetle and an inflatable tent, you stopped and pitched camp where you found yourself that evening. No one ever hassled or questioned you. Glorious freedom, almost frightening solitude.

The space where you felt the most free, however, was the beautiful, empty wilderness that is Norway. There everyone has the right to roam wherever they will and that roaming may be by shank's pony, on ski or in a canoe. It is easy to lose yourself in more senses than one in this lovely land. Your only fright was once coming face to face with a mountainously tall elg; at dusk sometimes, you experienced a delicious shudder imagining that those shapes and shadows in the forest were trolls watching you.

You worked and travelled in Sri Lanka and South India before the Tamil Tigers made parts of Ceylon, as it was called, a no go area. You always felt safe in India. Sometimes your blonde young wife had to put up with inquisitive children and even the occasional adult patting her hair out of curiosity. She never felt threatened. Later, when the assassinations and bombings began, you had moved on.

True, you were in Southern Sudan during its long civil

war, but most of the time you roamed freely and untroubled. You would encounter giraffe and hippo and elephant on some treks. Later the roads would be mined, the wild life slaughtered and the towns devastated. Then you did have to close your office and leave. Your last African country and the friendliest of all was Ghana.

The only place you have felt ill at ease was the USA. The sight of people walking on foot around town or in the residential areas, something you took for granted on other continents, seemed to unnerve the natives. Their attitude could be aggressive and you knew many Americans still carried guns long after they had 'conquered' the West.

You are now settled in Cumbria where you continue your daily walks along the many local footpaths. Once out of the friendly village you rarely meet anyone. If you do and they are local they will say, "How are you all reet?" Walking as therapy, as recreation, as meditation has become a neglected pleasure.

You were so lucky to have been brought up in a fear-free environment and to have developed the habit, nay the need, regularly just to walk out. It is a pleasure still to use this allotted space and time in tranquillity.

19

A Sense Of Relief

I t is said to be a relief when you stop banging your head against a brick wall. That must depend on what drove you to bang it in the first place, you suppose. But there are some kinds of relief that afford more than satisfaction, even some small pleasure: finishing a difficult job, leaving a noisy party, walking out of the dentist after uncomfortable treatment.

You vividly remember one such experience at the Kent and Sussex Hospital.

"But I'm not dying!" you said, while a horrible doubt surfaced. "Am I?"

"No," said the hospital receptionist with an ever-so-patient sigh, "but you are only in for the die."

"Oh, the *day* ward," you interpreted.

As one who breaks into a nervous sweat in a dentist's waiting room, and that just for a check-up, your confusion over the hospital admission procedures might have been forgiven. There were several offices and consulting rooms at the top end of Ward 10.

A nurse appeared from a room that smelled like a chemist's shop and asked if she could help. You told her the hospital had phoned to say there had been a cancellation and had asked you to come in at short notice. That had been yesterday.

"If you will go and sit in the waiting room, someone will be with you shortly."

Shortly is a word they use a lot in hospitals. It is their way of measuring the slow pulse of anxious hours.

For the best of ergonomic reasons, no doubt, the waiting room was at the bottom end of the ward. This at least gave new patients a Dante-esque preview of what lay in store; and it provided the maimed and the mutilated with live entertainment as the noviciates were ferried up and down this mall of suffering between the waiting room and the offices.

You were welcomed to the carpeted and comfortable waiting area by a huge sign: *Children. Do not play.* All the magazines were for a female readership, yet this was clearly a mixed ward; at least some of the male patients must also have been able to read. You have never understood why in all waiting rooms everywhere it is assumed the clientèle is semi-literate. Given the time spent waiting, perhaps the annotated works of Shakespeare would be more appropriate than the pap usually on offer.

You were in hospital for something called 'clerking'. In a nutshell this meant checking whether you were well enough to be ill. Otherwise they could not operate. You would have to come back the following day actually to be carved up. No need to worry yet, then. Only there was something about the rows of pasty faced men and women groaning and writhing in their unisex nighties that filled you with nauseous unease.

A thin, well scrubbed nurse entered and called out your name. She led you to a cubicle and pulled the curtain around the bed to ask the intimate question:

"Date of birth?" You told her. "Well done. Very good," she reassured you.

Not dementia then.

You felt quite pleased with yourself.

"Can I go now?"

She thought you were joking. "I'm going to tell you what will happen this morning." Your stomach turned over. You braced yourself for the worst, but it sounded fairly routine. Test heart, blood, urine – not state of mind fortunately. What she did not say was that during the course of the morning they were also going to test your patience and your nerve.

The frightening bit she kept for last. "Then you will see the consultant, who will run through your operation with you."

You wondered if this would be an illustrated slide show, whether perhaps you'd follow him into a theatre for a live demo. Would you be allowed, as you had heard on some consumer radio programme, to ask him where he stood on the league table of surgeons? Something like – operations performed: 300, survivors: 240, partially botched: 40, fatalities: 20. But how would you know if this was good or bad?

The nurse ended her briefing with what at first you took to be a conjuring trick. She pulled open a small, wrapped package in the way one tears the lid from a pot of yoghurt. Inside was a dinky container about the size of a bottle top.

"When you are ready," she said, "I want you to go to the toilet, wee a little, and fill this container from the middle of your wee."

This conjured up quite an acrobatic image before you grasped what she meant. Considering the size of the container, it might have been easier to shake off a drop or two when you had finished, but you guessed she had heard all the wisecracks. You thanked her and reverentially accepted the sacrament.

And then the testing began. You were to be shuttled up and down from the waiting area about every half hour for one of the procedures outlined. The patients were a bit like counters in a game of ludo: the player can either move one counter all the way round the board with each shake of the die (or should that be day?), or he can move a different counter each time, advancing his group together. The hospital was obviously intent on holding all its patients back as long as possible, an equality of suspense, so that you all progressed at a mind-numbingly slow pace.

Most striking was the lack of privacy. A curtain stops you seeing, but not hearing.

"Now please remove all your clothing below the waist and wait on the bed," you heard a voice saying on the other side. "A doctor will be with you shortly." When the doctor did arrive you heard him exclaim, "Goodness, how long has it been like this?" A nurse burst out through the curtains stifling laughter under the pretence of blowing her nose, and when the curtains were drawn back 'shortly' afterwards the eyes of everyone in the vicinity swivelled towards the occupant of that bed.

During another of your suffocating waits an older nurse came to talk to a woman sitting next to you. She was trying to keep her voice down while she broke bad news to the woman about her husband. Her late husband. You decided it was time to go for another wee, starting at the beginning and finishing at the end.

You would have preferred a coffee. You had got up early to reach the appointment on time, there had been a train journey and you had been sitting in sauna temperatures for two hours. Elevenses was long past. You could see no water dispenser, let alone a tea or coffee machine.

Dehydrated, you approached the final hurdle. A woman who was some kind of specialist came to accompany you to your consultant. Passing again between the bedridden carcasses, which even for you had now become wallpaper, she asked, "Have the pills been working?"

"No," you replied frankly. "They have not made the slightest difference."

She checked her step between a woman on a bed pan and a man trying helplessly to turn over.

"How long," she asked accusingly, "have you been taking them?"

"Two months," you said. "Why?"

She tore open a curtain to an empty cubicle and ordered you to wait inside. She would have to speak to the consultant. Why you were excluded you would never know. When she returned she told you to continue the pills for another six months. "You should never have come in," she complained, as though *you* were wasting *her* time.

"But the hospital phoned me yesterday."

"It's premature."

"It's lack of communication," you said, half expecting a lethal injection for expressing an unpalatable truth.

"I'll speak to the waiting list supervisor," she threatened.

You had wasted most of the day, not to mention the other business you had cancelled at short notice. The hospital had lengthened its waiting list. For the moment, though, you stepped out into the fresh air light-headed, as though the ordeal was finally over and you were cured: your only symptoms a modest pleasure.

20

Les Mots Justes

You woke early and a full moon, like the single eye of night curious to see what the new day might bring, shone in a blue and cloudless sky. The air held still with promise, summer perhaps having a few more days to run after all. You went down to the beach. The whole bay was as flat as a linen table cloth and bluer than the sky, sparkling with sunshine. It was so calm that no waves lapped the shore. The Mediterranean Sea could have been an unruffled lake, a mill pond.

Silence reigned. Few cars had yet arrived, the cafés were still closed, no jet skis roared, no water skiers thumped through their own wake; even the sailing boats floated motionless, tethered to their moorings or anchored out in the bay.

You walked on round the strand, enjoying the tranquil beauty and breathing in the scent of pine. When you reached the rocky headland at the end of the long beach of fine pale sand you climbed over to the first of many numerous small and intimate coves.

In the centre sat a middle-aged woman on a beach towel. She was wearing a swimsuit and talking into a mobile phone. Her voice was loud and hoarse and carried clearly in the general stillness. She was talking to her family back home in mainland France, making inquiries about individuals. Her eyes were staring fixedly out to sea, but her mind was totally on her phone call.

Her caller must then have asked about her holiday, about this little seaside village in Corsica, Ile de Beauté.

She paused a moment, relaxed and then said:

"C'est le bonheur complet."

This expression of her utter contentment was made with a deep sigh as evocative as her words. And you knew exactly how she felt. This moment, this place, this bubble you were both in was one of complete happiness. And hearing her declare it so, you knew it was true, and shed a little tear of joy yourself. She had encapsulated the moment for a stranger whom she had not even noticed passing.

21
On Returning Home From A Holiday

At first, relief. Relief and weary satisfaction that your journey home has gone according to plan, and that the travelling is over. Relief as you drive into Sheep Street Lane – in summer a leafy tunnel, where you pass through remnants of old woodland; in winter a ribbon winding through a more visible and familiar landscape – to find your terraced cottage rising like a ship above the hedgerow, still afloat, still intact. Relief as you turn into your driveway to find that no windows are broken, no doors forced. All is as you left it.

You note also that the lawn is knee high, the vegetable beds overgrown, the flowers choked by weeds. A few weeks' negligence and nature mocks your pretence at gardening.

You open up the house and step inside. No sign of break in, no squatters, water leaks or fire, wasps' nests or bee swarms. The air is cold and dead. You open a few windows to reanimate the old house, to breathe in fresh garden scents and to admit the sound of bird song. You turn on the hot water, plug in the computer and the TV. Red and green lights blink to welcome you home.

Before you even lug your suitcase upstairs you begin to download your emails, then turn your attention to the litter of letters heaped up inside the front door. Judging it from appearances you sort this into junk, business and personal piles. You put the kettle on, make a pot of tea and, clutching a big mug of it, return for closer inspection of your mail, selecting only the most private or the most urgent for immediate perusal. Satisfied, you do the same with your emails, deleting 60% of them. Messages on the telephone will have to wait, as you cannot hurry them along.

If it is still light you make a tour of the garden and look into the greenhouse. You water pots and tubs and trays, pick whatever is going for an evening meal, and wonder where and when to begin the serious work.

Finally you unpack your suitcase, flinging the dirty washing in the linen basket and stacking on a shelf the presents you have bought for friends and loved ones.

You are home, and it is good.

22

Uncertainty

I f certainty is defined as provable fact at one end of a spectrum, and belief as something unprovable at the other, then the line will run from certainty through probability, plausibility, possibility and guesswork to faith and belief.

Where does uncertainty lie? You are not sure, but most likely somewhere in the middle.

There are still people who hold unshakeable religious beliefs, but some of the greatest thinkers, religious and non-religious, have been doubters. As early as the 16th century Pascal let many off the hook with his famous *pari,* or bet. Since God's existence could not be proven Pascal calculated there was nothing to lose and all to gain by betting He did exist. You would need a pretty generous God, however, not to view this as a cop-out. Likewise Kierkegaard's leap of faith several centuries later. Where was commitment in all of this?

What is appealing about Pascal, although – and perhaps because – he was an outstanding mathematician, is that his motto was 'Q*ue sais-je?' – What do I know?* A healthy attitude in any age.

You find uncertainty a more satisfactory state of mind than blind belief. The road ahead for the uncertain may be more confusing than for those of strong faith, but it is always full of possibility, with or without a map.

Uncertain people have better conversations than those who believe they are always right. When a mother explains she cannot grieve for a lost child because its soul will already have transmigrated to another life, you can only wonder at such certainty. For you the loss of this life is the very reason to be grieving. The mother's attitude begs many questions that she will refuse to contemplate. She is consoled by her belief, though presumably for her there is no reason for consolation.

Uncertainty is the twin of doubt, and together they shape the questioning mind. If there is one thing to be certain about it is never to take anything on trust. This applies equally to get rich schemes, get fit regimes, find salvation plans, lotteries, diets, life style and even academic courses.

Your star sign is Libra, the balance or scales. However if there is one thing impossible to be uncertain about it must be that astrology is surely nonsense. Inconsistency of methodology and readings apart, our lives are more likely to be predetermined by our genes than by the stars. Nevertheless, you like to think of yourself as a balanced person, capable of seeing both sides, a point of view that in itself often leads to uncertainty.

Uncertainty does not mean you do not know the difference between right and wrong. You also have decided artistic, musical and literary likes and dislikes of your own. These latter are only tastes and may change, but even ethical values are not necessarily absolute. Take killing. It is wrong to kill, but is it always wrong? We kill to eat, we kill flies and mosquitoes and bacteria (unless we are Jain monks). We kill human foetuses and people dying in pain. How easy to take the absolutist line that all life is sacred and should never be terminated, until perhaps you become involved in the predicament of a friend or loved one. The uncertain would at least discuss each case on its merit.

Uncertainty does not prevent you coming to a decision if such is required. Uncertainty allows the problem to be aired. Being uncertain, you may never know if you reach the right decision, but uncertainty is not synonymous with immorality or unethical behaviour. It is broader and fairer than certainty. It is the application of reason and knowledge to intuition and belief. And who knows what motor drives our reason?

On the day to day level uncertainty makes a nonsense of many activities. Take those questionnaires and surveys so beloved of pollsters and market researchers. You are asked to tick boxes to show which newspapers you read, the detergents you use, where you shop and what you watch on TV. As though you were set in your ways; as though you lived life to a pattern. There is never a box for 'sometimes I do this and sometimes I do that' or for 'it depends.'

As for personality tests, the questions are ridiculously

hypothetical. *Someone is drowning, do you a) call for help, b) jump in, or c) ignore it and walk on by?*

You want to know first who is drowning, your child, a friend, a stranger, a criminal, a banker? You want to know how deep the water is, how cold it is, what are you wearing, is there anyone else around, where are the emergency services? In a real life situation you may well act immediately and without thinking, but you would not answer the call by putting a tick in a box.

Amongst those who think and act with certainty some may become heroes, others martyrs. Most will remain bigots and fools. You find uncertainty the best approach, indeed the only approach to most things. It offers greater possibilities, is more satisfying and safer. There is a small pleasure to be derived in the freedom from certainty.

23

On Being Hugged By A Tree

Having spent the morning scraping down and painting the inside of the shower door and surround, you went out after lunch in some wild weather to clear your lungs and sinuses of the toxic fumes.

It was brooding, windy and wet weather, and you were well wrapped up. Shod in gumboots and lost in thought you squelched over the field towards the railway line. After a while you found yourself standing on the first of the two wooden footbridges over the streams that feed the Rother. A single beam spanned each stream, and there were solid wooden handrails to hang onto should you lose your balance.

You stood right in the middle of the bridge, leaning on the slippery rail, and stared down at the turbulent, muddy torrent swollen by recent rain and dotted with the drops that were still falling. Gusts scoured the surface further.

All of a sudden you felt a hand on your shoulder, strong,

firm and friendly. You looked round in surprise and saw
it was the lower branch of one of the ash trees, standing
sentinel, that was greeting you. You smiled at the tree and
as it released its hold it seemed to wink back. "Good to see
you," it said.

"You too," you replied.

For almost thirty years you had been crossing this bridge
on average twice a week without exchanging so much as a
word with the ash. But nearly always you noticed it under
the different seasons. It is a familiar presence. Like some
people in the village, it obviously now considered you had
known one another long enough to make introductions.

You shook limbs. The tree remained rooted, but you
went on feeling in some way enriched.

24

Listening to the Torrent

You climbed steadily upwards: an easy stroll along
a stony track at first. At the head of the valley you
left the footpath and chose to follow the stream, if
follow is an appropriate term to describe clambering in the
opposite direction to the tumbling torrent. You stayed as
close as possible to the cascading water but as your ascent
became more acute the stream poured towards you over
waterfalls and the bare rocks were too wet and steep to
climb. You headed away and struggled sometimes through
waist high ferns, sometimes over thick grass set with bare
stones. Never, though, were you out of earshot of the beck.
There was no other sound in the landscape than the mountain stream. The air was still, the sheep silent, birds distant
and no sign of human presence.

As you neared the top of the climb there were more sheer
faces, more waterfalls before you reached your goal: a large,
black rock pool beneath a high and full curtain of crash-

ing water. Over the centuries the stream had worn into the mountainside and in its fierce career had dug a deep bed into the ground. Consequently on either side of the water course there was now a steep and grassy descent to its banks.

You lowered yourself down with care and found a slab of rock at the water's edge large and smooth enough to sit on. You settled down and began to eat your packed lunch.

Conversation here would have been impossible. The tons of water continuously falling into the deep pool kept up a constant splash and roar, the churning currents adding their own sound effects. But the outflow from the pool of this same mass of water made even more of a noise as it rushed over the boulder-strewn bed and through the rocks down a steep, winding cataract.

The rock basin was as large as a public swimming pool but more irregular in depth and shape. At the lower end where you sat the water was still and safe to swim in, though very cold. Towards the fall it was hard to swim against the strong flow and to approach the swirling maelstrom. From time to time a veil of spray covered the whole scene but did not mute the thudding growl.

Replete from your picnic and tired from your exertions you stretched out on your back and allowed the fitful bursts of sunshine to warm the rock and you.

Then you heard it. The sound, the voice of the mountainside, contained far more than you had hitherto taken in. There was the almost regular bass beat of the falling water and the counterpoint of its hurried exit down the mountain. If the waterfall itself was a double bass, the cascade was the timpani. But there was more. Indeed at first you thought you did hear human voices. You raised your head but realized it was only the ringing resonance of the rocks as they were struck and played by the heavy, rushing mass of water. The more you listened the more you heard and soon the most extraordinary perception became clear.

Closing your eyes you could imagine you were in the middle of a fairground. You listened to the lilting rhythms and the raucous music of the carrousel with its galloping horses rising and falling in harmony with the rising and falling roar of the big diesel-driven generators. The vulgar blasts from the sideshows and the hum and throb of the crowds created a muted symphony. The gurgle and babble of the mountain stream linked these disparate effects.

You knew you were miles from civilisation, from engines and electricity, but you felt that if you looked hard enough just round the corner of that grey rock, you would see the garish lights of the fairground with its seething crowds and its brash, distorted music. It was the hubbub that brought these two scenes together. Long before mankind had invented his noisy entertainment, nature had created this wonderful, chaotic cacophony.

25

The Old Mulberry Tree

The whole family loved the old mulberry tree. It is one your earliest and most enduring memories. The mulberry tree was part of your childhood, playing as important a role in your life as Mitten the cat and Buffin the dog. The tree had its own wise personality.

You were five years old when your parents moved into that white-painted Kentish weatherboard house, and it was the first time you had had a garden all around the house. There was a pond and an orchard, but it was the enormous mulberry tree that took your fancy from the first. Both house and tree were over two hundred years old and about the same height, which to a child was logical enough.

Some time before you all lived there the mulberry tree must have almost blown over. The first ten feet of the trunk, the girth of a water butt, leaned at an angle of 45°. A crutch hewn from another branch supported it, above which the tree had resumed its vertical and flourishing growth.

This sloping main stem, though rough on bare knees and feet, was easy to climb. You could scramble up on all fours and make camp in the Y-shaped depression where the tree divided. Climbing higher was more difficult as the branches were too widely spaced. If you wanted to get to the crown of the tree, you could cross the lawn and clamber up the magnificent copper beech that grew by the hedge. More slender than the mulberry tree, at the top of the beech you could feel the trunk swaying in the wind.

The old and stiff mulberry tree on the other hand offered much more than climbing opportunities. It had a skirt of low-hanging branches and when the pocket handkerchief-sized leaves formed in summer it made a tent-like cover, inside which you and your friends could hide and play and unless your memory is at fault, shelter from the hot sun; certainly from the rain.

On summer afternoons, serenaded by blackbird or song thrush, the family would take tea beside or beneath the mulberry tree, Mother carrying out the tea tray to take a break with her children. On his half day Father also joined you in his gardening clothes.

Over the summer you would watch the caterpillar-like fruit turn from green to yellow to pink, and when the berries were deep crimson you would place the sun-warmed fruit on your tongue, press them to your palate and slowly savour the delicate, sweet taste of this heavenly manna.

The mulberry tree also got you into trouble at school. When you were about nine years old, following a school trip to Canterbury Cathedral where the class had been shown the mulberry trees in the gardens there, originally planted for the silk trade, your teacher instigated a silkworm project in your classroom. She thought she could feed the silk worms on lettuce leaves, but very soon the larvae started to die.

"What we really need are mulberry leaves," she announced.

You stuck up your hand. "We've got a mulberry tree," you volunteered.

As a result it fell to your lot to supply the bugs with their breakfast every day. Not easy for a small boy to carry a sprig of leaves undamaged to school, though you soon perfected a technique of stripping and hiding the leaves in your lunch box. If you forgot you were scolded by the teacher and by your more committed classmates. However many of the silk worms did survive and pupate. Eventually a little silk was spun.

Disaster was revealed one autumn morning when you

were about twelve. There had been a violent storm in the night. The old house had creaked and groaned like a ship at sea. In the morning as usual you carried your clothes into your parents' bedroom to dress by their electric fire. It must have been a Saturday, for Mother and Father were still asleep. You went to the bay window, drew back a curtain and looked out over the lawn below. You could not believe what you saw and let out a shrill, involuntary cry. This woke both parents who stumbled to the window to see what was distressing you.

The whole, huge mulberry tree had been uprooted and now sprawled broken-limbed across the lawn. Your parents were as shocked as you were. You had all loved that tree. Standing there in your pyjamas you were all moist eyed. You are not sure you understand the concept of soul. Descartes did not believe animals had souls. Early missionaries did not believe native Australians had a soul. Well, if it turns out you are lucky enough to have a soul, then surely that old mulberry tree had one, too. The tree had always radiated a strong presence. You and your family were privileged to have shared its last years and felt bereft without it.

26

Respite

T he simplest of pleasures can come upon you unexpectedly. It was a last minute arrangement made for practical reasons. You had not slept in your own bed for three months; you had not been on your own for a single moment of those three months, care of erratic elderly parents being a round the clock job.

The first pleasure, then, was the peace and quiet, the tranquillity and your own undemanding company. Yes, your garden was overgrown and deep in damp leaf litter, but the little, manageable house was soon warm, spick and span. The contrast with the rotting, rambling ruin where you had been feeding the nonagenarians off chipped crockery, washing in a bathroom where wet wallpaper hung from the ceiling like a roost of fruit bats, where they would not contemplate buying a kettle that took less than ten minutes to boil, or throwing away broken handled pans, was akin to culture shock. It was refreshing simply to come home.

The second pleasure was the easy convenience of a jug kettle, an efficient toaster, thermostatic hot plates and a coffee machine. You had a clean, bright and functioning kitchen, a hygienic bathroom and shower, a tidy house, and all to yourself! Bliss! You could even turn on the TV or radio and listen to them at a sound level that did not fill the eardrums with pain and leave them tickling for hours afterwards.

Silence. No demands. After three months, responsible for a few hours for no one.

Then in the morning, what used to be a simple routine taken for granted now became an existential pleasure. A simple, Sunday breakfast: croissants with quince jelly, served with coffee ground to your preferred strength from your own percolator and dowsed in steamy hot milk. *Café au lait*. Best of all, you drank it from your big, yellow French bowl that you held with both hands as you brought it to your face, burying your nose in the warm aroma. No cat licking its bottom on the table, no complaints from a petulant old woman. For a few hours you could indulge yourself in absolute selfishness.

27

A Land Rover

A real Land Rover has nothing to do with the shiny, powerful, fuel-thirsty Chelsea Tractor; it is not the same vehicle that has spawned a dozen 4WD toddler and shopping transporters, city traffic jammers whose only encounter with mud comes from a spray can 'for that authentic look'. This last is the give-away, a remnant of that dream of a more rugged way of life, a kind of freedom away from the tarmac, 'off-road' as it is sold.

You have been lucky enough to have enjoyed the authentic – not as a look or a slogan, but as a reality. You have never needed spray-on mud any more than pre-stained or ripped jeans. A Land Rover has always been a workhorse, a necessity. Your closest encounters with death (your own and others) has been through one Land Rover or another.

The first Land Rover was almost a farm animal, a friendly, reliable, Series Two machine with a split windscreen that opened forward to allow a breeze, as if that were needed, and two goggle-head lamps set close together in front of the radiator. It was dark green. All Land Rovers were, in those days.

In it you helped hump bales of hay out to the sheep in winter, cart any manner of loads, from logs to livestock, in all seasons; tow trailers and horseboxes and even, once, a gang-mower to cut thistles in the paddock. Being an off-road vehicle, you learned to drive it around the farm before your twelfth birthday, five years before you would be permitted to drive on the roads.

In your teens a friend bought his own Land Rover pick-up, a short wheel base, and older than both of you. One summer's evening he drove over to your house. You had an Austrian exchange student staying. The three of you went for a spin, unaware how literally that term was to prove. Your friend drove; you and Anton (the Austrian boy) stood up in the back holding on to the cab roof.

On one sharp, downhill bend the Land Rover, unused perhaps to roads, did not respond to the steering and shot over the verge, dropping into a field. You remember being fired as if from a catapult, flying through the twigs and green leaves of birch and hazel before landing on soft grass.

The silence was broken by your friend's voice: "Are you all right?"

You did not know your ear was bleeding. You were stunned but rose shakily.

"Where's Anton?" Moments ago he had been standing beside you singing his head off.

A search discovered him beneath the door of the Land Rover, which was lying on its side. He was conscious but in pain. Later, in casualty, the doctors found that he had broken his shoulder. As a medical student, however, he proclaimed he'd been interested to see at first hand how the NHS worked.

Many years later, working in Africa, you had a small fleet of Land Rovers, petrol and diesel, short and long, open and covered. By now there were different colours. Yours were blue, green and a kind of desert beige, although these three different colours soon bleached and faded into a similar metallic hue under the African sun.

In the Southern Sudan there were only eight kilometres of bitumen, and this in Juba, the capital. All the other roads were red and hard and corrugated in the dry season, and often squidgy as wet cement in the rains. All bridges had collapsed, so you had to drive through the water when the flow allowed. You carried your own water, fuel, food and spare tyres. When the spares ran out you mended the tyres yourself with a hot patch. Authentic enough for the strongest man in such heat.

It is remarkable what terrain can be covered in a well driven Land Rover, what impossible gradients can be climbed and descended. But on a fast, straight road they are notoriously unstable. So many were rolled over. One colleague suffered a blow-out, her Land Rover capsized and she was crushed to death.

Your most frightening moment was in a big, heavily laden, long diesel Land Rover driving up a snake of a road into the Imatong Mountains between Sudan and Uganda. With altitude, a low cloud drizzled onto the baked mud, making it as slippery as ice. On a steep hairpin bend all four wheels were churning forwards but the vehicle was slowly losing ground, sliding backwards and outwards towards the precipice. Stopping would have made matters worse, creating a sledge ride; you knew from years driving in Norwegian snow that acceleration would increase wheel spin and loss of traction.

You remained in as high a gear as possible, kept the engine going, the wheels slowly turning, and you held your breath. Some moments you made ground, some you stayed in the same spot, and others you slipped back. The engine purred gently, some purchase was made and gradually, terrifyingly gradually, you pulled out of the corner, onto the straight and were safe.

Many years later, across the same continent, you had another mountain experience. Searching for a hill station you had asked the way of a cattle herder, who had pointed up a narrow track. After a while you realised this was very rough and very steep and probably only used by the most sure-footed of cattle. Your informant had not realised that normally cars cannot go where cows can.

But yours had to. There was nowhere to turn, no going back except in reverse. You plugged on up in first gear over rocks and boulders, the thorn bush and scrub scratching your paintwork.

You made it. Unbelievably you emerged through the goalposts of an improvised football pitch and drove out onto a plateau, where you found the real road again.

But this was in a Land Rover Discovery, the first to be imported to Ghana, a new breed. A vehicle designed for leisure, and the end of the authentic dream.

28

Maupassant: Quinze Contes

ou still have the book. It runs to 123 pages, bound
in a blue hard cover. Though worn and faded it has
aged well. The label on the inside of the front cover
reminds you that six fifth formers had been issued with
this copy before you were given custody by the school book
exchange. Their names, form, date of issue and return and
the master's initials are written in ink in their own writing.
One, surprisingly for 1958, used red biro.

Your name, as you signed it in blue ink in 1959, stands
at the bottom of the list. There is no date of return, for this
book is the first (and, as far as you can remember, the last)
you have ever stolen. Originally handed out as part of your
'O' Level French curriculum, you did not then know that it
would influence what you would subsequently study, where
you would travel, work, who you would meet and what you
would read for the next fifty years.

The fifteen stories in this slim volume are selected and
introduced by FC Green, Professor of French literature at
the University of Cambridge. Cambridge University Press
published the book in 1943, when Maupassant had been
dead only fifty years: quite a radical move at the time,
particularly as it was also the middle of the Second World
War. It must have been a successful venture, for your copy
was a 1954 reprint.

The introduction is short, giving a concise account of
Maupassant's life including his death from syphilis. There
follows a brief and workmanlike appraisal of his *oeuvre*. The
stories themselves, of course, are in French, but the Professor adds helpful footnotes translating what he surmises
sixteen-year-olds might not know. It is revealing. Many
pages have no footnotes at all and at most there are four
notes to a page; yet you remember no difficulty in reading
the text and you have pencilled in no translations of your
own.

In English you read and enjoyed *Great Expectations*, but it was Maupassant who fired your imagination, who made you want to read more, who led you back to Flaubert and forward to Somerset Maugham. More importantly he made you want to attempt to write your own short stories, an absorbing, anti-social and time wasting habit that you have never shaken off.

Your faded blue book of these fifteen selected stories of Maupassant is a symbol of a lifetime's aspirations unrealised. Maupassant would have liked that.

29

Alice Revisited

The original 1865 edition of *Alice's Adventures in Wonderland* was printed from electrotypes taken from original wood blocks and sold for 4 shillings. In 1896 fresh electrotypes were made from the same immaculate blocks and the book re-set. It sold for 6 shillings.

This is the book you have in front of you, and you note that even in 1896 authors felt they did not receive enough money for their work. Here is Lewis Carroll justifying the cost of the first edition and the re-edition:

"Four shillings was a perfectly reasonable price to charge, considering the very heavy initial outlay I had incurred: still, as the public have practically said, 'We will not give more than a shilling for a picture-book, however artistically got up', I am content to reckon my outlay on the book as so much dead loss, and, rather than let the little ones, for whom it was written, go without it, I am selling it at a price which is, to me, much the same as giving it away."

Your copy smells like an old book, the pages held in place by thread are now yellowed, but the binding, if stained and shabby, is still firm. Considering the book has been read by four or five generations, it is remarkably unsullied by scribble, sticky fingers or spilled liquids. The original owner, your grandmother-in-law has written her name four times in pencil across the inside cover. It is still a childish hand and she must have felt very proud and possessive of her book. She writes her name again on the flyleaf, this time in black crayon and twice underlined. You can trace that stubborn, determined streak down the female line through to your own children today.

Since that first childish signature your late mother-in-law must have treasured the book and, books in those days being much respected objects, seems not to have left a mark on it. It must however have made its mark on her, for she read it to her daughter, the little girl who has become your wife and a granny herself. But she was brought up as a Norwegian and did not pay much attention to Alice. Subsequently you have rescued and read it to your own daughters and now they have children of their own. But will the book continue its march on down the generations?

On the very first page Alice thinks, "… what is the use of a book without pictures or conversations?" For the Victorians Tenniel's illustrations sufficed; for your generation his drawings of Alice, of the Mad Hatter, of the caterpillar and the Cheshire Cat defined and fixed their images in your mind's eye. For a child in 2013 with limited attention span and a head crammed with multi-coloured and moving images, these sparse black-and-white pictures may hardly register. Modern children's books, excellent though many are, are more illustration than text. Though perhaps this is truer of books for the very young such as *The Gruffalo* etc. Even so Dahl's *Matilda* has more pictures than Carroll's *Alice*. This does not prevent an intelligent child today from finding the conversations in both books amusing.

You have a sneaking suspicion, though, that *Alice's Adventures in Wonderland* was always better appreciated by the adults reading it than by the children upon whom it was inflicted. The absurdity prefigures the Goon Show and Monty Python by a hundred years, and the surrealism was also way ahead of its time. Alice, though, is timeless. She is a tough little nut, quite independent and strong-willed, though perhaps a mite more polite and better behaved than the modern young miss.

These random thoughts lead you, not for the first time,

to wonder what a book is. It is both more and less than the story it contains. Your father could recite Alice's adventures by heart. He had no need of the intermediary of print. Yet this peppery smelling, faded, red-bound book beside you as you type has been read and touched by five generations from 1896 to 2013, and for all of them it is *Alice in Wonderland.* Each child could have bought a different edition and today the story can be downloaded on Kindle. It is the same tale. There are also other illustrators painting quite a different portrait of Alice.

There have been many versions of the story in film, even a ballet, but as far as you know Alice has not suffered the same fate as *Winnie the Pooh* and become an American speaking cartoon. What would Great Granny have made of that?

What you have in front of you is multi-layered: it is first and foremost an artefact, a book, containing a classic story; it also, for you alone, contains family history and memories, traces of having been kept on shelves in different homes and countries. Who knows whether it will continue its trajectory down this family line or end up in an Oxfam Shop, perhaps to start a new existence with another family altogether?

One thing is for sure. You can read it as a grown-up with as much, though perhaps different, pleasure as when you first read it as a child. And come to think of it, you must have read the story in quite a different book.

30

Literary Surprises

In Molière's 17th Century comedy, *Le Bourgeois Gentil-homme*, the eponymous Monsieur Jourdain, who is striving to become accomplished in the arts, says, *"Par ma foi, il y a plus de quarante ans que je dis la prose sans que je n'en susse rien."* (By my faith, for more than forty years I have been speaking prose without realizing it.)

In the same way you realize that for an equivalent length of time you have been writing not pieces or articles: you have been writing essays. In your mind the greatest essayist was Montaigne, the 16th Century philosopher whose motto was *'Que sais-je?'* (What do I know?) What a contrast, by the by, with the certainties of today's bigots.

When you picked up a second-hand English book, *Essays of Elia* by Charles Lamb, published in 1901, it was out of curiosity to see how essays should be written in English. It was certainly an eclectic collection, but what startled you was Lamb's essay on Modern Gallantry. It is about the proper respect of men for women and could, apart from the sober and gentle tone, have been written by a 21st Century feminist. He despises the conventional attitude many men had, and some today still have, towards women; he depre-cates the hypocrisy of insincere flattery as much as the abusive language used to denigrate women.

He believed furthermore that a gentleman should be as civil to the poorest servant girl as to 'females in the drawing room'. He criticises fine speeches and false compliments and proposes kindness and sincerity to all classes of women. In fact he proposes treating everyone, men and women kindly. Not surprising, but read his whole essay and you will find it both ahead of its time, possibly ahead of ours, and certainly still relevant.

Another surprise discovery was a book, by odd coinci-dence published the same year as Lamb's essays, entitled *The Garden of Kama*. It could not have been more different.

Perhaps it is well known but you had not heard of it. It could not have been more different from Lamb. Indeed, when you first leafed through this large volume, glancing at the illustrations, you wondered whether you had stumbled upon a work of Victorian erotica, though in truth the pictures by Byan Shaw were as much exotic as erotic. Besides, on the first blank page of the book one Horatio White-Abbot had written in pencil, "To my sister Daisy Carrick with much love." It puzzled you that a brother should have considered this a suitable work for his sister.

You started to read the poems. Daisy would undoubtedly found have found these Indian love lyrics racy but heart felt. You, too, found them sensuous and filled with passion. There was a great variety of mood and circumstance. One lyric was in the voice of an Indian woman who had given birth to a baby by her absent white lover. She loves the little boy because he reminds her of the man she still loves, though it is clear to the reader that to him she was just a plaything.

There are other songs of lament and of betrayal, and many by men and women of unrequited love, of separation, and of death. Some anticipate the arrival of a lover or celebrate a brief night of love. Many recall the physical pleasures of love, some even recounting what today would be considered forced sex. All the poems are set in India but there is a Persian feel about some of them. The collection plays the gamut of emotions, some scenes being vividly captured in the illustrations by Byam Shaw – himself a lover of India and a respected artist of the time – that first caught your attention.

The book was published by Laurence Hope, who claimed he had translated the lyrics from Indian sources. Who was this Laurence Hope, then, you wondered? (You will leave a biography of Byam Shaw aside for another day). You quickly discovered that Laurence Hope was in fact a woman, and a remarkable one at that. She had composed and written all the verse herself. All the poems were the original work of Adela Florence Nicolson.

She must have been a lively character, you thought, for the poems were so heartfelt and some almost confessional. Romantic, yes, but there was nothing Mills and Boone or Gillian Ayres about them. You dug further and found that Adele was born in India but educated in England. Her awakening came through her marriage to an Indian Army officer who introduced her to 'the real India' in more ways than one. The couple seemed to have led a wild life. It must have been quite an open marriage, unusual at the time, but one poem sent a chill through you when you read it, and when you re-read it now, too. Here it is:

kashmiri song

You never loved me; and yet to save me
One unforgettable night you gave me
such chill embraces as the snow-covered heights
receive from clouds in northern auroral nights:
such keen communion as the frozen mere
has with immaculate moonlight; cold and clear:
and all desire;
like failing fire;
died slowly; faded surely; and sank to rest
against the delicate chillness of your breast.

Adela Nicolson herself committed suicide in India aged 39. Her book was a best seller.

31

A Cabin In The Mountains (Summer)

This was a *hytte*, a Norwegian log cabin. On the outside it was planked with vertical weatherboard. It had a grass roof from which small trees and bushes sometimes grew. It was isolated and accessible only on foot. It stood in a clearing surrounded by silver birch, Scots pine and Norwegian spruce, with an undercover of sprawling mountain willow.

Much of the clearing was springy with bilberry bushes. Cranberry flowers peeped through in the wetter places. The barer patches of mountainside were ribbed and veined with lichen-covered roots. Pine cones piled randomly up; later you would collect and burn them against the evening chill.

Here and there butterwort raised long purple stalks to allow their leaves to catch passing insects. To reach this spot you have had to walk through clouds of wild lupins and delphiniums. The only sound you could hear was the donk and tinkle of sheep bells on the higher slopes. The scent was of warm rock and pine.

The *hytte,* long and low, looked a natural part of the scene. You removed your heavy rucksack and took the ladder away from the porch where, horizontal, it had been keeping the sheep away. Here there were racks for boots and skis and pegs for articles of outer clothing. To your right a wooden door into the longdrop toilet, with a bag of birch bark to sprinkle over your deposits. To the left the entrance to the cabin.

The English word 'cabin' was apt, for in its economy of space this family *hytte* inside resembled the cabin of a large sailing boat. The three bedrooms each contained two bunk beds, one above the other, with storage space beneath and a small wash basin in the corner by the window. From the compact galley, with its own trap door into a tiny cellar in the mountain floor where food and milk could be kept cool, a broad hatch opened onto the main living space (or cockpit). In summer you could even open the doors and walk out onto the ant- and needle-strewn deck, a barbecue area.

The interior was heated by an open wood-burning stove, not necessary in summer. You had an electricity supply now, though the old oil and hurricane lamps were still in evidence; your water was piped in fresh and clean from a nearby fast-tumbling stream.

But you had only just arrived and there were chores to do before you could properly settle in. You turned the water on and filled the pipes that you had to remember to drain again when you were ready to leave. You took down the shutters, opened windows, switched on the power; you put some water on to boil. Later, to wash, you would fill the big copper kettle that required all your strength and both your hands to lift onto the hob.

For now you just wanted to sit down with a cup of coffee, some crispbread and goat's cheese and relax after your hike. You looked around the room and took in again the rose-painted, pewter-blue corner cupboard, the reindeer skin stretched on the wall; you counted the different products made from antlers – from pegs, to door and walking stick handles, to sheer decoration. You remembered the weaving of the curtains, the knotting of rugs and the varnishing of the wooden floor. You admired again the porcelain shade on the lamp that swung on its long chain over the low, pine coffee table.

You recalled that under the seats were board games and packs of cards and drawing materials; that in the book-shelves volumes had been left behind by many guests over the years: an eclectic collection; and that the outside store attached to the cabin contained paints and tools, choppers and axes, fishing and skiing tackle and all that could be needed for running repairs.

Later perhaps you would browse through the *hyttebok,* an album of photos and accounts of family holidays in the cabin. Tomorrow you would trample down through the white tufted glade of bog cotton; you would step over dried lichen as though crunching on brittle bird skulls; you would sink into soft sphagnum moss and peat bog until you found a suitable rock from which to launch yourself naked into the black waters of the sparkling lake for a pre-breakfast swim.

For the moment you had your rucksack to unpack, supplies to store away – and the prospect of solitude to savour.

32

A Cabin In The Mountains (Winter)

E ven though you could not park your car closer than
five miles from the cabin, it was easier in winter on
skis to reach it, and when necessary with a *pulk* or
a sledge, to bring in supplies than it was to carry them or
wheel them there in the summer. You had come only for
the weekend, and skied down with just a rucksack of provi-
sions. Nevertheless you felt exercised on arrival.

Your first task was to light the boiler and dispel ten degrees
of frost. Then you went out with a broom to sweep the snow
from the stream, and an axe to hack through the ice for a
bucket of water. The physical activity lifted your spirits.

Next day was bright and sparkling, the temperature a
dry, invigorating -8°. Ideal for a ski tour in the mountains
above the tree-line. You pocketed an orange and a bar of
chocolate, fastened on your skis and set off up the slope.
The *hytte* was quite isolated. No one in the city knew you
had come away for the weekend. You were on your own
and you intended to break yourself in gently with a short,
circular route. You would not be out more than a couple of
hours. Or so you thought.

You saw the herd of reindeer a second before they saw
you. Two hundred, three. They fled like startled sheep,
drumming out their panic on the hard snow. Then they
slowed down and the drumming receded like a wave on
a beach. You caught your breath. As if you had struck a
common nerve they stirred again as one. The wave of sound
broke over you, receded. It was still, quite still.

Overawed at the spectacle, you had made one simple
mistake. It took you a while to realise anything was wrong.
When you did, you knew you had broken all the rules.

The reindeer were not a complete surprise. You had
crossed their tracks soon after climbing out of the woods. It
was like skiing over an enormous waffle iron. You bumped
over the same grid of hoof prints further up when you were

warm with exertion. In all that white desolation there were two colours: shadows frozen blue in the deeper depressions, and clusters of brown droppings glistening in the snow.

Nevertheless when you crested the brow and saw the whole herd a second before they noticed you, you gasped a mouthful of cold air. The reindeer formed a semicircle above you. Frozen in awe, you could not move a step further.

With great assurance and enormous curiosity they all turned their heads towards you in one synchronised movement. As they did so a collective clicking of antlers filled the air like a scurry of hailstones, a salvo of gunfire or the ticking of a vast machine. A petrified forest of antlers masked the skyline, darkened the sharp edge between the white snow and the blue. The reindeer peered down on you like gods. You looked at them and they stared on.

For a moment you thought they were going to charge, but their big eyes conveyed a deeper message. You were intruding. You should not have entered their kingdom. You let your ski tips fall away down the slope and slipped around the shoulder of the mountain.

This was your second mistake. Exultant from your encounter, you did not know how long you had dropped blindly down. You were still thinking of the drumming of feet on hard snow and the warm, sweet smell of hundreds of bodies and breaths, when you realised you were lost. This was not your valley. You recognised none of it. The foothills rolled down to a vast plain of snow-capped fir trees that stretched towards the distant Jotunheim mountains, caught in the sinking sun.

You were not worried. Not yet. You had only to go back up, retrace your tracks and return to the valley that sheltered your cabin. But looking up you could not tell where you had come from. Your light, cross-country skis had made no impression on the icy mantle of glazed snow.

You discovered your third mistake. You had come out without your map and compass, essential furnishings of any cabin. You had not intended getting lost.

Panic is a strange emotion. It floods reason. It sets the mind spinning free of rational thought. It is a monster in the head and in the bowels. It is not the situation you have to control. It is your panic. It is yourself. If you can regain calm you have a good chance of winning through.

You understood this now. You took your orange from your pocket. Removing your gloves you peeled it slowly. This act of concentration stilled the fly-wheel of panic. You assessed your situation.

You were cold and hungry. You had no map, no compass and – your fourth mistake – no extra clothing. That you had intended only a quick climb up the mountain and an easy run back in the afternoon sunlight was no excuse. Even under the best conditions a skier could be injured.

There could be no question of a search party. No one would know you were missing until Monday, and one day off work might not ring alarm bells in the office. Even if it did, your colleagues would still not know where you had gone.

You considered the positive points. You were fit, well and mobile. You had a bar of chocolate and at least half an hour of sunshine left. Even after the sun went down and the temperature plummeted to below -15° you could keep warm if you kept moving. This was not the North Pole. It was the middle of a populated country.

If you failed to find the cabin you would simply have to travel across country. Between you and the distant Jotunheim range a road ran from Gol to Fagerness. If you kept a straight line you were bound to cross it.

You pocketed your orange peel, pulled on your gloves. You had been standing still all of five minutes and were already stiff and cold. You set off again fast to warm up, hugging the side of the slope, searching for a way off the bare mountain.

Carefully you dropped into the scrub that poked through the crust of snow above the tree-line. If you were to find the road, you needed to make as much progress as possible in daylight. Few cars passed that way. Even if you struck the road you would have a long trek ahead.

To add to your worries the skies began to cloud over.

You were shaken out of these thoughts by a lone dwarf birch. Nothing exceptional, but one, remote brain cell sent out the message, *There's something familiar about that bush.* Other evidence corroborated this. You came across reindeer droppings and then, a little lower in softer snow, you saw an extraordinary sight. Man Friday's footprint was nothing compared with the set of ski tracks that appeared in this vast, untrammelled whiteness.

71

Your heart leaped like a trout. You could hardly breathe.

Now you were faced with an agonising choice. In the hour or so of daylight that remained after sundown you could forge on with the sensible plan of finding a road, or you could follow the ski tracks in the hope they would lead you to a cabin, even to a settlement.

It was a risk. What if the tracks faded out? What if it snowed? What if it grew dark too quickly?

If reason is submerged by panic, instinct sometimes throws it a lifeline. You followed the ski tracks.

In no time you were back in familiar territory. The trail you were following was your own. It led you back to your own cabin.

Just as you caught sight of the roof below you through the trees, the first flakes fell. In all that silence the snow dropped soundless, softer than a bursting bubble. It muffled the land, obliterating with its quiet kiss the tracks you had been following and the tracks you were making.

You kicked off your boots in the porch and entered the cabin. Despite its welcome embrace you were shaking with relief. You prepared a hot meal, ate it in abstraction. There was no better place than a warm cabin in winter.

33

Ostehøvel

They are as common in a Norwegian kitchen as teapots once were in Britain. Everyone there has one, even two or three. Breakfast would be inconceivable without an *ostehøvel*. You have to use the Norwegian name for it. It is not affectation. There just seems to be no suitable English translation. Cheese slice conjures up the slice of cheese rather than the slicer and cheese slicer would denote the person who draws this simple implement across the block of cheese to lift a flap of this sweet, moist nourishment.

You have also seen the literal translation, cheese plane, but this evokes images of carpentry, of an old fashioned box plane, of shaving a wooden surface smooth. And shaver would not do either.

The first time you saw an *ostehøvel* you wondered what it was for. Then you discovered *geitost,* the brown Norwegian goat cheese and wondered how to eat it. It did not take long to put two and two together.

These *ostehøvler* (to use the plural), although simple tools, come in many shapes, sizes and materials. They are usually made of steel with wooden or plastic handles. The silver ones are usually formed in one piece. The handle is long enough to grasp and a broad flat blade, like a wide spatula, has a slot across it near the top or handle end. In this way it does resemble a plane, though it needs no extra blade. The cutting edge which protrudes from the lower surface like a sharp, pouting lip can be smooth or serrated, depending whether you like your cheese plain or corrugated.

The blade section itself can be heart shaped, almost pointed, nearly square or any combination. The width of the cut varies, the depth you can adjust yourself with more or less tilt and pressure of the wrist.

Your favourite *ostehøvel* was beautiful in its simplicity. You bought it in the newly opened IKEA near Oslo, long before the Swedish store came to British shores. It had a bright yellow plastic handle and a strong, flexible blade. It was lighter than the conventional planes sold then in the tourist shops.

You never had any problem bringing presents home from Norway. Everyone, once introduced, became addicted to the rich fudge of genuine goat cheese and even to the sweeter, blander mixture called G35 (35% goats' milk and 65% cows') that for you lacked the tang of real goat. Then, having bought whichever cheese, you added an *ostehøvel* as an essential and enduring extra.

Other Nordic countries no doubt use a cheese slice, but like the names Liv, Mette and Bente or Bjarne, Egil and Odd, this ordinary Norwegian kitchen tool has always seemed to you to encapsulate a unique and untranslateable experience. Five happy years in the palm of your hand.

34

A Wife's Arrival

During your peripatetic career there have been many farewells: partings from parents, lovers, wives and children, theirs and yours, leave-takings at railway stations, ports and airports, often dread-filled, always painful. Then there were friends and colleagues left behind never to be seen again.

Most loved-ones, however, you knew you would see again in the long or short term and there have been many joyful and memorable reunions. One of the most nail biting and curious of these took place in the unpredictable Southern Sudan, where your wife and baby daughter were trying to reach you, having flown out from Norway.

The Sudan Airways flight flew from Khartoum to Nairobi and back, stopping half way in Juba when it was safe to do so. These flights themselves were not without risk. One colleague of yours went to the toilet and fell through the floor into the baggage department beneath. Another flight landed in the Nile by mistake. This would have been all right in the 1950s when the old Sunderland flying boats had a scheduled stop on the Nile just outside Juba on their way to East Africa, but a Boeing is supposed to land on terra firma.

You had this in mind when arranging your wife's flight. The last surviving Boeing had been operating on Mondays to Nairobi for some time. The previous week for a change, and unannounced, it had flown on the Sunday – thereby stranding all Juba-bound passengers who turned up in Nairobi on the Monday expecting the usual flight to Juba and Khartoum.

With no telephone or radio link you had no means of warning Anna, your wife, of the change; indeed no one knew which day the flight would resume the following week anyway. This was normal. Sunday came however and with it the Monday Boeing again. Your heart sank as you thought of Anna just setting off from Oslo and expecting to board the Juba-bound Sudan Airways flight in Kenya the next day, after a night in the air with British Airways from Heathrow. She would now arrive a day late with the prospect of an uncertain week in Nairobi.

On Monday however the President of the then Southern Region of Sudan was due to return to Juba from Khartoum and therefore the Boeing had to do the trip again. The president was expected in Juba at 8 am. This gave the plane plenty of time to fly on to Kenya and pick up all the scheduled passengers. However, this meant making the return journey before sunset, after which the airport closed. Like the rest of the town the airport had no power and therefore no lights.

From early morning crowds were cajoled and bullied 'spontaneously' to welcome their beloved president home from his negotiations with the North. They were not to know that he had been demoted to Governor of Equatoria. Amid the cheering rentacrowd you were allowing yourself to hope that on the return leg you might actually be welcoming your own beloved wife and daughter.

The humiliated President did not arrive. The crowds dispersed. Your hopes fell. Then at about 11 am, and back in your office, you heard the sound of the plane. It had landed. When it took off just after 2 pm in the direction of Kenya, so you were told, your hopes were raised. It just had to land in Nairobi and turn around quickly enough to reach Juba before dark. Otherwise it would overfly and Juba passengers would be stranded in Khartoum instead of Nairobi, a far less attractive option. It was also far more difficult to get a seat on the plane, whenever it flew, from Khartoum to Juba because of the obstructive and uncooperative officials suspicious of their troublesome southern neighbours.

Juba was a small town with few vehicles and the arrival and departure of aircraft could be heard all over. That afternoon you imagined every lorry, every passing Land Rover to be the sound of the returning plane, even though you knew the earliest it could arrive would be 5 pm.

At five, half excited, half not daring to be excited, you drove out to the airport. The Arab merchants in their white jallabiahs and white Toyota pickups were also waiting. The plane was expected. By 5.30 however, people began to drift away. With tropical darkness falling at 6 pm the plane would be unable to land. It was too late.

Stronger than your disappointment was anxiety for Anna and Emily if they arrived, unexpected and unmet, in the filth that is Khartoum airport. You walked back to your Land Rover remembering the excrement and vomit on the floor of the airport and the unhelpfulness of the staff. Then you spotted the Boeing low in the late evening sky.

Usually it would circle the airport, sweep low over the runway to make sure there were no stray cattle on it before turning and straightening into a final approach for landing. This time in the failing light it was trying for a direct landing, taking the chance the landing strip was clear. Even the old fire engine was taken by surprise and coughed out angry black smoke as it lurched towards the runway, a pointless precaution because it rarely contained water or chemicals.

The jet landed a bit too far up the short strip and its motors screamed in maximum reverse thrust, throwing up so much dust you thought the plane must have crashed. But the silver machine, the last of the ill-fated fleet of three, re-emerged and raced towards the terminal building. Boarding passengers were lined up ready to run to the aircraft steps. It was the first organised queue you had seen in Africa. Officials actually hurried to mount the aircraft, open the door, expel disembarking passengers and hurl off their luggage to make way for passengers and *their* luggage joining the flight.

There was a scream of engines again and a lot of smoke and dust. When the smoke had cleared and the dust settled, there, standing on the only bit of tarmac in Southern Sudan, stood your wife and child. You waved and they waved back. Soon, after all the uncertainty and separation, you were reunited. The words of greeting from your already much-travelled toddler were, "Mummy can do the passports and luggage and everything and we can go home to our house."

You have described this as a small pleasure. Rather it was a huge relief to be safely together again.

35

The BTF

S trictly speaking (and strictly they do speak), '*la BTF*' stands for *la vraie baguette de tradition française*. It is a baguette made in a particular way from particular ingredients and with no additives. Since 1993 the BTF, like wine, has even had its own *appellation contrôlée,* a label guaranteeing its origin and quality.

Well, bully for the American professor and bread buff who has campaigned so hard for the independent bakers of Paris. Even the French face the degradation of industrial bakeries and levelling by vast supermarkets.

Nevertheless your own definition would not be so strict; and it would be more historical and personal.

A sixth former, you travelled to Paris for an Easter course at the Sorbonne. In England at that time the only foreign food was Heinz curried beans. There were certainly no baguettes at the baker's or at the grocer's and wine was not so widely available. France was still a foreign country. An exotic land.

You still have a photo of yourself in the Luxembourg gardens, holding your bottle of cheap vin rouge and a baguette. Had you enjoyed smoking, no doubt a damp Gitane would have been hanging from your lower lip.

Your mind was similarly cluttered with clichés. Paris was the Left Bank, was Sartre, Camus, Les Deux Magots café; it was Juliette Greco in black, Ionesco and Anouilh in the theatres; it was still the culturally important language.

Sitting on the wooden seats by the boating pool hungrily breaking off hunks of baguette, you soaked up the mostly imaginary atmosphere and thought you were in heaven. After the age of twenty you would never again attain quite that mixture of passion and naiveté, but even today a faint flavour of it returns when you snatch a crust of baguette.

There were earlier associations, too. You had been on family holidays in Normandy, Brittany and further south.

They usually began and ended with long car journeys down empty, tree-lined highways. There were stops for roadside picnics. The food was simple and delicious. A fresh baguette, local cheese, tomatoes, peaches; and at the seaside when you had learned it from French children, a baguette filled with a bar of chocolate. Wonderfully sustaining after a long swim!

Mostly these baguettes, and those you regularly consumed during subsequent visits to France, were baked on the premises. To that extent they might have qualified as BTFs.

A good baguette needs to be bought early in the morning while still warm. It should radiate a freshly baked aroma and should have a firm but not tooth-breaking crust. The bread should be slightly moist, like the inside of your lover's thigh. You have always felt, too, that there was something soapy about the after taste of a good baguette.

In recent decades when all over the world we have come to wear the same clothes, are shod in identical trainers, buy similar food and watch 24-hour TV news in a variety of Englishes, the baguette too has become universally available, sliced as an accompaniment to meals in most restaurants, or whole from all manner of retail outlets. Even British supermarkets sell them, including a half baked dough that you can take home to heat up. Like the ever increasing digital TV and Radio channels, the more you get the less you get.

Perhaps today then, even more so than in the past, it is necessary to go to France again. It is now so much easier. For a genuine BTF you can simply hop on a Eurostar train to Paris. And when you get there the baguette will cost you all of one Euro.

36

Café Au Lait

I t is difficult to find a good bowl of *café au lait*. You will not find it in London and probably not in Paris either; certainly not served in a *bol*.

Yet a good bowl of *café au lait* is so simple, so satisfying, a breakfast in itself, even without the indulgence of dipping your warm croissant in it.

It is important to drink your *café au lait* in the right setting. A plain café with a football table in one corner and a solitary labourer in blue overalls taking a glass at the zinc bar is a good place to hunt down a real coffee; or a single star hotel in the country. Often the two are combined.

Your coffee must be served in the aforementioned *bol*, preferably of plain white china, chipped with use and big as a chamber pot. A bowl with two flat handles like ears is acceptable, too, as is a more patterned piece of faïence if you are in somewhere like Brittany.

You are sitting in the bare, anonymous café at an uncovered cane table with a practical surface. You have your bowl. All you need now is the milk and the coffee. The milk should have come direct from the cow in a metal pail or in a red plastic bucket, not from a lorry or from a carton, or even from a bottle. It should not have been pasteurised, homogenised or mistreated in any other way; it should simply have been boiled and served hot and frothing in a big jug, big enough to fill half your bowl at least twice. The coffee should be scalding, strong and aromatic, served in similar quantities in an identical jug.

It may be early or late morning, you may have eaten heartily the previous night or you may be ravenous; you may still be sleepy or you may just have returned refreshed from an early swim. Whatever the case, it is time to focus your attention on the highlight of the morning.

You lift both jugs, one in either hand, and pour the contents together while they are piping hot. You like it half and half but sometimes it is necessary to pour a larger proportion of the coffee.

With a spoon you remove the bits of milk skin that should be floating on the surface. You lean forward over your bowl and breathe in the strong, warm scent. You spread your fingers round the bowl, careful not to burn them; you lift the bowl to your lips and take a first sip; you tilt the bowl more and take a deep draught, properly wetting your throat. You feel it sink down into your stomach.

Already you are restored.

37

Things That Might Come In Useful

You are no hoarder. You do not collect coins or stamps; you do not keep birthday or postcards or save the labels off wine bottles. On the contrary, you have been known to discard the odd sock with an irreparable hole in the heel, frayed shirts and moth-eaten pullovers. You throw out electrical goods too expensive to mend and watches that no longer tell the time. However you never get rid of anything, or part of anything, that might come in useful.

Some of these are mundane. A stained but robust old kettle that you kept 'just in case' has been retrieved from the garage every two years when the latest glass jug kettle broke down; the single cylinder, rusting camping gas ring is occasionally called into service when your all-electric house suffers a periodic power cut.

Then there are used yoghurt pots, jam jars and containers of all shapes and sizes that might have a variety of future uses, from storing food in the freezer to bulbs or seeds for the garden, not to mention screws and washers. There are paper clips, padded envelopes, sheets of paper blank on one side; first and subsequent drafts and printouts of your novels, poetry collections and other documentation that were first written on the backs of forms from exam boards; junk mail, financial reports and begging letters.

This very piece is being written by hand on the other side of a letter soliciting your presence at an expensive hotel for a seminar, where they hope to sell you a timeshare or advise you on inheritance tax. A forlorn hope, but the creamy verso of this luxury note paper was too inviting to jettison. You can only hope that your words are rich enough to match it.

Once, when clothes were garments to keep you warm and worn until they fell apart, you saved buttons, zips, and even pockets, but since you have no skill with the needle and your better half no interest you now keep only the most useful buttons. You put them in a stud box along with the pins and collar stiffeners that fall out of new shirts, and they do come in useful from time to time. Only last week you retrieved a pin to remove a splinter from your thumb.

Shoe laces and pyjama cords are always useful after their host garment has been composted or binned: rose bushes, climbing plants, vegetables – all need to be tied up, tied back or tied down. You rarely have to buy garden twine for these tasks when you have just the thing in your string bin.

You never know when something might come in useful – but there is always pleasure when it does. Only the other day a light switch on the sitting room wall had to be replaced. The new one was smaller and left an unpainted patch around itself. One solution would have been to redecorate the whole wall, which in turn would have meant the whole room to get a match, but you had just the thing in the garage.

You had kept the last few centimetres of the last tin of paint used on that room – just in case. You brushed off the cobwebs and the rust, opened the dented can and broke through a thick crust. There was still enough liquid paint beneath, as fresh smelling and spreadable as when you had first used it years ago. You stirred it with a stick, a useful piece of dowelling rod you had kept, as it happens; painted around the new switch (there was enough for two coats), and finally discarded the can with great satisfaction. You had avoided the stress of shopping and the distress of spending a bucketful of money.

Of course, you cleaned and kept the brushes and rod.

Other things you keep and occasionally use are old tools, parts from cars, bicycles, electrical goods; nuts and bolts, hooks and hinges. You have consequently never had to shop for these latter items, sorted in the aforementioned jam jars. You frequently find yourself ferreting in those jars to retrieve the hooks. There are all sorts, from picture hooks with a slender pin which you lightly tap into a wall, and many of the screw-in variety you select when putting up a new washing line or when you need somewhere to hang up a string of onions in the back porch.

The only objects more ubiquitously useful than hooks, perhaps, are bricks. Individual bricks are so varied and beautiful, and can be put to so many different uses quite apart from building walls and houses, that they deserve their own chapter, along with tiles, in the same way as they have their own dedicated space in your garden.

Sometimes you make a real find in your useful pile. When you employed a carpenter to replace some ugly matchboard doors with handmade wooden ones, he said he would have to go out and search for suitable fittings to go with those on the older, authentic doors in your cottage. Bells rang in your head and you led him to the garage.

From under a metal wall rack you pulled out a drawer you had kept from an old chest. In it, buried now beneath leaves and mice nests, you uncovered a heavy heap of door furniture kept from previous demolition and extension projects. The carpenter's eyes lit up and he whistled his appreciation. These were, in his words, "lovely Victorian hinges and latches, just the right size, too, and a bolt to match."

After some vigorous work with a wire brush and some rust remover, followed by a paint stripper and careful oiling and repainting, he attached these fittings to his hand-crafted doors and for the first time in thirty years you and your visitors could not only shut a lavatory door worthy of contemplation, but you could draw a bolt as well. Privacy at last; and with brass knobs on.

Most things that may come in useful are those you are reluctant to throw out in the first place. But another category comes from the odd item you might pick up on a country walk or along the beach. Tennis balls always come in useful for visiting dogs and grandchildren; some bottles, sea glass, ropes or spent brass shell cases are worth taking home, but not sea shells – which fall into the same category as stamps and postcards. These are unlikely to come in useful except as pastimes. You plead an exception for the sea glass, which has a decorative function.

Once you carried a very heavy cast iron brazier two miles on your shoulder along a shingle beach. It had either fallen or had been thrown from the cliff above. Since you rescued it from the rock pool where it rested submerged it has served as a barbecue, a bonfire base, and is now what mail order magazines – ignorant of colonial history – call a 'planter', ie you have planted a hanging pansy in it, the ensuing cascade of fire making a strong garden feature.

Another time, after floods along the river, you retrieved a very serviceable stepladder. More of an indulgence, perhaps, was bringing home a set of antlers, ornamental rather than useful, but also educational, and it is amazing the games your grandchildren play with them.

A balance has to be drawn. In these days of throw-away consumerism and waste, you could daily visit the local rubbish tip (or 'recycling centre' as it is now called) and salvage enough unwanted but hardly used articles to furnish house and garden. But this is not quite the same. The best *objets trouvés* are literally just that. Not something sought but something you just stumble across by chance; and the real satisfaction lies with a find you thought twenty years ago might come in useful and which suddenly becomes essential: that sundial which perfectly fills the space in a newly cleared patch of garden; the big old black telephone that the local dramatic society wishes to borrow; or that long-cherished oak floor board that now you need to reshape to replace a broken tread in the staircase.

38

Objects That Follow You Around

Many people with attics and lofts accumulate trunks and boxes of household and personal items. Garages, too, are a magnet for old tools, mowers, hinges, screws, nails and useful bits of wood. In your case, however, during your working life you moved to a different country every three or four years and as a result are relatively unencumbered.

When you emigrated to Australia as a £10 Pom you carried all your possessions in a suitcase. You furnished your first house in Melbourne with soap boxes and planks found on the beach. When you went to live in Norway some years and many experiences later you still managed to fit all your worldly possessions into your car, including a carpet bought in India and stolen on your next posting in Belgium.

Of course over the years all kinds of junk accumulated as gramophones gave way to stereo systems, TV became coloured, CD players and MPVs replaced walkmen while phones, cameras, typewriters, pens and latterly books became obsolete. Boxes of vinyl records, audio cassettes, CDs and VHS tapes filled crates and were cherry picked by collectors before being dumped. Books are another matter. They are like old friends and they lodge in four rooms of your house. You still talk to them and they to you. You share memories quite apart from the content. You have not the heart to turn them out.

Despite a fairly Spartan and nomadic life, however, quite unconsciously certain objects have remained with you throughout. From your youthful beachcombing days in Australia one *objet trouvé* sits on your Sussex sideboard. It is a piece of twisted driftwood, pale and hard as ivory and retaining a simple and beautiful shape. There is also a particular breadboard from this era, not particularly attractive but obviously practical, because it still sits in your kitchen. Dark, scoured by a million knife cuts, it is just the right size to handle and presumably to pack.

A couple of things are more to do with your childhood, passed on by parents. There is a brown mug. It is not the memories it contains, though it brims with those, but again the simple shape and feel of the mug that appeals. When you first handled it you must have been quite small. Drinking hot chocolate from it perhaps, you had to clutch it half way down with both hands, warming them at its waist, for it is concave in shape. Solid, dark brown on the outside, lighter inside, the mug is practical and strong enough to have lasted unchipped for 70 years. Yet in its way it is simple and elegant. The rim curves out slightly in a mild pout and feels as good as it meets your lips as its body does wrapped in your fist. It is now lodged in your daughter's house in France and you have the familiar pleasure of its use when you visit.

While clothes, even belts and boots, wear out and you have never been interested in fashion anyway, there are one or two articles you seem to have kept. When you went to university, and fewer did then, all students wore a university scarf as a badge of honour or achievement, or (though I hope not) as a sign of belonging. A scarf was one of your first purchases and for reasons not to be divulged here, you have kept it unworn for years to this day in a plastic box. You also have a woven, dark blue Norwegian tweed busserull, a traditional, folksy jacket that you still wear from time to time. Neither formal nor informal, it suits most occasions when you have to attempt to look respectable. And though no one wears ties any longer you have one or two of special significance that you occasionally put on, among them a grey African one with the Asante peace symbol.

In your travels you have picked up many artefacts that seemed important at the time: Indian bronzes and miniatures, African baskets and carvings, an Australian didgeridoo and wooden bowl and although some of these are dotted about the house, many are packed away in boxes and others have been sold or given to charity shops.

There are two or three you would be reluctant to part with. In Sudan you were guarded by a night watchman armed only with a bow and arrows. You still have the authentic bow, a very simple wooden weapon strung with the original fibre. The iron-barbed arrows, deemed too dangerous for

85

children, have long since disappeared.

Of your Indian bronzes only one matters, and that for sentimental and superstitious reasons. It was a gift from a close Indian friend so much more educated than you in Western and Indian culture. Succeeding effortlessly in almost all she did, the one thing she could never understand was the Western obsession with ambition and progress. In your own life, too, your desire to write always took precedence over the brown-nosing necessary for career advancement, therefore to some extent you could agree with her priorities. You did, though, dream of an alternative literary career. You wanted to create something worthwhile. Accordingly your fond and indulgent muse gave you a tiny bronze of Ganesh, the elephant-headed god of the Hindus. Amongst the gifts Ganesh could bestow upon mortals, she explained dead pan, was inspiration in the arts. For you no more than a lucky charm little larger than an Oxo cube, the bronze has sat on your writing desk now for more decades than you care to remember. You have yet to create your masterpiece together, but then perhaps you do not believe enough!

These objects, gifts or purchases, have been kept because in some way or another they still matter. Other things accumulate by accident or by the workings of the subconscious. Every so often you pick something up and realize it has always been in your life, probably having travelled the world with you. None of them are elaborate. Paintings and works of art are another kettle of fish. What you have in mind are everyday objects, a penknife, a shoe horn, a bill hook and a watch. And of course your toolbox, though its contents have changed over time, but have been just sufficient in whatever clime to do those minor running repairs to house and home. Like the handkerchief in your pocket, you could not imagine life without your toolbox.

You have bought, broken and discarded many kitchen implements and tableware. One simple earthenware bowl, you noticed only the other day, endures. Like the brown mug and, come to think of it, a little brown milk jug, this is simple, practical and pleasing to touch and use. The glaze is crazed but still smooth to the touch, and there is on the inside a hairbreadth fissure invisible from the outside. It may be its well used and worn look that is the attraction of this small, oven proof suet pudding bowl. Otherwise it is utterly unpretentious, and unlike the expensive silver cutlery left over from the days you had to give dinner parties, it is without any monetary value. You have hardly been aware of it until now but it is always in the kitchen cupboard and almost constantly in use. Perhaps this multi-purpose crock would make a fitting receptacle for your ashes.

39

The Red Telephone Box

Your first active memory of the phone box is as an occasional source of pocket money. Two red-painted, cast iron kiosks stood side by side by the village green. They were well used. Local calls cost 4d (four old pennies); callers would insert the coins and when they got through would press button A for a connection. Should they not get a line or should their call be very short, they would press button B for their money back or for some change. Sometimes distracted callers forgot to press button B.

On your way to your friend's house, or he on his way to yours, you never passed the kiosks without popping in to press button B. Even a penny bought a gobstopper or sixteen aniseed balls; more could buy four ounces of sherbet lemons or a bottle of Tizer. This habit lasted long into adulthood and the advent of the modern grey BT telephone booths, so long as they remained coin operated. At busy airports, a cluster of phone boxes used by hundreds of confused foreigners could yield enough for a coffee (even at inflated airport prices) and *à la rigeur* provide the change for a phone call of your own.

But the phone box that sticks in your mind is the one that stood and still stands down the lane from your present home. When you first moved, like many other people in the lane, you had no phone in the house. You calculated that rental would cost more than the occasional use of the public phone; before BT and Maureen Lipmann told us that it was 'good to talk', brevity was a virtue: you noted down the points you had to make and never indulged in unnecessary chat. The half mile walk to the phone box was always for a good reason. Besides, a letter, posted even closer to home, would always get there the next day.

Your fondness for this particular box, however, stems from the events of one late summer's day twenty-five years ago – events which in the longer term led to your getting a phone of your own, a two way phone, and now a line that brings Broadband into your house and TV and radio stations from around the world.

That morning the weather changed violently. You and your toddler daughter were caught in a heavy rainstorm on the way to the phone box half a mile along the lane. The rain fell so thickly and incessantly that the inside lining of your substantial raincoat was wet before you reached the shelter of the booth.

Even then, despite the reasons for the call, you felt a calm within. You would have expected a not quite two year old to be frightened by such violence. The rain bounced off the road higher than her knees. She sat in her pushchair in a waterproof anorak, cocooned against the dancing, flying rain by a red nylon cover. The back of your shirt beneath your Mac was now sodden as you leaned almost horizontally to push the buggy through the wet. You were intent on reaching the shelter of the phone box. No meandering for blackberries, examining of stones or dropping sticks down drains; and puddles were not yet part of the child's experience. It had been a long, dry Indian summer, her first English summer. Now her first rain.

She wasn't frightened because you named the rain and so rendered it harmless. You told her matter-of-factly, calmly, "Look at the rain. Like big, wet sticks."

She reached a hand out of the zip-up cover, unafraid of the torrent. "Rain. Sticks," she summarised happily. "Wet," she discovered and told you, imparting her observation in return for yours.

On the way back from the telephone booth you did meander, picked rain-washed blackberries in the hedgerow, studied the gurgling drains and stomped in unstill puddles. Unhurriedly and sodden you both relished the incipient storm.

Curiously, as the weather and the day's news grew melodramatically more violent, so your own serenity increased, spread, calmed you. Perhaps a burst of sunshine, too bright suddenly like eyes laughing after tears, presaged this mood.

You saw three simultaneous rainbows and showed them to your daughter. The first formed a perfect arch, spanning the black sky, one end in a steaming field of charred stubble, the other burning into a wood. The second, a fainter copy, was repeated above it. The third was unrelated, a miniature glint in a garden momentarily lit by a flash of sunlight and caught only in the corner of your eye. You wondered what this meant. Three rainbows. And the child whom you lifted to show the big, bright rainbow arch over the trees which filled your dripping foreground said only, looking along your pointing finger, "Sky," and noticing rather the shining blackberries in the uncut hedge added, "More."

Did you alone see the three rainbows that morning?

Despite the rain, and the night's warning on the radio of storm force gales; despite the bad news from the hospital – news which, worse than bringing about a change of plans, brought an uncertainty against which no planning could guard – despite all this, after the long journey to London and back, the hospital, getting food and fire on your return, the child and you spent an hour of rare calm and happiness before she went peacefully to bed.

Rare, that is, in both senses. Unusual for her to be still, for she was normally so active, happy but boisterous. But that night you looked deep into one another's eyes and held a long, slow smile of some mutual, shared.... what? Love, contentment – or just peace after the rattling Land Rover, the novelty of the hospital and seeing her mother in a big, high bed. For you, too, relief that your daughter was not upset by her mother's absence, by the strenuous travelling and enforced constraint of four hours strapped to a hard seat.

You did romp. You played with glove puppets. But the storm outside outdid you both. It blew open the letter box, rat-a-tat-tat, and you looked to see who was knocking and there was no one. You gazed out at the sticks of rain, at the frenzied trees, at the woods that surrounded your garden on two sides.

"Windin'," said Emily

"The wind is blowing, woo-oo," you agreed, and you fell silent, watched the turbulent tree-tops, felt the glow from the fire on your backs.

The storm raged all night, but it was not a real rage, it was a benign energy. It drew out your agitation, your apprehensions, the anxieties which so often used to hurl you about in your dreams, and in the eye of the storm you were still, for after so much planning, so much preparation, so much living in a future which was not after all to be, there was nothing to be done but live on from moment to moment, and wait.

This time yesterday, only yesterday, you were set, the packing finally done, the coming weeks arranged in detail, the next three years accounted for. The windows were all open on the night, as they had been open night and day through five weeks of summer leave. Now the windows were closed, although they still rattled furiously against the slanting rain, the gathering storm force winds; closed on certainty, a planned future, security.

You should not still have been here, but away with the other children you loved, children held to ransom in a northern city by a weak, possessive woman. Your eldest daughter who, when once she came here, asked:

"Daddy, what's that?" pointing to the clear night sky.

"What?"

"All those little dots."

"Dots. Those are the stars."

"Oh yes," said your son, "so they are. We only have street lights in Leeds."

All of you were amazed. You at the extent of their deprivation, they wonderstruck by the tiny seeds of brilliance carelessly strewn across the sky, so different from the picture book illustrations.

What would they now, five years later, have made of this night? In Leeds could they hear the rain beating down on their roof? The cottage here was all but submerged in the roar and hiss. The night was now quite black outside. You could make out nothing below roof top level, but imagined you could discern a lighter shade of darkness about there, where you knew the treetops to end and the sky begin, where one summer the children and you watched the bats and listened to the owls screech before dawn.

If they had been there then, all those you loved, your wife in her hospital bed suffering with babies perhaps now never to be born alive, your star-starved children in a distant city, you would have held the window open with all your strength and from that porthole on the night you would have braved the spray to listen again, to watch in wonder. Alone, infant daughter sleeping, you dreamed you were in a submarine world, you dreamed you were already drowned.

And now you are alone again, the children fledged, the house empty. But down the lane, although it is not a blue police phone box, the time capsule still stands. The cast iron is sometimes repainted, the money collected from it at long intervals, so little is it used. You walked down to it the other day for old time's sake, thinking to ring someone up. You dialled home. You were not there.

40

On Going Out Without A Phone

Sixty years ago a stockbroker acquaintance of your parents who commuted from his village to the City every day, arriving at his desk at the civilised hour of 10:30, would consider his work-load and send a post card by the midday mail to inform his wife which train he would take home in the evening. She received the card in the afternoon mail.

Fifty years ago you drove your VW Beetle from Melbourne to Perth around the coast and across the Nullabor Plain. Most of the roads were then dirt, you took a tent and your time, spending four months on the journey. Four months without a telephone or radio.

Forty years ago public areas in towns and cities had phone boxes and the first motorways had emergency telephones along the hard shoulder.

Thirty years ago you worked in offices in Africa with no electricity and communication by the weekly mail bag. When you went on trek you took plenty of water, fruit and fuel in the Land Rover. If you broke down or got stuck you fixed it or waited; if you had an accident you died.

Twenty years ago your eldest children did their 'year out' before the phrase was coined. You felt lucky to receive an aerogramme or a postcard every month or so, by which time of course the writer had moved on to new countries, new adventures, new perils.

Ten years ago your younger children were travelling in the electronic age and you felt alarmed if a week passed without an email. This was the precursor of the epidemic, nay the phobia that seems to have swept the whole world and now affects us all: the mobile phone syndrome.

You kept your first one in the car 'in case of breakdown' but otherwise never used it. Gradually, like everyone else you began carrying one around. You only realised what a comfort it must be to so many people when on a longish hike in the Lake District you discovered with a shock that you had left your mobile behind.

You were for a moment a child without a dummy to suck. Now this was hardly darkest Africa or Mount Everest and you were surprised and disgusted at how insecure you suddenly felt. You even debated turning back. It was another 'just in case' situation. But in case of what? Getting lost? Breaking a leg? A heart attack? Did you need to know the breaking news or the state of the stock market?

You pulled yourself together. You did not actually tell or text anyone, *I might be some time.* How could you, without a phone? But as you strode on up over the Cat Bells towards Great Gable you did feel like an explorer again. You felt emboldened, relying only on your own resources. You felt free. A mere ten years ago you would not have been able to experience this: you would have taken it all for granted.

41

A Shopping Basket

I t is a Ghanaian basket, hand-woven from cane and rush, very light and immensely strong. It is about a foot deep, a little less across the top from handle to handle and a little more from end to end. It has faded to a straw colour and groans when you pick it up. Its beauty lies in its functionality and its simple design, no doubt tried and tested over generations. The reason it has lasted is that it is so well made.

The base consists of five narrow woody strips of cane (you suppose) running lengthwise. Woven across them are narrow strips of similar material alternating with strips of tough reed the width of your middle finger. Although the basket, empty and laden, has been stood on these strips on wooden and concrete floors, in the boots of cars and Land Rovers, in the damp and the dry, in the humidity of the tropics and in the raw cold of English frosts and has collected the dust of droughts in both countries, the underneath shows little sign of wear and tear.

The sides of the basket consist entirely of the reed woven across vertical canes. The exception, whether for strength or decoration, is three narrow rows top and bottom of a naturally black, fibrous cane that makes a border. The whole is topped with a rim of attractively plaited cane.

The excellence of the design lies in the handles. Usually with a straw or cane or wicker basket the handles are the first to go, rendering the basket useless. These handles, however, one on either side, have a loop within a loop, joined at the top for your comfortable grip, but separating at the bottom to give four anchor points on either side. You can consequently lift great weights in your basket without exerting undue strain on the handles.

To your amazement you have been using this basket weekly now for over ten years: before that it was used daily in Africa for five years, sometimes carried on a black woman's head, sometimes in a white woman's hands. Then it contained bananas, papayas and pineapples, mangoes, avocados and aubergines, tomatoes, peppers and sweet potatoes and green leaves from the roadside market; today you bring back from the farm shop bananas, tomatoes, Maris Piper and Desirée potatoes, rhubarb, broccoli and kale, parsnips and turnips, red green and yellow peppers, cucumbers, purple aubergine, red cherries, white cherries, gooseberries and soft fruit, peaches and pears, Coxes, Bramleys and orange Pippins, and salad according to the season.

You cannot remember where you bought the basket. It cannot have made any special mark at the time. Perhaps you got it at the central market from amongst a pile of baskets, or perhaps from a roadside stall supplied by one or two basket makers. You must have been impressed by its usefulness, though, because when the time came to move house you bought two more identical baskets to pack things into. It is now impossible to say which of the three is the original.

Two of them, not necessarily the same two, serve a different purpose now. One you stack with old newspapers, magazines and junk mail, a far heavier load than it was designed for, the other you fill with empty bottles, glass jars and tin cans. In Ghana these would have been treasures that disappeared before ever being considered rubbish. Here, once a week, you are obliged to drive to the recycling point to empty your waste.

You probably paid pennies for these baskets. You have had many years of use out of them with perhaps many more to come: these baskets are the warp and weft of your past, your present and your future.

42

Elephant Bag

I t is small enough to be accepted as hand baggage on an airline; it fits in the overhead lockers or beneath the seat; it is large enough to carry your essentials for a weekend, and with a zipped top, secure eonough to contain your valuables. Two side pockets, one zipped, usually contains your luggage, house or car keys, one – open topped – is handy for papers to which you need easy access. On the outside of each pocket, now faded with use, is stitched a panel of lighter material displaying the logo (though the word did not then exist) of *Travelling Light,* one of the few companies that catered for off-season travellers to warmer climes. The logo is a blue and white swallow, and beneath it the boast that the elephant bag, as it was described in the catalogue, was made in the UK. Nowadays, like everything else, it would probably have been imported from China.

Such bags have since become commonplace. Everyone travels and everyone changes their bag with the fashion. It is necessary, it seems, not to have something that is useful or durable, but something in the latest style, colour or shape. Last year's bag is discarded. There is no rapport between owner and bag. The last bag is about as memorable as the last meal out; the last package holiday embrace.

Your affair with your black bag is long lasting. Together you have travelled the world; you have survived the toughest hotspots and you have relaxed on the sunniest beaches. Sometimes the bag contained passports, documents, airline tickets and currency; other times it held a picnic, a beach towel, a swimming costume, a bottle of water and the car keys.

Your bag has travelled on trains and planes and buses. To the far north and to the tropics. It has become indispensable and is always ready, be it for an examiners' meeting in Manchester, a holiday weekend across the sea or a family emergency almost anywhere. And yet they mock you. *Dad's still got that ugly old bag. Why don't you get a new one? How can you be seen with...?* etc.

They understand nothing, these throwaway people. The bag is not worn out. Not in any way. It is not even shabby and any dirt can easily be sponged off. You have no idea what material it is made of, but the bag is thicker skinned than you. You will wear out first. The elephant bag will be something to leave behind.

43

An Ordnance Survey Map

A musician friend said he preferred reading the score of a symphony rather than going to a performance. This may be hyperbole; however, the next best thing to going for a hike is to sit down with an ordnance survey map. You do not get the fresh air, the smells, the sounds, the aching limbs and lungs and the delicious physical tiredness at the end of it: but you nearly do, in some kinetic way; and you can travel much further.

It does not have to be one or the other, of course. In unfamiliar territory you will take your map with you. It will jog your memory and guide you on your way. You are far more self reliant with a trusty map than with GPS, which is too much like a spy in the sky. Or perhaps more like a guide dog for the blind, only you are not blind and you like to make your own decisions. With a map you are free to choose your own mistakes with your eyes wide open..

The most remarkable thing about the map is its language. Long before the widespread use of road signs, signing in public buildings, street furniture and computer screen icons, the Ordnance Survey had developed its economic and picturesque symbols which enabled the user to read a map without recourse to the written word.

Looking at an OS map, you can distinguish at a glance a beacon from a lighthouse, an orchard from a non-conif-

erous wood, from coppice or from heath land. Marsh reeds
and saltings are different, domed churches are distinct
from churches with a tower, and some houses are more
important than others.

In mountainous areas you are made aware of scree,
loose rock or boulders; for the historically minded battle
sites and places of antiquity are marked. At the coast the
map will inform you whether you will be walking on sand or
shingle, cliff top or mud.

All these symbols, combined with the different types of
roads, railways and boundaries provide us visually with
information, thereby short-circuiting language. But what
richness the written language also provides in the place
names. Your local map alone contains descriptive names
such as Wet Wood, Mousehall, Froghole Farm, Twelve Acre
Ghyll and Snowdrop Copse; historical names like Clayland
Shaw, Glebe House, Coneyburrow Wood, Prior's Plot; then
there are names that suggest tales of struggle or despair
such as Wish End Farm, Sliding Field Wood, Gallow's
Cross, Deadman's Wood, Hope Cottages.

All these names are within walking distance of your
own unimportant house, but the most telling features are
the changes. The map confirms your memories that what
is now a dumping ground for manure and slurry hardly a
mile away along the lane was only ten years ago a healthy,
deciduous wood. Across the road an even larger part of that
same wood has made way for large silage pits and a store
for stacks of giant, plastic wrapped bales of hay.

The large front garden of a well known TV environmen-
talist, like those of many of your other neighbours, has gone
under half an acre of tarmac and bitumen; large trees have
been felled to make way for garages and extensions, for
engine sheds or in a futile attempt to prevent subsidence
to houses. The strip of woodland parallel to the lane on the
map and dotted with small houses has all but disappeared.

To compensate for this vandalism another area shown
on the map as arable farmland and which you remember
twenty years ago as bean fields, has been set aside and is
already almost an impenetrable wilderness, sheltering deer,
boar, badger and fox and increasingly home and hunting
ground to birds of prey.

A similar picture of change for the better or for the worse

could be got anywhere within the country, tracing maps back for centuries.

But your major interest in the maps lies in the planning of walks. Underlying all the symbols and colours and names are the thinly but clearly drawn contour lines. From these you can judge the steepness of the climb, the number of ascents and descents you will have to make and estimate the length of your ramble. Much satisfaction can be derived from this exercise alone, long before you pull on your walking boots. And if you are in a lazy mood, what does it matter if a footpath is overgrown, a bridleway no longer accessible? After all, you had no real intention of leaving your armchair.

44

A Bird Table

A bird table is not primarily for the welfare of the birds. A bird table is put there for the observer. While some people watch daytime TV, practice meditation, sketch, take photographs or simply make lists, you have your bird table. If you wished, it would offer the opportunity of doing any or all of these other things at one fell swoop, but you just like to have it there.

Your first bird table was a stake driven into the lawn with a flat, wooden platform hammered onto the stake. All you fed to the birds were the scraps from your table. Like a new restaurant it attracted a number of curious diners and given the right menu they kept coming back.

There were however disadvantages to this simple design. Your initial modification was to fix a strip of beading around the platform to prevent the smaller crumbs, titbits you might say, from spilling over. For birds are messy eaters. Starlings, even blackbirds and robins, will throw their food from side to side like a dog worrying a rabbit it has caught, before swallowing it down. Why swallow?

The biggest birds that land on the bird table are the jackdaws. Despite their size they are much more careful than many of the smaller birds. They live in the chimney and have presumably observed human comings and goings all their lives, but they do not descend directly to the breakfast table. They will fly first to a high branch, then to a lower one, and then descend perhaps to a shrub or a climbing rose before flopping onto the bird table like a black shadow. With a final look around they will then concentrate on the food. With great urgency they load up their beaks from back to front until they are full of whatever the day offers, sliced fruit, bread, cheese rinds, fat, meat or seeds. How or in what order they deliver or consume their shopping you have been unable to see since this takes place within the intimacy of the chimney pot.

A second disadvantage to your pre-garden centre, pre-mail order catalogue prototype was that, having no roof, the smaller birds were exposed to danger. A streak of brown along the hedgerow like a silent jet stream, a steep turn, a shriek and an explosion of feathers above the table, bird panic and silence. A sparrow hawk, like a fighter bomber, has raided the feeding birds and carried one off before its attack was even noticed.

Being roofless, on the few days a year when it rained and the fewer still when it snowed, the bird food got sodden or covered. And it is in harsh conditions of frost and snow that the birds most need this sustenance.

So the final modification was a roof, high enough to allow jackdaws in, but low enough to discourage the moorhen from a neighbour's pond from flying up. That and their white doves are no more acceptable than geese or chicken would be; the cock pheasant that strolls in and out with his harem of distinctively different hens is borderline. The party pick up only spillages and since the garden offers them asylum from the £250 a day city gunmen, it seems wrong to drive them away.

The action is live, in colour and incessant. Sitting watching, your mind may observe, wonder or wander at the same time. You can monitor the constant comings and goings of great, blue, coal and long tail tits; you can observe solitary, fearless birds like the small but well armed nuthatch take possession of the table, you can watch blackbirds fighting so much over possession as to lose sight of the banquet altogether, you spot raiding parties of chaffinches on, over and around the table; less often but more violently a gang of starlings will invade and take temporary possession; greenfinches also believe in safety in numbers. House sparrows fight for nesting rights in bird boxes around the garden, for this accommodation offers bed and breakfast, but once on the table they are cooperative. In the lulls a robin, a pied wagtail, a wren might drop in for a quick inspection and a snack. The thrushes never seem quite to pluck up courage to expose themselves to the dangers of eating in public, preferring to scavenge beneath the shrubs, and in summer knock out snails on the brick path.

The pattern of activity on and around the table can be subtly changed by the food you give to the birds. Nuts and fat can be hung from the platform or strewn across it for the huge variety of tits; seeds are eaten by most birds but preferred by the finches; chopped windfall apples, currants and other scraps will bring on the blackbirds who seem to have an internet all of their own. When it is very cold, however, it would seem that all birds will eat all things.

The bird table is a part of your routine. Get up, bathroom, feed birds, breakfast. During the day you frequently look out to see what is going on and in the coldest weather you dash out to replenish supplies several times a day. And in so doing you are replenishing a spiritual need of your own. Your offerings are perhaps to a higher force than these small, feathered bodies.

45

The Royal Continental Hotel

Y ou have been to a few more expensive and to many cheaper hotels around the country and around the world, most of them in far more exotic locations than Manchester. None of them, however, was as odd as The Royal Continental Hotel.

Royal is a misnomer. The only palatial thing about it is the vast, glass-domed entry lobby and the size and condition of some of the rooms: but we'll come to that. Besides, monumental would be a better description than palatial.

Access off Oxford Street is the first surprise. You have walked the lower length of Whitworth Street to find a way in: suddenly around the corner, hidden behind students and shoppers queuing on the pavement for buses, you find an entrance.

But once you have found the fairly modest sign and walked through the glass doors, you no longer doubt that you have arrived. You still have another hundred yards to go, across the chequered, marble floor and the circular central carpet directly beneath the dome, before you reach the efficiently manned modern reception desk. This is the first real evidence that the Victorian insurance edifice has been converted to a hotel.

After the familiar check-in ritual you are given a time-coded key and directed (but not helped) to your room. There is only one, very slow lift. When it stops at your floor it takes you by surprise, the exit door opening behind you, for it is a walk through lift like the one in London Underground's Leicester Square. Later you discover a hidden, and despite the labyrinthine corridors, much quicker route: the original staircase, a broad stone spiral with wide brass handrails, marble walls and steps and porthole windows between each floor that look down into the central lobby. In each window is a heraldic device in stained glass.

Tracking down your room number you insert your key

and push open the door. What a surprise! Your 'single' room contains two double beds, two bulky armchairs, a writing desk and chair (a real luxury these days), internet connections, TV and telephone, not to mention the kettle with its tray of instant drink powders, the hair dryer and trouser press and of course a Gideon Bible tucked away like pornography in a bedside drawer.

Despite all the paraphernalia there is still room to hold a party in here. Moreover the room is as high as a two storey house. From the central light fitting a thick flex hangs down, ending in an inverted, opaque shield of a lamp, a flying saucer that might house several aliens. Between the beds is a pair of wall mounted lights with age stained shades.

The part of the room that was the original insurance office remains largely intact. The walls are built of shiny bricks, some green, some white, broken up with marble pillars and decorated with elaborate cornices. But where the room is partitioned off it is finished in common hardboard and paint with an air conditioning grill and a central heating thermostat inserted into it.

Two huge windows, higher than a bus, look out, one onto a central courtyard and incidentally into other people's rooms, the other onto a railway only metres away. Each window contains many panes, none of which have been cleaned in decades, inside or out. It does not matter. To ensure privacy you have to shut them out behind drapes that would not be out of place in the proscenium arch of an average sized theatre. Each curtain is topped with a pelmet of the same fussy material, a green and red pattern that picks out the green of the brick wall and the well trodden green and red flecked carpet.

This is not the only room. A lobby with a Narnia-sized wardrobe leads to a large, comparatively modern bathroom with a gutsy shower in the bath and a wash basin providing space to spread more grooming aids than you have ever possessed.

The rooms are grand, imposing but also comfortable. What adds to the homely touch is that it is all so downright shabby. There are no concessions to trend or fashion here. The dirty windows, the faded and tattered beds, the worn chairs with their broken springs and arms smoothed black with use (the rest of its upholstery being red), belie the pretensions of the place.

The marbled brick is chipped and riddled with rawlplug-filled holes in one corner where perhaps some fixture once stood. The wire connecting you to the internet is boxed in and painted over on its long journey around the room, but where it reaches a corner pillar it straggles across the stone like tired knicker elastic and disappears through a hole in the partition. The frayed carpet is full of holes, especially beside the bed. Desk tops have suffered scalding from the kettle.

The hotel itself, however, offers all you need for your meeting and your sustenance; your room is clean, spacious and comfortable. You even smile in your sleep when the goods trains rattle through your dreams at one and two and three in the morning, and there is small risk of oversleeping once the morning rush hour clanks under way. You miss only the pad of a barefoot but uniformed bearer across the floor bringing you your bed tea, but that *was* in a royal continental palace – in Mysore, not in Manchester.

46

Cellar

A cellar for many will evoke vineyards or pubs where wine, liqueurs or beer are stored in glass bottles and in oak barrels, in firkins and in flasks.

In your mind the cellar is a private place, two dark and private spaces beneath your childhood home. The wine cellar and the coal cellar were separated only by a brick wall but each had its own entrance.

Access to the coal cellar was from the kitchen down a dank, brick staircase. When you opened the trap a cold, sour breath thick with damp coal dust gasped across your ankles. The dark cellar was divided into stalls for the different fuels; big irregular lumps of coal for the open fires, smooth, uniform cakes of anthracite for the kitchen range, and lighter, jagged bits of coke for the stoves. These were replenished through two hatches that opened into the garden.

On the outside was a wooden, hinged lid beneath which was set a heavy iron grill to keep intruders out. It took the two hands of a strong man to lift and fasten the grill. Men your grandmother called coal heavers, grimy, black-faced goblins would hump twenty or more sacks each weighing a hundredweight from their Bedford lorry parked in the drive and pour them with a whoosh and roar like waves breaking on a shingle beach down the chutes into the cellar. They wore brass studded, leather waistcoats so the greasy sacks would not slip from their shoulders.

Before breakfast every day you would hear the sound of a shovel beneath the kitchen as your father filled the coal buckets and lugged them upstairs; as you grew up you began to share these chores, remembering to wipe your slag wet feet on the coconut matting of the top step before crossing the tiled kitchen floor with the fresh smelling lumps of coal that glistened like precious stones. You never played or hid in the coal cellar.

The wine cellar, on the other hand, was a place of excitement, of awe and adventure. The door to the wine cellar, a big, solid oak door with a huge, black iron bolt, opened off a downstairs passage. One bare bulb lit the steps, beyond which stretched a musty, cavernous and empty space. Empty because your parents kept no wine, though sometimes the alcoves were filled with wooden crates of apples picked in the garden. In winter these ripe and often rotting apples filled the damp air with a pungent sweetness. The bare floor was brick and from the ceiling hung hundreds of years of spiders' webs and the skeletons, if that is the word for the age old and withered corpses of the brittle and whitened spiders themselves.

During the Second World War the cellar had been used as an air raid shelter and an entrance made into the garden. From outside this secret panel six foot below ground level was hidden by a thick growth of lavender bushes, but you children knew you could squeeze between the weatherboard house and drop down into the square pit from which you might gain access to the cellar and introduce a shaft of daylight and some warmer air into the creepy depths. The pit sometimes filled with creatures, dead and alive, that had fallen in and could not escape. You frequently rescued frogs and newts which you would put back in the pond.

Because the cellar was unlit the dangling webs could take you by surprise and cling to your face, making the furthest recesses frightening places to explore, but what brought you and your friends down here were the smugglers' tales.

You knew from local history and hearsay that during Napoleonic times smugglers gangs had operated in your village. And not to get too Enid Blyton about it, there were stories of secret passages linking your parents' house to the church one way and to a farm house further down the hill. Part of the passage at Cockshott Farm had been explored and casks of brandy discovered but most of the tunnel beyond had collapsed. What excited you and your friends was this end, the cellar of your own house.

The cellar walls were brick lined and at one end was a roman arch over a recess which looked as though it must once have been a doorway, only this, too, was bricked up. You were convinced that if you removed a few bricks you would find the opening to a secret passage. It was hard work. For days you and a friend laboured away in the dark. You had graduated from a screw driver and mallet to real coal chisels, both broad and narrow bladed, and a masonry hammer.

Getting the first brick out was the toughest of all, but after that, you reasoned, it should be easy to prise the others away. Only that first brick and all the others in the wall had stood there for 250 years and it was not going to yield so easily to a couple of puny kids. Besides, it was summer outside and since it was your childhood the sun must perpetually have been shining. Your friend drifted off and you soon followed.

Then came a really exciting discovery. The twelfth century village church had been bombed during the war and now, fifteen years later, it was being repaired. Workers in the crypt found what they took to be an underground passage leading off beneath the cemetery in the direction of your house. This news reached you first by bush telegraph and later there was an article in the local newspaper, linking the tunnel perhaps to the notorious Hawkhurst gang of smugglers.

The bad news was that further exploration was deemed too costly and too dangerous and the decision was taken to fill the tunnel with the rubble from the ruins and to seal it off for good. You were appalled. You dragged your father into his own cellar and showed him your excavations. He laughed at the damaged bricks and pooh-poohed your theory that the buttress not only concealed a doorway but most probably the other entrance to a smugglers' hideaway, if not to the network of tunnels themselves.

"I wondered what all the banging was about," was all he said, and this was the first time in your young life that you encountered the lack of curiosity and imagination of the adult world. You vowed never to lose yours.

47

A Pocket Handkerchief

A weekend newspaper interviews minor celebrities of the moment to a strict formula. One of the questions is, "What objects do you always carry with you?" Answers vary from the predictable, "my mobile phone," through the medical, "my asthma inhaler" to the sentimental, "photos of my children." No one so far has mentioned a pocket handkerchief. Perhaps instead they lug a box of tissues around with them. More waste, fewer forests.

The use of a handkerchief is a cultural matter. You remember walking through an African market with a Ghanaian friend when in mid conversation he sniffed, grunted, gripped the bridge of his nose and deftly sent a string of snot into the gutter. Startling at the time you recalled this not uncommon habit when another African acquaintance visiting you in London reacted with obvious disgust when a man on the tube emptied the contents of his nose into a grubby handkerchief, folded it up and crammed it back into his pocket.

The difference in our cultures might partially be explained by the differences in rural and urban living and by centuries of evolving manners. It was not so long ago the British spat and spread their tuberculosis on the trams and in the streets. Footballers still do spit publicly. Proficiency in gobbing is one of the prerequisites for getting into a premier division team. Perhaps we cannot expect footballers to carry a little hankie in their shorts (though imagine the advertising possibilities). In any case a pocket handkerchief is much more than just a snot rag, though that remains its primary function. Ever since your first pair of shorts you have always carried a handkerchief in your right hand pocket.

Throughout life, long trousers, jeans, uniforms, suits, beach shorts, and ski pants – that hankie has been your comfort blanket and your emergency kit.

Think of the uses of a handkerchief: in childhood you need it to clean wounds from falls and scrapes, to stem a nose bleed, to use as a blindfold, to carry home small creatures in, as a sieve for pond searches, to tie aniseed balls up in; as a grown up to flick over your toecaps before an interview, to mop your brow after the interview, to clean your glasses, to knot and protect your bald patch during that break in the sun, to wipe the mist from your car windscreen in the damp, to clean a nib, soak up a spill, protect your clothes. As child and man there have also been numerous occasions when a handkerchief was essential to dry your tears; or to hide them.

A pocket handkerchief can also become a fashion accessory. In this case it is worn in the breast pocket and is often a white silk handkerchief if that pocket belongs to a dinner jacket or dress suit. In other jackets it can be of any colour. If there is gypsy blood in your veins a dark red kerchief can be worn around the neck but then it ceases to be a handkerchief.

The important thing about a pocket handkerchief is that it is just that. When you go out in the morning you might check you have your wallet, your season ticket or pass, your keys and last but not least a clean handkerchief in your pocket. A pocket handkerchief is the psychological battery that powers you, a clean energy source at that.

48

A Bodge

E very child needs a 'bodge'. It provides good exercise, it develops muscles and spatial skills and co-operation, it is dangerous and it is fun. Moreover a boy's imagination transforms this wooden frame on wheels into a safari vehicle, a formula one racing machine or a get-away car.

You thought you had invented the bodge, bringing it on through various prototypes, though the name and the concept came from your father's memory of his childhood; he, too, bought the pram wheels for the first bodge and helped you construct the chassis.

On an early model you lay flat on your stomach, hands gripping the wooden, centrally bolted cross strut that supported and steered the front wheels. You bent your knees, folding your legs over your buttocks and your friend propelled you by pushing on your ankles. Both faces were therefore close to the ground and the driver's in particular was horribly exposed. Although it felt fast and exciting, the next model was a much improved version.

In this you sat up between the rear wheels and steered with a rope attached to the front axle. It was easier for the pusher and better for the driver. As you grew stronger and more daring you got through many pairs of wheels of various sizes until one day your father came home with some sturdy pram wheels that lasted many years.

Your favourite circuit was around the house, a mostly flat but challenging course over a lawn, between flower beds, through an S-bend that separated house and garage and out onto a long, sloping gravel drive. If you turned right it swept up to the front door but if you carried on it led into the main road.

This last bend was the climax of your ride. The panting pusher summoned up all his energy for a final, frantic effort and shoved you off down the slope with the last of his strength. Thus catapulted you sped towards the road, holding a straight course for as long as you dared, then you leant over and pulled the steering to your right and drifted round the corner scattering gravel through the spokes. If you got it wrong you overturned or collided with the rockery. If you judged it right you coasted up to the front door and it was your turn to push.

When you tired of the bodge you would do the same thing on your bikes. Forbidden to eat between meals you were always ravenous when you came in.

One day, however, you got a surprise. You were aware of the existence of other bodges since friends had copied what you considered was your invention. Then, opening your Eagle comic, you read an illustrated article about the Soapbox Derby. In London a bodge was called a soapbox because many of them were literally soapboxes on wheels with more or less modification. The competition in which children raced them down a hill somewhere had apparently been going on for years. You looked at the pictures in disbelief and scorn. Boxes! You had long since abandoned any sides to your own bodges as being an encumbrance. And coasting down a hill! Where was the fun in that? Even at that age you associated pleasure with effort, with getting puffed out, with running and climbing or pushing a bodge.

There is a postscript to this piece. In later, lazier teenage years your friend, who was to become a mechanic, thought it would be a good idea if your bodge had an engine. He quickly realised something more substantial was needed than wood and string and pram wheels, so began converting an old pedal car which had strong pneumatic tyres and a rigid chassis. He installed a motor mower engine and the finishing touches were done with the help of a local garage. The car, unreliable, noisy and dirty, was far more dangerous than the bodge. It must have infuriated the neighbours with its noise on the days it could be got going. When some time later the go-kart came onto the scene, we said in dismay and disbelief, "But we invented that years ago!"

49

A Push Mower

The only mower you have ever coveted was a gang mower drawn by an ox in sacking slippers. The beast was being led by a *mali* over the well-watered lawn of a large house in New Delhi. This trio, the mower, the *mali* and the ox, would hardly be practical in your English cottage garden. Indeed, for most people, a hand propelled mower is the most appropriate tool.

If the lawn is not larger than a tennis court, then the only suitable mower is the simple push mower. Little changed in design for a hundred years, though with some variations over the number and position of rollers, cylinders, chains, grass box and the materials these parts are made from, they are light, easy and silent except for the pleasant click of the blades that, to take a common model, send up a green arc of finely cut grass into the metal box in front.

As early as 1850 there was a model called *'silens messor'* which in Latin means 'silent cutter'. The simplest push mower today is hardly more than a revolving cylinder on a handle, a cutting roller on a stick. Most machines cost less than a tank of petrol for a small family car.

Not only is the hand propelled mower environmentally friendly, but it will give you a gentle workout before lunch or tea. Twenty minutes, that's all you need to get a heap of sweet grass, a trim lawn and a decent thirst.

Most important of all, you will not have disturbed your neighbours.

Some people unaccountably use an electric mower, even though this requires as much effort as a push mower to propel and to hold on course. Moreover, it is limited in range by the length of the cable. You also have to perform elaborate acrobatics to avoid tripping over the cable or more dangerously cutting it with the mower. Worst of all is the noise, ranging from a high pitched whine to a crunching roar, depending on its power and the thickness of the grass.

Less excusable still are petrol mowers. They are unfriendly to the environment and to anyone living within half a mile of them. Some still have to be pushed, most whether rotary or cylinder drive themselves while you walk behind breathing in the fumes and disturbing the neighbours' Sunday lunch on their patio, or afternoon tea in the garden. For the only time half the people get out their mowers is when the weather is fine; and when the weather is fine the other half wants to sit out and enjoy the peace and quiet of their gardens or labour meditatively in them.

There should be set hours when everyone has to cut their grass. For a short while there would be one almighty cacophony, then peace! Or if this sounds far-fetched, there should, as in most enlightened countries, be a total ban on the use of all machines at the weekend, hedge cutters, leaf blowers, chain saws and strimmers included.

In this country, however, where we are obsessed with lawns, we are heading in the opposite direction. There is an ever more popular and quite unnecessary piece of equipment for the domestic garden: the sit on mower or as it is described in a give-away piece of marketing, the garden tractor. It promotes unfitness and pollution in equal measure, bringing the drone of the motorway to your own backyard. It is the Humvi of garden appliances.

The only sensible solution would be to pass a law decreeing that those incapable of cutting their grass with a push mower should move to a smaller house. A similar law should apply to hedges and shears. But you had better not let your hobby horse bolt with you. No, it's time to get behind that green painted metal handle and clatter quietly away behind your people friendly, ecofriendly push mower. Besides, if you leave it too much longer you will need to borrow your neighbour's powerful dragon of a Flymo even to cut a swathe through the tall grass.

111

50

A Bicycle Bell

A mail order catalogue known for its forward looking products has just discovered the bicycle bell. To their amazement it "will fit any handlebars" and can be used to "enhance your bike." They further boast that it is practical "taking only a few minutes to fit." They even tell consumers how to use the bell and why. "A movement of the thumb causes the two clones of the bell to rotate, two clappers inside produce the typical dual ringing sound, ensuring your safety on every bike ride."

This is something of an exaggeration if the careless motorist bearing down on you is on her phone, listening to loud music or towing a large trailer too fast. In China, perhaps, before the motor car became available it might have been true that "ringing the bell alerts people's attention to you – even when they are metres away." In this country how many metres would the tone carry? Two, three? To the inside of the cab of a tractor or dustbin lorry?

In the end this well written if unlikely description of a bicycle bell concedes that you will probably buy it as a collector's item, that it will look decorative in a display cabinet. The company is selling a fashion accessory with a three year guarantee.

You have never owned a Chinese bell with a dual chime, though you did buy a Chinese Flying Pigeon bicycle in Sudan and you have always owned a bicycle at home. That bicycle has always had a bell on it.

For a period of five years, when you commuted from your local, rural railway station into London, you would cycle down the narrow lane in the morning and toil back up every evening. For many months of the year it was dark when you went down and dark when you came home. You had to allow time when leaving the station to remove your lamps, pump, and to lock the wheels to the cycle park stand. While fellow commuters carried important papers in their red, leather brief cases, you bore your cycle accessories and a packed lunch. But it never occurred to you to remove the bell. No trophy hunters would have wanted to nick that.

Yet your bicycle bell was as important to your safety then as the lights and the fluorescent reflecting strips you wore in the winter. It was certainly fastened to your handle bars so that you might alert people's attention to you. In fact it was not so much to protect you from inattentive motorists but from two enormous dogs. For whatever train you returned on, walkers from the kennels were exercising their dogs, two at a time up and down your route home. In the summer, when they were coming towards you, the minders were able, sometimes with difficulty, to hold the German shepherds in check as you pedalled by, their breath scorching your ankles.

If they were going in the same direction as you it was a different story. A bicycle is a fast, silent and efficient means of transport. The dogs would not hear your approach from the rear, light or dark. And in the dark, whichever way they were walking, you were always fearful of colliding with them. A bicycle lamp is dull and feeble. So you would ring your bell at the very hint of a darker shadow in the night and if it was the dog walker, she would gather her charges to the verge while you swept past.

It was similar with horses: not that the horses were inclined to attack you as if you were some fleeting hare, but that by swishing into their vision from the rear you might startle them into bolting. After all a paper bag in the hedge or a frightened pheasant was enough to send some horses skittering and sliding across the tarmac. But with one press on your trigger both horses and riders soon learned what to expect. You could pass them in safety.

Whether you were sailing on your way to a day's work or struggling back up the hill to supper, that little bell on the handle bars was both a comfort and a necessity. Perhaps now you should remove it and place it in a display cabinet.

51

Flip-Flops

Y ou first heard the word flip-flop in France. Spoken with a Gallic pout and a shrug it was even more onomatopoeic than in English, echoing the suck and slap of rubber on bare flesh; or wet sand. At the time the current French words for flip-flop were *nu-pieds (bare-feet)* and *tong*. You liked the symmetry of this for you had first worn flip-flops in Australia in the days when that country had been a distant and foreign land and where they still called flip-flops 'thongs' in the same way that they called vests 'spencers'.

The thong refers to the rubber strip that runs between your big toe and second toe to hug the flat sole so snugly and effectively to the ball of your foot. Only decades later did it come to mean the piece of string women wear between their buttocks, or by association the minimal attire both women and men use as a *cache-sexe*.

The term flip-flop or flip-flap has been in use since the 1900s but the first mass produced flip-flops did not appear until half way through the century. They were cheap, simple, practical and durable. In warm climates, on bare-foot summer holidays, they were easy to slip on to walk over pebbles, gravel and hot sand.

Perhaps not so good in the wet when they would stick to the surface or gloop up mud and splash the back of your legs and the seat of your shorts. It was not long before they became a fashion accessory and took on colour and trimmings. Leather versions became available and some were studded with jewels.

But nothing beat the basic, no-nonsense green rubber flip-flop, except perhaps the even cruder African version created from old car tyres. Recycling here was a necessity long before it became a virtue. These shoes, in West Africa at least, were known as Charley Woteys, words you first heard from your daughters who attended school in Accra and who were able to talk and indeed to bargain most vigorously in Ghanaian English.

But even Ghana could produce a luxury version. You possess a pair of Asante sandals, crudely ornate with rubber soles onto which a leather platform has been both stapled and tacked, the leather thong covered in silver material and topped with a round, glittering bauble. They are more decorative than practical, and were given to you as a leaving gift from a university colleague. They are still unworn. Souvenirs of a happy time.

You also have an old pair of original rubber flip-flops, now worn wafer thin, which in the summer you sometimes use when stepping out into the garden. When you once put them on in the bedroom their smooth underside slid on the top tread of the stairs and sent you surfing down to the kitchen tiles below. You paid for that for two years with a painful frozen shoulder, but the flip-flops remain in your wardrobe, stacked with memory molecules of Australian barbecues, French seaside holidays, a time before the tyranny of leisure wear and fashion. Flip-flops mean more simple days.

52

A Fountain Pen

For the last ten years at least you have barely written more than the odd personal letter by hand. The keyboard has taken over our lives. Everyone knows how to type and more and more of us have lost the physical fluency of writing by hand.

Then came the gift of a fountain pen, a birthday present from a daughter. It arrived in a strong brown carton marked Gucci. You had never bought or used an expensive brand name before, let alone anything fashionable. Inside the cardboard box was an etui that might have contained a diamond necklace or an expensive watch. It had a leather feel to it and was lined with velvet. Inside this was a velvet pouch like a slim sleeping bag and inside this the pearl in the oyster, a fountain pen.

All these layers were irrelevant to the function of the pen. You were not going to wrap it up, tuck it up and box it up after every use. Their sole purpose was to enhance the unveiling of a luxury gift.

A clearly written little booklet explained how to use the pen. The language was so clear and simple that it alone deserved a prize from the plain English lobby. You should not have been surprised that there were people today who needed instructions on how to prime a pen with ink, how to substitute the cartridge for the converter; people who were unfamiliar with the old button filler and lever filler pens, let alone how to prime the modern ink reservoir.

The moment you handled the Gucci pen you realised how special it was. It fitted into the hand like a sixth finger, comfortable and easy to control. It felt a natural part of you. You could not wait to fill it. You had none of the recommended Gucci ink but risked your own bottle of Quink, the washable ink you had used since your school days – possibly the same bottle.

Carefully you unscrewed the pen, separating the body from what you learned was the writing unit. The nib end. As instructed you removed the converter and plunged, lovely word for dipping, the tip into the ink. You carefully rotated the grooved part and siphoned up the black liquid. You were advised to fill and re-empty the chamber several times to expel any air bubbles.

You replaced the converter in the writing unit, screwed the body of the pen clockwise and your pen was whole again. You were ready to write your first words.

The feeling of comfort and control returned as you held the nib over a fresh sheet of paper. What you wrote was banal but your surprise was spontaneous. The thick flow of ink, the broad and fluid characters transformed your sometimes cramped handwriting into something legible and generous. The fatness of the pen opened up your style. Your trite phrase looked like a piece of poetry. This fountain pen was a toy and a tool to treasure.

Soon you sought out better paper: vellum, white laid,

cream wove, manila, watermarked, Nile blue, and even handmade, to do justice to your pen. Normal writing pads and cheap envelopes absorbed and spread the ink like blotting paper, making the handwriting look crazed or spidery. You did in any case require real blotting paper in all its shades of aubergine, salmon and spinach, and a soft cloth to clean the pen which was supposed to be rinsed through with cold water after every third or fourth use. And you remembered that, if travelling on a plane, the pen must be either quite full or quite empty.

But this fancy pen carried within it memories of all the other pens you had owned.

At school you first learned to write with a wooden dip pen. The ink was mixed from powder and poured by the ink monitor into the china wells set in each wooden desk. Sometimes the ink was lumpy like custard at school dinner. Sometimes it was too runny, also like the custard. The addition of the sugar from lemon sherbet could cause a dramatic reaction, but even under normal conditions writing was a scratchy, blotchy business. You were allowed one new brass nib and a clean sheet of blotting paper a week. The blotch never lasted more than a few days. Books, your hands and your cuffs were permanently ink stained.

There followed the Parker 51, a workhorse of a pen on sale cheaply in the chain stores. Sometimes it leaked in your pocket and of course needed to be refilled from a glass bottle every so often, but it saw you through your early days. The invention of plastic, ink-filled cartridges did away with the inconvenience of a bottle, but using a cartridge somehow felt like cheating. Other pens came along. Your mother lent you her green marbled Conway Stewart to see you through your 'A' Levels and at university you may have used a Waterman or a Sheaffer, although by then the Hungarian Biró brothers had revolutionised the writing habits of many.

Nevertheless serious written work still had to be submitted in pen and ink. For your finals you bought a new, more continent pen that could hold out for three hours of frantic writing in any language without needing attention.

Later you lapsed into using biros of all kinds, ball points, roller balls, felt tips, the word processor and the personal computer. All so much easier, so much cleaner.

Or so you thought, until this last birthday when you were given the present with which this piece is lovingly drafted and crafted.

53

The Red Shower

I t is easy to take it for granted: you use it every morning and often your thoughts are elsewhere. But the red shower is something special.

For a start, like Harry Potter's 'Platform 9½' or Dr. Who's 'Tardis', you would not know it was there at all. A wooden door in the kitchen that looks as though it might reveal a larder or a cupboard in reality conceals the magic box. Open the door, draw the stiff silvery curtain aside, snap the light cord down and you reveal a red-tiled space containing an adjustable shower-head, a cage of hair and body potions, and a white tray to stand in. The cord that switched the light on has also set a fan in motion; its whirring adds to the intimacy of the pulsing enclosure, and when you close the shower curtain to the light clatter of plastic curtain rings on their aluminium rod, and you have set the heavy fall of water to your preferred height and body temperature, you are swallowed down into the belly of another world.

On some days you may soap and rinse yourself within a minute without thinking about it. On others you luxuriate in the steaming water, turn your back to the stream and feel it massage your neck, your shoulders, and wash the worries and stiffness away, invigorating you for the day ahead. You might choose to wash your hair and stand and soak a while in the full knowledge that, unless you are very slow, the shower will use less than half the amount of water required to fill a bath, and all the water that touches you is clean.

But the shower can be a temptress, a seductress. You

may be caught up in the embrace of her watery tresses, your head may swim in the warmth and the fragrance of this little cell and you may forget time and place. Your mind will run over yesterday's events, will review today's challenges or get lost in the intricacies of some plot you are working out. For the shower, the singing, humming, hissing shower so relaxes your body and numbs your anxieties that the mind is released to float free in a dream, in a bubble of its own making. Eventually you will shake free of the spell, turn off the water, crash aside the curtain, thud open the door and rub yourself down on the cold tiles of the kitchen floor, or wrapping a towel around your waist hurry back up to the privacy of your bedroom.

The red shower also has stories of its own to follow. The air vent gives out into the garden and in wet weather spiders come in out of the rain. Although many are washed away when you turn on the tap, others learn that the area above the shower head remains dry, albeit beaded with condensation at times. One spider laid her eggs in the top corner beneath the red tiled ceiling, depositing them in a cobwebby sack. She stood over them for months. You watched them develop and one morning discovered hundreds of thousands of tiny black spiders spreading like a stain across the tiles. For a while their mother fussed over them, shepherded them, and when disturbed by the shower would, like a mother hen, gather them in beneath her. The little specks of pepper became more clearly recognisable as spiders and then one morning they were all gone. Only the adult female remained, a dried out skeletal corpse.

The red shower is not only a necessity and an indulgence for cold mornings. On hot afternoons, particularly if you have been working in the garden or have returned from a stuffy drive, you can strip off and step into its dark cavern, turn on the cold tap only and let the water shock and cool you down until you start to shiver. Then you can step out into the light and let the sunshine warm you up; or you can stay and thaw under the hot tap.

Sometimes when you have been out in the cold and wet of winter or your hands and feet are numbed you can turn on the hot water in darkness so as not to activate the fan, fill the kiosk with steam and step in, breathe in the humid air and soak up a river of warmth. And when you do pull the cord and switch on the light the red tiles emerge gradually through the steam and you feel restored.

There is something complete and comforting about the red shower that no draughty cubicle, no thin piddle of bathroom shower can provide. Your pulsating red womb of a shower is a secret and always a surprise.

54

Pulling The Chain

This is another visit to the barber, for you go there not only to have your haircut but to be entertained. Today unusually there were no stories, no jokes, but the encounter was as instructive as usual and it dredged up a forgotten memory.

It was a cold day with a biting wind. Hardly the day for a haircut but you had the time and the opportunity. When you entered the barber shop you found Graham toasting a piece of bread at a blazing fire. There were more dogs than usual, four lurchers, which between them occupied all the seats once-upon-a-time intended for his customers. You are used to squeezing in next to one or two lurchers, but four great gangly sprawling creatures did rather fill the little cottage room with their smell and their presence.

"My wife asked me to take the four biggest boys out of the house," he explained, removing the toast from the fork, "while she got the new curtains measured up."

You crouched down beside him to warm your hands at the coals and to enjoy the hot glow of the fire on your face and chest. While he finished his toast and apropos of nothing in particular, and as the dogs snored and fidgeted in their slumber, you discussed vinaigrettes, those silver containers filled with scents that ladies of yore held to their noses to counteract the foul smells from the streets.

Eventually you climbed into the chair; he robed you,

pumped the chair to a convenient height and set to work on your head. He never asks what you want. You never tell him. He snips away with his scissors, pausing minutes at a time while he tells one of his stories. Today, though, was different. He had been doing some home repairs in his bathroom and he launched on an enthusiastic description of the Victorian lavatory cistern; how pulling a chain to release a gallon and a half of water five foot down a pipe, made for a much more effective flush than you get from a modern cistern built in just above or behind the lavatory pan. The modern ball cock, too, was inferior and nothing like as long-lasting as the Victorian original.

He waxed lyrical on the virtues of the cast iron tank, the metal bell that both released water and created a suction to gush it away, the chain the user pulled and released to set it all in motion; he recalled the various handles, wooden, porcelain or other at the bottom of these chains. He went into raptures over the robust simplicity of Victorian engineering and compared it unfavourably with the light-weight but short lived plumbing of today.

Between the stanzas of this ode to the water closet he did cut your hair, but left you feeling quite nostalgic. It was a long time since you had 'pulled the chain', once a regular occurrence in the house where you grew up. You remembered clearly the decisive pull of the chain, letting go of it at the lowest point to allow it to rise back up on the iron lever. There came a clank, a rattle and a whoosh and while the bowl was still whirlpooling you could hear the ballcock in the ceiling high cistern open to the sharp hiss of its own refill.

While you retrieved your duffel coat from beneath one of the lurchers the barber made up the fire that had died down during his impromptu recital. You fished out your wallet, warm as dog's blood, to pay the bill. As usual you felt you were paying not just for a haircut but for a splash of wisdom and an almost kinetic memory. It was cheap at the price.

55

Real Money

Y ou read in the papers today that Sweden aims to be the first cashless country. Certainly in cities it is convenient to be able to pay with the swipe of a card when travelling on public transport, making small purchases or buying coffee; and paying larger sums by credit card makes the expenditure somehow seem less painful. It may be another month before your money leaves your account.

There is nevertheless something safe and comforting about real money; something easier to control, to keep tabs on. There is nothing like the reassurance of the pound in your pocket, though there was a time when a pound was worth so much that it would not have been in your pocket as a coin, rather in your wallet as a banknote.

Your first pocket money was 6d (sixpence in old money) a week. Even so you saved up most of it. You had a post office account and a pay-in book. When you went to secondary school your pocket money rose to half a crown (two shillings and sixpence) a week. Your best friend got only two shillings and you felt embarrassed for him. However you occasionally contributed to the cost of airgun pellets with which you shot squirrels on the farm. You would earn two shillings for the tail of each of this vermin you posted off.

Your pocket money did not increase when you were a boarder in the VIth Form. Boys would queue up every Friday night at the housemaster's study to withdraw what they needed. The bespectacled master would count the coins out from a metal cash box and enter the sum in a ledger with his fountain pen. Most boys received the same pocket money.

Mind you, half a crown went a long way. You could buy one gobstopper for a penny. True to its name it entirely filled the mouth and lasted for hours. It changed colour as you sucked it, which tempted you to remove it every so often for examination. You could also buy sixteen aniseed balls for a penny, and when you were hard up the shopkeeper would sell you four for a farthing including the paper bag. There were four farthings to a penny. Halfpenny pieces were also quite useful.

It was always exciting to go abroad and count out, examine and compare the different coins in the different countries, and before the Euro there were so many with their various shapes, weights and sizes. With a few wafer-light French centimes you would go into the patisserie and buy a handful of hard and chewy carambars which the shopkeeper lifted from a big, scented glass jar, in the same way as you bought gobstoppers in England.

When you returned home the English coins always seemed bigger and heavier than the foreign ones. There were silver coins and there were coppers, or that's what you called them, and it all had great value to a schoolboy.

Your saving habit continued. At the end of term you had never withdrawn quite the whole amount. On the last day of term you would withdraw the balance and pocket it with satisfaction. Occasionally, when grandparents or other visitors gave you money you would pay it straight into your post office account. One day, you had been told, you would need those savings.

On a particular occasion your savings received a huge boost. Your father, a doctor, had a few private patients whom he treated in his consulting room in the house. One old lady on emerging saw you in the hallway, introduced herself, took a large piece of paper from her bag and handed it to you. When she had left you unfolded the paper and asked your parents what it was. Your father was flabbergasted.

"Good God," he said, "a five pound note!"

£5 was a lot of money and the notes were huge. If you remember rightly they were very white with blue printing, but you might be mistaken.

Before you went to university you opened a bank account after a paternalistic interview with the tweed-suited bank manager in your village. Your annual grant was around £300 and you calculated you needed £3 a week in cash for everyday expenditure. There were no credit cards or ATMs so you had to look after your cash until you next got an opportunity to go to a bank. You knew where you stood with the money in your pocket and were careful not to let it run out. You never used the coffee bar in the Union when you could make your own in your room much cheaper. Anyway drinkable coffee, let alone real coffee shops, would not arrive in the UK for another fifty years.

Only once in your three undergraduate years did you eat out. It was to celebrate the rash decision to get married. At the end of the meal in some kind of a steakhouse under a glitter ball you found that you had too little cash between you to pay the bill. Your girlfriend rummaged in her untidy bag and fished out a few more pennies. You searched all your pockets. You made piles of your coins but could not get them to add up to the total bill. You offered to wash up but the waiter said it did not matter because you looked so much in love.

All the money you had saved since childhood went on that love. You withdrew all your savings and it was just enough to buy a second hand diamond engagement ring. You hoped second hand would not bring bad luck, but it did. When later your wife deserted you she sold the ring and bought a TV set.

To come up to date, you still like to have a few real coins about your person. They remain useful for parking and public toilets, though recently in Norway you found that even to go to the loo was so expensive that you needed a credit card to open the door, and for almost everything else. Perhaps Norway will beat Sweden in the dash from cash.

What a pleasure, then, to return to an English village where it is still the norm to pay for coffee, beer or even your shopping in real money; and – illegally perhaps – to slip the occasional tradesman or odd job man real, countable (though perhaps unaccountable) dosh. But you would not go quite so far as one of your daughter's more louche suitors who would use nothing but cash and who carried big rolls of banknotes in his pocket like a 1930s gangster. You sometimes wonder what happened to him.

56

An Old Tree

You are fortunate to live in a county, albeit an over-crowded one, that still contains much woodland. In the depths of some of these woods a few ancient trees remain. There is one you visit from time to time when you seek repose and a calming of your spirit. It is a magnificent old beech.

This tree stands in a clearing of its own making, the ground beneath carpeted in its debris of discarded mast, husks, bark, old leaves and broken twigs. The even ground is swollen here and there by some of the roots that have raised themselves above the surface or have been uncovered by long forgotten rain storms. Moss grows on some of them and in one damp place ferns struggle up through the thick, organic bedding.

At the edge of the circle, larger than a circus ring, holly bushes straggle and grow. Beyond them is a dense wood of birch, hornbeam and chestnut, once coppiced but now growing thick and tall from the stools. In places rhododendrons, introduced long ago for adornment, have grown so thick as to have become impenetrable, stifling all other growth. But beneath the great beech you feel you are standing inside a circus tent, an open space within the neglected woodland. The central tent pole, the tree trunk is of vast girth, thicker than a Martello tower, large enough to fill a conventional circus ring itself.

The first colossal branch is ten foot up and larger than most individual trees. On the other side of the tree trunk an even older, original branch has died and started shedding lengths of its leafless timber, but five feet above that another large branch reaches out. Each of these lower limbs themselves branch into scores more. After about forty feet it is difficult to trace which was the original trunk and which are newer branches growing vertically. A dozen torsos each sprout a score of arms, a hundred fingers, thousands of leaves.

This huge, heavy body, its central bulk rigid and unswaying, is nevertheless dressed by the smaller, leaf-covered fronds and branches that spread and dance in the breeze. The massive presence of the tree is often softened by the sun-dappled foliage.

The tree's great age is evident at ground level. Parts of the trunk are decaying and covered in lichen and fungi even as it pumps sap up to its extremities hundreds of feet distant. On close inspection the trunk seems to be made up of lots of huge limbs, twisted and compressed, as though consisting of more than one tree. Between their individual rotundity a gap has appeared. You imagine it as a doorway into its secret interior, though this heavyweight is far from hollow.

The bark on the lower trunk is rough and flaky like an old man's legs and it is disfigured by warts and whorls, bumps and bruises. Only the smaller, higher branches are still smooth, as young beech trees usually are.

Standing beneath this venerable old tree you can understand why ancient peoples believed in tree spirits. Even in your own sceptical age you can experience a sense of wonder and if you are lucky enjoy a few moments of contemplation and serenity.

57

Hop String

When hops were widely grown over Kent and Sussex, the rough ginger string was used by everyone. String *was* hop string. It was found not only on the hop farms, but every village store and ironmonger stocked it. A ball or a hank of it was sure to be kept in most garages and garden sheds, too.

With the demise of hop farming in the Garden of England the supply of the string dried up and now it is difficult to find. When you ran out yourself you went on the internet in consternation only to find you would have to order it by the ship load – literally. Jute from Bangladesh was among the products listed, but there were no small suppliers of hop string. Fortunately you were told of a traditional iron-monger in Tenterden that still sold it. There you bought two tightly wound hanks suffocated in cling film and labelled coir bean string. You tore off the superfluous wrapping, sniffed the contents, sought the end of the string, pulled it out enjoying its roughness to the touch and you rejoiced: it was still hop string.

You use this twine in your garden for everything from marking straight lines in March to sow your seeds to string-ing the runner bean poles in April and for tying up, tying back, tidying, staking and fastening everything else the rest of the year.

Decades before Velcro, hop string was a non-slip fixer. For the beauty of hop string is that you can fling it round the most robust of bushes and the most wayward of branches, pull it tight, make the first loop of a reef knot and the hop string will grip fast while you inevitably release the pres-sure and position your fingers to make the knot secure with a second tie. Any other, smoother string would have slipped and catapulted the branches out of your grasp. Thin green garden string and its variations are nothing like as strong, as tactile and as versatile as rough old hop string.

Babies are sometimes given swatches of materials to experience the different feel of things: silks, velvets, plas-tics, papers. All such books should contain a length of hop string. It is almost prickly stuff, gingery brown in colour and whiskery as a witch's chin. It consists of two main strands of coir – fibre from the coconut husk – twisted the one round the other, but each of those strands is made up of scores of others, rather like fuse wire. It is uneven in overall thickness changing in the way a moving worm shifts shape. Unravel a hank of it and you will find thinner and thicker, darker and lighter sections, but it is universally strong and resistant. Unlike the designer strings from garden centres that rot after a season, the hop string which your runner beans climbed last year can be recycled for the sweet peas next. The rain, the frost, the sun may fade or darken the string but it will weaken only after several years of use.

Hop string is well and truly entwined with the fibres of your memory. Your father used it in the lean post-war years in his garden much as you do in yours, spoilt for choice these days, but still choosing this. As a child you watched ragged men on stilts string the tall hop poles. To earn money as a student you drove a tractor in the hop fields: you would steer between the rows of hops while gypsy gangs slashed the bines and laid them out in your trailer. This you towed to the shed where women fed the bines into the deafening picking machine.

Hop string was the first thing that came to hand when you had mislaid the dog lead, needed a harness for the sledge after a surprise overnight snowfall, or when you needed to lash a mattress to a car roof rack.

Hop string is like an unemotional, trusted friend. It is there for you in times of stress and distress, more effective than an executive toy, more comforting than the believer's worry beads. For just to hold a piece of hop string and to run it through your fingers is a pleasure in itself.

58

Tale Of Two Laguiole Knives

Once following Robert Louis Stevenson's route from *Travels With A Donkey in the Auvergne* you found a pocket knife in the grass beside a stream. You picked it up and it felt good to handle. It was dirty, well used but, once you cleaned it up, fully functional. You took it home and used it for several years until it got lost again. You remembered the name, *Laguiole,* moulded into one side of the steel blade – but you knew nothing of its significance.

Years later you were in the Aveyron region of France, where these knives are made and displayed in many of the shop windows. Laguiole, pronounced 'La Yole' locally and with the g sounded by other Frenchmen, refers to the type of knife. It is not a trademark and this has meant that many Asian-made imitations of inferior quality are on the market. But your knife (for you did indeed obtain a new *Laguiole* single-bladed pocket knife as a surprise birthday gift) was made in Aubrac and has the L symbol and a bull stamped into on one side of the steel blade. On the spring at the top of the olive wood handle is the insect that might be either a fly of the sort that pester local cattle, or a bee that was an imperial symbol bestowed by Napoleon. No one knows which.

It took 109 steps to assemble your knife and you had a choice of scores of different wood, from rose to box, for the handle. The olive wood looks good and feels just right in the hand, whether the knife is open or closed. The implement has accompanied you on many picnics, helped in the garden and in the kitchen and never been far away, even when you lost it.

For one fine day you could not find it. You searched high and low, sieved through dustbins and compost, emptied drawers and shelves all without success. Several years later you were cutting your hedge when you caught sight of something glittering at the foot of an overgrown gate. There, almost covered by weeds and undergrowth, lay your knife, the point of its blade catching the sun. And you suddenly remembered years previously thrusting the knife into the top of the gatepost when, working on something out there, you were called into the house on an emergency. It was days later that you returned to your gardening job, during which time the knife must have fallen down and become concealed. Remarkably it had lain unseen all these years.

The knife had rusted and its handle was covered with earth and worm casts, but it cleaned up well with a good wash and several sprayings of WD 40. After a bit of care it was as good as new and is now here in front of you again as you write this. To pick it up is like shaking the hand of an old friend.

59

Walking In A Puddle

After many dry months heavy rain fell. In a clay depression in the corner of a field it formed a broad, shallow puddle. A horse squelched over the wet grass to investigate, walked into the puddle, lowered its head and blew softly through flared nostrils. The puddle seemed to puzzle the horse. It pawed at the water with its right hoof, but however much the horse pawed and scraped and scooped, the water kept on running back. The horse stood in the rain, wet mane hanging forward, neck lowered, soft nose just above the surface of the puddle, pawing, pawing, deep in concentration.

We are all fascinated by puddles. Almost as soon as he can walk a toddler will splash through a puddle in his red Wellington boots. He may stumble and sit down in it but usually this does not deter his delight. Babies are used to wet bottoms. Later he will discover other pleasures, kicking through drifts of fallen leaves in the Autumn, walking barefoot through the sand, egg timer dry and loose or low tide damp and hard, he will discover roller boarding, skating and skiing. But walking in a puddle is where it all begins.

It is also his first creative act. He makes waves, sends up sparkling curtains of spray, flings droplets of water through the air, moves oceans. And when he has gone it all reforms behind him, becoming a puddle again, a blank sheet.

Parents, if they are sufficiently shod, grandparents and even great-grandparents will follow, indeed they will often lead and support a child into a puddle. It might be shallow and good for a stamp; it might be slippery, long and deep, nearly reaching the top of the toddler's wellies. This requires careful exploration, tentative steps, control and the relief of emerging the other side safe and dry: an early expedition.

Sometimes puddles can be put to practical use. You might wash your boots in them after a muddy, country walk. At the seaside, if you find a fresh water puddle at the top of a beach, you will wash the salt and sand from your feet before putting your shoes on. Birds will regard a puddle as an opportunity for a bath, ducks will have a swim; dogs will always drink from a puddle, the muddier the better. Only a cat will avoid a puddle.

For people, though, those still young at heart, a puddle is mostly for walking in, or simply for standing in and smiling.

60

Walking In Maize

The rows of maize were just wide enough apart for you and your dog to walk between them unimpeded, but in many places weeds covered the clay soil and nettles grew high in the shade of the corn. Shod in sturdy boots and protected by thick cord trousers you blazed the trail. The lurcher followed, stepping cautiously like a ballet dancer but impervious nonetheless to the stings.

On either side the thick, green stalks topped with dry, yellow wisps rose like bamboo well above your head, each plant shooting forth several blades that appeared from below as starbursts. The cobs on a level with your thighs were breaking out of their pale, green sheaths that had split to reveal the ripening corn inside. Each husk grew a brown beard at its tip.

You had to push vigorously to pass through the rough leaves of the maize. So stiff and sharp were they as almost to cut your bare arms and throat. They grew at waist height, chest height and above. No recent rain having rinsed them, these green scythes were stained brown with dust and pollen. Soon you and the dog received a coating of it, too, the dog sneezing and biting at a tuft of medicinal green grass.

It was difficult to navigate the field and to work out precisely how far in you were, though you had stuck to the one, straight row, confident it would cross the field. Sure enough, at the corner the row turned, you pushed to your left through some stems, whistling to your dog to follow and broke out through the perimeter of the field. Released, too, the dog ran around in happy circles in the open ground.

61

Being On Water

There is more to it than messing about in boats, though – as Ratty knew – that is a pleasure in itself. Simply being afloat is a pleasure. It might be the rising and falling and rocking from side to side that contributes to the peculiar sensation of being on water. For whether you are on a cruise ship in the ocean, a ferry in the Channel, in a canoe on a river or in a millpond on a raft, you are aware of the motion of being at sea or of floating on fresh water. Even if you only stretch out on a lilo in a swimming pool your slightest movement will make it react on the membrane of water in quite a different way from on the solidity of terra firma. What you are travelling on, playing on, resting on is animated in a way the earth is not. You are floating on something that is alive and breathing, seductive and deadly; only the thin skin of a hull, a few oil drums or inflated rubber keep you from this creature's kiss.

Floating is different from swimming. It is an effort to swim through the water and reach the diving raft anchored one hundred metres off the beach. You are contending with the water, fording your way through it, battling against it. Once you climb aboard the raft you relax, you give yourself up to the moods of the sea, calm and soothing, rocking you under the warm sun, or spitting at you windblown and angry, pitching and tossing and wetting you with whipped wave crests.

Turn on your belly and peer down, enjoy the giddying

rise and fall and as you regain strength after your swim out, recover from the salt and giddiness, watch the seaweeds swaying, the fish that pass so effortlessly, the crab perhaps or the lobster on the rocky bottom. Or in a fresh water pond quietly look for roach and pike, silent as a dream.

Sailing a yacht, rowing a boat, paddling a canoe, all immense pleasures in their own right, are more akin to swimming. A certain amount of exertion is involved. You are either battling the elements or making use of them. But let down the sails, ship the oars, stow the paddles and drift. Let your craft simply float.

You are afloat in a different way. You are on the water, you are of the water. You no longer have to concentrate on a course or a landmark; no longer must you maintain a regular rhythm. Given space and the right conditions you can sail away into a daydream. You are lulled, lullabyed, entranced.

There is one way in which the worlds of in the water and of the water come together, a way in which sailing and swimming meet the joy of floating. If you are very, very relaxed, you can enter the water, turn on your back, pillow your head in the sea, let it sink as far as it needs to to achieve buoyancy; your face will remain above the surface if you really let go. Trust it.

Now spread your arms wide, palms up, allow your legs and thighs to float apart, suspended independently. Relax, relax. There are no boards, no decking, no hull between you and the water now. Only your own skin. Once you are confident, you can enjoy the rising and the falling, the tipping and the splashing, the sliding sideways perhaps, the rotating, even the current. And it is even better if you are naked.

62

The Raft

Y ou worked on the raft that whole summer. You learned by trial, error and occasional duckings. You began simply by lashing two oil drums together with hop string but they floated apart under your weight. You got hold of an old door and tied the drums beneath it. Stability remained precarious.

Eventually you had constructed a solid deck supported on struts over four tightly secured drums. Not only did your raft float evenly but you could walk about on board. Soon you learned to punt with a slim hop pole. The Ice House Pond became your Seven Seas, the woods around it your New World.

Named after the building where in a colder century ice from the pond had been sawn and stored, the pond was kidney shaped, deep enough for your raft and abundant in roach. Occasionally a large pike glided through the deeps.

One day that summer changed your whole perception. Revelation would not be too strong a word. It was one of those mornings full of promise and you went down early to the pond. The raft was moored to the bank. You untied the knot, coiled the rope and threw it aboard, leaping on after it. Your momentum nearly capsised the craft, but it righted itself and shot out rocking into the pond. Clinging tight you watched the shock waves ripple across the still water and disappear in a series of little kisses on the opposite bank.

From the stern you pushed the pole into the soggy mud. Bubbles and gaseous rot rose through the black water until you got properly underway. The raft was light and difficult to steer across the breeze.

After one circumnavigation of the pond you fell into a steady rhythm. For the first time in your young life you began to take in your surroundings as something more than a hiding place for rabbits and squirrels, more than a playground. It was beautiful. You sat and gazed and let the raft drift. The lapping of the wavelets on the oil drums ceased, the only sounds were the dripping of water beneath you, the wind in the rushes and scattered birdsong above.

"Beautiful," you said, examining the word for the first time like a precious stone.

You lay on your stomach and stared down into the pond. So engrossed did you become in watching water boatmen, beetles and tiny fish that you paid no attention to the raft's drift. A scraping sound warned that you had come up against reeds. The drums bumped on the bottom which had rapidly risen to meet them.

You looked up straight into the eyes of a snake only two hand spans from your face. It lay coiled on the sunny, clay bank. Equally startled, you held one another's looks. To this day you remember the flicking tongue. You kept still while the reptile slowly unwound and glided out clear of the raft, periscope head aloft, body painting an ephemeral arabesque across the pond's face.

Ever since, being on water, whether in a punt in a poplar lined river in Charente, on a houseboat in Kashmir, in a canoe on the river Eden, or in a sailing dinghy on a disused gravel pit at Rye Harbour, that memory is the palimpsest over which each new experience has been drawn.

63

An Oil Painting

I t is a large but, to most observers, an uninteresting oil painting, for no visitor ever remarks upon it. It is hanging on the wall opposite you as you write this and has done for some time. Only because you have been thinking of repositioning some of your paintings do you now realize that this picture has been part of your life for over half of it. Despite its size and its heavy frame you have had it with you in parts of the world as varied as Norway and Ghana. For this English landscape painting has special significance for you.

What does it depict? It is a view over a field of mown hay, across a meadow the far side of which, though you would not know from the painting, the Kent Ditch divides that county from Sussex. Behind the stream the woodland rises up. Between the brown hayfield and the green meadow is a fence and a row of trees: three young oaks and a taller elm. It is a summer scene and the trees cast dark shadows. The sunny hayfield is brightly lit. The sky is hazy blue. That's all. All that meets the eye, that is. There is no wild life, no animals grazing, no human figure, no tractor. It is a peaceful scene devoid of incident and dull to the casual observer.

To you, though, the picture is crammed with life, anecdote and memory. For this is part of a farm you knew and loved, a second home where you and your best friend grew up together and for him the family farm that he left in the 1960s to seek his fortune in Australia. There you explored the Kent Ditch and the woods with your dog, and in those days of food rationing shot rabbits for the pot; you also bagged squirrels for the two shilling bounty on their tails. When you were old enough you helped with haymaking, with bringing the cows in for milking, you cut hedges and did any other chore for pocket money or sometimes in summer for a glass or two of ice cold, home-made elderflower cordial.

Once when cutting thistles one wet autumn you ran the heavy old Fordson tractor into a boggy area of the field that looks so dry and sunny in the painting. It took half an afternoon and another tractor to pull it out.

You know and can still smell the rocky track that leads from the centre left of the painting to its middle. Like the stream, it is screened in the painting by the summer vegetation but you know it is there. There was a rookery in the top field behind the viewer, and walking across the green five-acre field in the middle ground you would disturb teal and snipe; the field that was last ploughed in living memory by Dolly the Shire horse. She had already retired when you first met her and you were warned to keep clear. Dolly could be irritable and she did not take kindly to small boys.

The Kent Ditch originated from Lloyds Lake, just out of the picture to the right. Even then the lake was more a huge swamp full of pungent bull rushes than a proper open expanse. Older generations, though, remembered winter ice skating parties there. What little surface water there was left the lake down a well-like hole and emerged through a long brick tunnel to form the stream below. During dry summers you could wade up this dark and slippery tunnel to the hollow echo of dripping water and the cautious swish of your own boots. When you were bold enough you walked the length of the tunnel and gazed up at the water slipping towards you over the lip. Returning downstream you re-entered the sunshine with a shudder of relief; thereby you also re-entered the painting.

It was the first art work you ever bought, painted by an artist and family friend ten years older than you. She went on to make a name for herself as a portrait painter as well as landscape artist. Should she return to the scene today she would find it not so very different. The farm has been split up, some of the buildings converted and sold off, but the view in your painting is almost unaltered. The elm has blown down, all the single standing shade trees, including the majestic oaks, were felled and sold for cash, but the lay-out is the same and new trees and shrubs have grown up. Or so you hear.

You have not been back, you do not believe in going back, except like Alice stepping through her looking glass, by entering the oil painting on your wall. If you did return to the actual scene, you would probably still recognize the chrysalis from which you emerged.

64

Log Fire(s)

Yesterday's crumpled up newspaper accepts the flame from the match, sucks it up and breathes it ever more boldly over the kindling you chopped last week and dried above the boiler. The wood crackles, the flames begin a tentative dance and soon grow stronger. They consume the parched smell of burned paper and exude, depending on whether it is apple, beech, birch, oak or hornbeam, a more or less sweet perfume seasoned with an acrid cough of smoke.

By the time the kindling burns black, red and fierce, the flames have caught the logs above, leaping ahead and scorching the bark before biting into the pith and flesh of the tree. Split logs catch the flames quicker; the heat increases and a throat of rising smoke fills the chimney.

Very soon you find yourself staring into the hot heart of a glowing fire, a child again making pictures in the embers. The flat, split sides of the red burning brands are patterned and criss-crossed with lines and cracks, with countries and continents, rivers and lakes. This fiery landscape is an image of the blood pumping in your heart and in your brain, a picture of your thoughts and fantasies.

Nor are these pictures silent. Bright yellow flames from the tinder make a dry, licking sound like the tongues of lizards and snakes, the greener logs exude sap and their burning proceeds with a kiss and a song. Every so often a spurt of gas squeals out of its woody tomb only to be consumed in green or blue flame.

And there is the scent, the acrid smoke and the sweet sap and the lick of warmth that bathes your face as pleasantly as any shower of summer sunshine. As the blaze settles into a steady hum accompanied every so often by the soft fall of ash through the grate, your ancestral memory perceives that mankind in its infancy must have sat and stared into a fire much as you are doing now. For them it meant the promise of hot food at the entrance to a cave, protection from the cold and from harm.

From them then, and for you now, to sit by a log fire is a meditation and a relaxation, surrender to an ever present and simultaneously distant mystery. You acknowledge Jung's 'million year old man within' and feel the same sense of long continuity as when pacing a solitary seashore or gnawing on a bone. You are content.

L ooking into a log fire is a kind of meditation, the steady, pulsing flame a visual mantra that draws you into a trance, setting free your thoughts. But there is also the practical side, the present reality.

Watching the flames devour yesterday's *Guardian* you took apart and loosely crumpled to light the fire you remember one page held a striking piece of news, one a thoughtful review or another the usual self-pitying piece by some London-centric, trend conscious columnist. All those words, yesterday so fresh, now up in flames.

The kindling catches and you recall splitting all those chips last weekend in the frost. Hunkered over the block, chopper in one gloved hand, log in the other, you sliced each one into a score of naked sticks until the trug was full. You brought them in to dry and each morning when you laid the fire you used half a dozen of these pieces of firewood.

And now the logs themselves are ablaze. Others in the copper scuttle in the grate, more stacked beside the fireplace, await their turn. Some you recognise from the twisted shape, from a knot or from the particular hues and patterns of their veins. For you have over the summer sawn and split all these logs yourself, multiplying each one into four with two blows of the big axe. A satisfying swing, thump and rip. You have created these logs, you have handled them three times, once to stack, once to bring them indoors six or seven at a time in the scoop of your elbow, and you have carefully chosen individual logs to feed to the flames.

As you watch them burn you recall that these logs themselves came from a branch that came from a tree that once grew in the woods near your house. Some of these fallen branches you also remember well, the oak split by lightning, the hornbeam topped and shattered by an autumn gale or the birch that toppled and fell of its own accord. All these at one time or another, in one season or another you lopped and trimmed and carried home sawn to convenient lengths. To birdsong or in the rain, to the mechanical sound of fair-weather neighbours on sunny Sundays trimming their hedges, mowing their lawns or blowing fallen leaves about, you sawed up your logs, not with a noise polluting, anti-social chainsaw, but with a good old orange-handled, sharp-toothed, blue-bladed bow saw. Steadily you drew it back and forth, watched it spitting sawdust on the forward thrust, until limbs and branches became a stack of many hued, differently shaped and scented logs, drying for the winter.

And now it is winter and you watch them burn and warm you for the second time. You stretch out and enjoy the fruits of your labour.

65

Guy Fawkes Night

The bonfire heap grew on the green right opposite the house you were renting. For the past week you had watched it increase in size as people brought in wooden pallets, garden waste, lopped branches, felled trees and cardboard boxes; anything in fact that would burn. By Saturday evening the heap was taller than your house.

At 6 p.m. in total darkness the fire was lit and the flames climbed rapidly through the briars and brambles, the timber and the cardboard to lick hungrily at the thick night. You could have watched the blaze from your bedroom window but you braved the northerly wind and walked the hundred yards across the sheep-cropped, tussocky grass. Soon you felt the warmth radiate but kept your distance in case you were snatched by a wayward tongue of fire carried on a wilder gust.

You turned around and for a moment it looked as though

your house and all the others facing the green were on fire, for every glass windowpane reflected the huge, flickering bonfire. And over your own house a cold, sharp moon cut its crescent into the black, star-perforated sky.

You returned briefly indoors to look at the scene from a distance. The big, naked horse chestnut tree only recently stripped of its yellow and brown and russet leaves stood now, an intricate black silhouette motionless against the deep red, pulsing inferno.

Around the fire well-wrapped and booted villagers grouped, dark figures lit only by the fire. Children darted around like fireflies, waving sparklers. Some responsible adults set off the firework display and faces in caps and hoods and berets and woolly hats turned skywards.

An hour later those so inclined walked across the bridge over the river to shed boots and coats and enter the village hall for drinks and hot food.

Next morning when you drew the curtains in your bedroom large rags of sleet were dropping gently outside like wet handkerchiefs, and smoke was still rising from the embers of the bonfire. From hot white ash white strands curling up through white snow falling. Silence.

66

A Morning Shave

You have been doing it every morning of your life since your schooldays, except for a decade or so when you wore a beard. In those early days razors were clumsy contraptions. Gillette blades, double sided, came in paper packets. Each blade had to be extracted from the packet, unwrapped with care and fitted into the razor, the razor reassembled and screwed together. The risks of cuts to the fingers during this process were higher perhaps than cuts to the face when shaving. Disposal of the used, naked blades was also hazardous. Being a teenager you were too spotty for such butchery.

No, your first razor was a Philishave, an electric razor, the Ipod of its day. It was quick, clean and relatively efficient on pubescent bristles. You were later to learn that this was by no means a proper shave, however. Not by today's standards. A dry shave, despite the application afterwards of stinging Old Spice aftershave cannot be compared with the ease of a wet shave with a modern manual razor.

Then, as now, electric razors were more cumbersome. They need plugs, extensions, adaptors, or at least recharging along with mobile phones, digital cameras, laptops and torches.

The death knell of these Model T Fords of grooming was the one-sided Bic disposable razor. Bright yellow plastic handles and blue blade guard at first it lead to a new concept in shaving. Wilkinson and Gillette designed razors with disposable single blade sections. These were refined to two and three tiered blades for a supposedly closer shave. And, hey presto! a morning shave today is the simplest and the cleanest it has ever been. You never feel clean until you have shaved, for at a stroke, or at several swift and practised strokes, you sweep away the sleep and nightmare, you stiffen your upper lip and prepare chin up to face another day.

Those politicians, male models and tie-less actors who cultivate two days stubble do not realise what their scruffy look shouts about their personal hygiene, their lifestyle and their habits. Come clean, you want to whisper to them.

So how to shave? The operation itself is simple but the preparations are various. Least satisfactory are the lazy, spray on foams. Some are as dry and rubbery as marshmallow, others wet, white and slimy as tortoise piss. For travel minute bottles of nevertheless inexhaustible shaving oil are handy. You shake two drops into the palms of your hands and rub it into your dampened face. The best are lavender scented and refreshing, but all oils have one disadvantage. You cannot see where you have shaved. The strength of foam over oil is that you remove it as you quarter your face, so you know what is left to do.

There is, however, only one real way to prepare yourself, as the Barber of Seville might have told you. You need a bowl of good shaving soap and a badger's hair shaving brush. Wet the brush thoroughly in hot water, stir it in the soap and apply it vigorously to your face until you have a light, aromatic layer that will not clog the blade of the razor, but rather float away the overnight stubble.

Where do you start? It has become such an automatic process that the question is akin to asking how you ride a bike. Usually you position the blade at the hairline in front of your ear and sweep down to your jaw bone. You work inwards to your cheek bone and in three swipes you have completed one profile. Same on the other side. This leaves top lip and front chin, the easiest of all the surfaces. So far all your strokes have been downwards.

Now you raise your chin, bare your neck and work your way round with bold upward strokes. All the soap has gone. You are clean-shaven. It has taken less than two minutes but it has set you up for the day.

67

Getting The Hang Of It

Y ou do not remember learning to walk and you have never really learned to talk well, which is perhaps why you prefer the written word. You do remember vividly the sense of achievement when you learned to ride a bike. You were all five or six years old: Pete the farmer's son with a robust but second-hand bicycle, Mike the only child of a local, chain smoking band leader with a flash new two-wheeler and you with a fairy cycle as it was embarrassingly known.

You were all learning to ride your bikes together on the gravel drive of your parents' house. You took it in turn running behind a friend, holding the cycle upright by its carrier, even pushing off, until a wobbly independence was gradually and painfully gained. Pete, slow and sure, mastered it first, then to your shame the spoilt and rather silly child, Michael got the knack and rode round in circles metaphorically thumping his chest, though had he literally done so he would have buckled in a spray of gravel there and then.

For you there followed hours of despair and humiliation and just when you were on the point of giving up, your patient friend Pete launched you with a resigned last shove and hey presto you found the trick of balancing a bike, something that once learned is never forgotten, even after decades of neglect. In fact getting back on a bike or a horse after a long time is a kind of homecoming. A familiar, but at first slightly strange pleasure.

There is one earlier memory. You quite clearly recall in primary school being taught to tie a bow with a thick yellow ribbon on the back of a chair and then, miracle of miracles, transferring this skill to your own shoe laces. This lesson saved you hours of time waiting for a parent or a teacher to do up your shoes. It was a first step towards independence.

From that same time you remember, but less clearly, learning the alphabet and from that to reading and writing. A reminder of the initial difficulty of this fundamental skill was forcefully thrust upon you when in later life you variously tried to learn the Hebrew, the Tamil and the Arabic alphabets. There is a lot of learning by heart and much drawing practice involved, but getting the hang of it is when somehow you crack the code, chance upon the password, gain access and it all hangs together at last.

Other skills like driving a car or getting dressed can be taught without the need to acquire any real knack. Practice makes perfect, or at least helps you do it better. Still others also require practice but only after you get the hang of them. When you first learned to swim, to ride a horse, especially the rising trot, to ski and to water ski and later to paddle a kayak the experience and the reward were much the same as when you had learned to ride a bike. Getting the hang goes along with building the confidence necessary to perform the task.

There is much you never could get the hang of and there seems to be no rhyme or reason why some things you can and many others you cannot do. You were never able to keep a hoola hoop up or, despite careful tuition from a clown friend and the gift of three coloured and solid rubber balls, have you ever got the hang of juggling. On the other hand you were born with the ability to stand on your head and not only to climb a rope but to anchor yourself effortlessly at the top.

Something really complicated like playing the piano seems to require so many skills as to be utterly daunting. You have to be able to read and interpret two different lines of musical notation at once, play the different sequences of notes at the same time with quite different hands and in time not only with each other but perhaps with a soloist or an orchestra. Having no musical ear and no sense of rhythm you abandoned the piano with such relief that the freedom from lessons and practice remains in your mind as one of the pleasures of your childhood, a pleasure and an escape through failure.

Lacking that sense of rhythm, dancing has always been more of an ordeal than a pleasure. You know that in ball-room dancing the waltz is the tune that goes one-two-three, one-two-three; you were taught that your feet were meant to go forward, side, step, and together, but there was no together about any of your clumsy movements. You never got the hang of catching the beat, surfing that wave of sound and actually getting started. As you floundered becalmed on the dance floor sweatily clutching a bemused partner, the very music seemed to get in the way of your intense but useless concentration.

This rhythm deafness, lameness, call it what you will, translates into your appreciation and practice of poetry, which otherwise you adore. Classical prosody never made sense. Yes, you could distinguish a dactyl from a trochee or a spondee and you could measure out the easy beat of a French alexandrine or an English iambic pentameter, but you could never figure out quite how the rules of a dead language adapted to living verse. Analysis and parsing seemed so forced and rigid and inappropriate. You were content to listen to the beauty of the words and let the verse pulse to a beat of its own.

Language and languages you love to study and try to use, puzzling out the different ways they are organised, wondering at the myriad ways in which different cultures view the world. While you instantly recognised the ablative absolute in Latin as a nifty and efficient device and you never had any difficulty in French with the various agreements of the past participle, the abstractions of mathematics was quite beyond your grasp. Quadratic equations, calculus and how to use a slide rule, precursor to calculators and in general use when you were in school, remained out of your reach. As for higher mathematics and philosophy, they demanded a mindset, a competence you never acquired. Another failure, something else you never got the hang of. You will never know if your life has been the poorer for this. Perhaps if you had persevered you might now have been able to understand Stephen Hawking.

Some things are very simple and can be taught, but even the simplest can defeat you. With patience and after more than fifty years you can now thread a needle, but not as deftly as your grandmother could when you were only ten and she seemed very old. A quick lick, a push and she could ease the most wayward thread through the smallest eye of a needle. Several decades went by before you had the patience to master this simple trick. That is when you realised that it was neither the needle nor the thread you had to convince and control, but yourself.

68

On Finding Something That Works

When city dwellers write about the countryside they use the same clichés: mud and green wellies are uppermost. There is always truth in clichés, which is what brought them into being before they became overused. There is no denying, particularly this year, that there is a lot of mud in the countryside and that Wellington boots are the default outdoor footwear much of the time.

Your wellies, however, are not green. You were persuaded to buy a famous brand. Black, topped with a red band and with the name printed on the front, for some these boots are a fashion statement. Your motivation was to purchase a pair that would actually last and you made the mistake of thinking that price equated with quality. You were soon to be disappointed. Since production was moved from Scotland to China, the boot seems to have deteriorated.

When one boot sprang a leak it was not through a gash ripped by stumbling through brambles or a hole from the misdirected prong of a garden fork. It simply came apart at the seam where the upper boot meets the sole. You had not even noticed before that there was a join, imagining a Wellington boot to be a complete moulded entity.

The split seam was like a shut mouth when the boot was empty, but when you put your foot in it, the pressure of walking made it open with a gasp. In mud and puddles it choked and the water seeped in.

You could not afford a new pair of boots, having splashed out on this expensive pair. You thought, however, that it would be simple to patch it up. When no glue, however super, would hold the seam together you tried rubber solution and an orange patch from your cycle repair kit. Your botch up, though it gave the boot a certain piratical look, lasted less than a week.

This was ridiculous, you thought; people must get holes in their wellies all the time. Someone must have the answer.

You returned to the shop where you had bought the Wellingtons in the first place. It was a large agricultural concern that sold everything from tractors and other machinery, chainsaws and tools, to shirts, sticks, sweaters and hats; and trousers and jackets; and boots and shoes. You asked for a kit, or at least a tube of really strong glue to mend wellies. The young man at the counter must have had this request before because his reply was firm and immediate.

"No, there's nothing can be done."

You were not going to buy another pair from a salesman who could not be bothered with a sale of anything smaller than a quad bike. There was one last hope: the Internet. Googling 'repair wellies', the name of a product came up immediately: 'Stormsure'. It seemed too good to be true. It could be used for boots and inflatable boats, bouncy castles, convertible car roofs and a dozen other applications. One tube was inexpensive. There was nothing to lose. You placed an order.

When the product arrived you cleaned and dried the damaged boot and squeezed the sealant over the split seam. It spread itself out like a second skin, forming a membrane over the whole area. Having left it to dry for twelve hours in the airing cupboard, you somewhat sceptically pulled the boot on and went for a walk in the floods. When you returned home your foot was still dry. At the time of writing and after the wettest winter on record your boot is still watertight.

It is very satisfying when something does, to use another cliché, what it says on the tin. Stormsure actually works, and no, you are not being paid to say so.

69

On Reaching The Summit

Y ou are not talking about reaching Everest or about mountaineering. You might go for a tough trek, even for a bit of a scramble, but not actually for climbing with ropes and crash helmets and all that accompanying clobber. No, you are talking about hiking, rambling towards an objective and coming down again.

Perhaps it is a modest hill top near your home or a cliff top along the South Downs; perhaps you are in the Lake District and decide to make a day of it climbing Great Gable or Scafell; or in the Alps, scrambling up La Pinéade or one of the many peaks from which you can look in one direction towards Mont Blanc towering above the whole range or the other way down over Grenoble in its sheltered pocket by the Isère; or Norway with the punishing trek up Gaustatoppen in summer with its views of a wilderness in all directions.

Why bother? The stock reply is, "because it's there" – but that is not the whole answer. It is not as if you look at a peak and say to yourself, "I must conquer that." Rather a peak stands out, it is an obvious feature, it is a logical place to aim for, to rest, to eat your picnic before turning back.

If you were canoeing you might head for a particular bend in the river or island in the lake; in town you might go to a certain pub or restaurant for lunch and return home satisfied. Hiking, your objective is the summit. The essential is that your climb requires effort. There seems little point, as on Mount Wilson in the American White Mountains, the Schneeberg outside Vienna or Snowdon in Wales, in taking the cog railway.

There is even less point in riding the funicular up Hastings East Cliff, when you can walk up the stone steps between the old houses and emerge at the beginning of a roller coaster hike.

You might get the same views at the top but you feel none of the physical rewards of having made it under your own steam. A helicopter would be worse still and as for ski lifts, their sole purpose is to allow you to come back down again as quickly as possible.

A climb will usually be varied, even if the ascent takes under a couple of hours. You may begin alongside a stream below the tree line or up a farm track. The start may be gentle enabling you to set your pace and gain your second wind. It may be grassy all the way at first and an easy ramble, but the high peaks will emerge above the tree line, the paths will be stony, will cross rock and scree.

You may see wild flowers or there may be nothing at all, but your legs will feel the climb and your lungs will pump fresh air. As the Norwegians put it, you will 'know' your muscles.

On the more demanding climbs it seems that you will never arrive. From the ground base the peak seems too far away to be reached and too steep to climb unaided. When you struggle over the 'last' ridge you are confronted with another and then another. You plod on and while your body toils your mind spins free only to re-engage when you are really there, when there is nowhere higher to go.

You sit with your back to a cairn, sheltering from the breeze and unpack your rucksack. Depending on the weather you will unstopper a flask of hot coffee or snap open a can of something cold and reviving. Then you will bite into a thick and well filled sandwich.

It is too easy and trite to see all this as an allegory of life, to read hiking as a metaphor for the peaks and troughs of our hopes and ambitions. This is too far-fetched. On a ramble you can map out where you are going; in life there are more unexpected twists and turns, paths you cannot map.

Besides, what dreams have you achieved? You never won Wimbledon or became a concert pianist. Mind you, neither did you climb Mount Everest.

As Tagore put it:

"My offerings are not for the temple
at the end of the road
but for the wayside shrines
that surprise me at every bend."

70

An Everyday Journey

For once the ticket office was open and the computer was coping with the issue of tickets. The electronic indicator boards informed an empty platform that the 10:15 was expected at 10:28. By this revised time quite a group of passengers were waiting, foreigners with suitcases optimistically bound for airports, local people going to town on this the first offpeak train and a few delayed businessmen and women in power suits.

A fine drizzle enveloped the scene, but when the bell rang and the automatic level crossing gates fell shaking into place, the bunch of passengers straggled out from the shelter of the station proper and along the unswept platform. Then when the train came it consisted of only four coaches, so they rebunched, anxious about getting a seat on the slow one and a half hour journey to London.

The train filled at every little station, Stonegate, Wadhurst, Frant and by Tunbridge Wells it was full with still an hour to go before it reached London. At Tonbridge more coaches were added and at last there was space for everyone. By the time the train arrived in Charing Cross it had made up the lost ten minutes. An auspicious start to a longer journey.

You had twenty minutes to get to Euston before the next train left. Worth a try at any rate, but the exit gates at Charing Cross refused your ticket, resulting in a queue for the manned gate where a bored official nodded you through without inspecting the ticket. On arriving at the underground platform you found the next train on the Northern Line was not due for eight minutes. During each and every minute of that wait the platform filled to capacity. Trying not to think too much about bombs you squeezed onto the train which miraculously emptied at Tottenham Court Road.

There was no chance of hurrying from Euston underground to the main line station. Fat people walked abreast of one another, small people with big suitcases blocked the narrow tunnels and you just had to swim slowly and laboriously along with the crowd, corridor after corridor until the final escalator up to the station. You emerged at noon and saw that a train was due to leave platform seven at 12:05. By 12:03 you had located the platform and the train and were running past the four first class carriages. You lunged into the fifth carriage to find all seats reserved. Eventually a green light above one seat in the next carriage indicated that the place was free. You removed your coat, put your bag in the overhead rack and sat down. The train moved off.

Only now is there time to look around. Under the seat in front, near your feet in the close packed seats of this new Pendolino train, squirms an agitated dog. It yaps and fidgets ignored by its owner, a middle-aged woman. She is unperturbed even when the dog breaks into a series of sharp, concentration busting yelps. You did not know dogs were allowed to travel on trains other than in the guards van. All the passengers are in for two hours and twenty minutes of disturbance. By way of distraction a happy thought enters your head: this is twice the time of the journey from your home station to London but covers more than four times the distance.

Railways north of London are a different world from your familiar rural line. Fast, clean, comfortable except for the lack of space, and they are staffed. A shop offers practical travelling needs like tissues and headache pills, drinks and snacks and even a few books and magazines.

The dog becomes frantic and emerges from under the seat to bark and foam in the aisle. It is a young, black and glossy creature. With the owner's tacit consent another woman sitting over the way takes it to her seat and talks to it. The dog wags its tail enthusiastically. It seems to be thirsty and laps up water the woman offers it in a plastic cup.

After ten minutes quiet, if not rest, the dog is returned to its clueless owner. The yelping and barking starts up again. The owner intersperses a few barely audible shushes as though afraid she might irritate the passengers herself. The dog becomes increasingly agitated, jumping up and climbing all over her. The ticket collector and other train staff ignore the problem or else do not recognise it as such. A young man trying to work on his computer keeps turning and giving disapproving looks but says nothing. Not even a sigh.

As a minor diversion from the canine disturbance one of the cabin crew runs through your carriage to tell a colleague that a passenger has collapsed in car C. A few minutes later a special announcement is made appealing for any doctor on board to make himself or herself known to the train manager. Well, *there's* a title for you.

Four or five minutes later a forty year old Asian man in a dark suit tells the shop attendant he is a doctor but where is the train manager and what is the problem? The shop attendant hands over her till to the ticket collector and goes off in search of the train manager who has disappeared. The doctor follows her and you never learn the outcome of this incident.

The dog becomes more and more frantic and now the ticket collector pets it and talks to the owner. He learns that it is half setter and half collie. The dog likes the atten-tion but will not settle down. It pulls on its lead and comes round to where you are sitting, trying to get on your lap. You push it away.

Another passenger accepts the dog and starts feeding it jelly babies from a paper bag. The train, which was making steady progress comes to a stop in the middle of nowhere. Only now are you aware that during the whole journey a baby has been crying and now it yells its head off in competition with the dog. The train is still motionless.

In an announcement you are informed there has been a 'bridge brush' and that the bridge ahead is being inspected. They hope to be on the move again in five minutes. The woman with the dog takes the opportunity to walk her pet up and down the train.

Five minutes later the train has moved a few hundred yards when an alarm bell sounds. Someone is stuck in the toilets. "Probably pushing the wrong button," says a scouse crewman and like the medical incident you hear no more. After this excitement the train crawls over a bridge and you spot fire engines beneath it. The train soon picks up speed again and the old momentum is regained.

Just before Macclesfield the dog owner, a weak woman in her late fifties starts crawling under her table. A black man opposite who has stoically put up with the dog for two hours asks if she is all right. She is looking for a part of her shoe that the dog has bitten off. It is, she explains, an ornamental leather bow. She finds it, gets ready to leave the train, the dog grows more and more impatient as do the remaining passengers. Finally dog and woman make their exit to a collective sigh of relief.

You now have fifteen minutes to read the book, write the letter, do the work you had intended doing on the journey. The train rolls into Manchester Piccadilly only a few minutes late. An ambulance is waiting to meet the train. You collect your hold-all and stroll out through the modern station and down to your hotel. Journey's end.

71

Abstinence

Many small pleasures may be derived from abstinence or if not in the act of abstinence itself so much as in the resumption of your regular life at the end of it. For abstinence need not be a permanent state except for adherents to certain faiths. Even for them abstinence may sometimes be chosen, sometimes enforced, as at the end of Lent or Ramadan when feast follows fasting. Then there is an element of celebration.

Much abstinence is attempted as a result of illness, allergy or addiction. You have never smoked and rarely drink, so abstinence in these areas is no hardship. Once you tried giving up tea and coffee for a year. At first it was difficult, partly because it meant breaking habits, routines and escape routes; mainly because the herbal alternatives to real tea and coffee are so insipid and characterless and their effect emasculated of caffeine so weak that you might just as well have imbibed warm water. After a few weeks without coffee you did not miss it, though. Walking past a coffee shop the scent of freshly ground beans would come as a brief pleasure rather than as a temptation. However when you concluded that abstinence from these beverages offered no improvement to your health, in your case headaches, you began to drink a morning coffee and an afternoon tea again with the enjoyment of a clear conscience and a piece of research well done.

For heavy smokers and alcoholics, not to mention addicts of other drugs, you realise that abstinence from their particular fix is a much harder struggle, if it is a realistic option in the first place. But you can imagine that if successful the smoker or the drinker must reap great rewards: the pleasure of tasting food again, of being able to smell the scent of wildflowers and pine trees, the ability to breathe freely and to exercise are in themselves pleasures to be measured and repeated, pleasures the rest of us take for granted.

Sometimes abstinence is thrust upon us by injury or surgery. After slow healing the pleasure of walking again, of lifting and carrying, of planting and harvesting after enforced idleness are pleasures to be savoured upon resumption. Once you injured your back and only months later were you able to step into and pull up underpants and trousers and put on your own socks and shoes. In so doing these everyday activities afforded you much satisfaction and no little pleasure.

On another occasion you were forbidden to drive while a scar healed. In the countryside this was a sentence, albeit to a pleasant and open prison. Escape on foot was too painful so when you got back behind the wheel again and drove into town you felt like a teenager in his first car, the whole world waiting for you.

Perhaps the activity or lack of it that springs to most people's minds when you speak of abstinence is sex. Celibacy, originally meaning the condition of being unmarried, has come to be synonymous with chastity, a state with a more religious intent. Perhaps, too, you are chaste only once, if like virginity it is not a condition you can return to, so let's use the word celibacy in its looser, modern sense: refraining from sex. This for many is a deprivation rather than a pleasure, but most of us experience temporary celibacy at some time or another during the absence of a partner, during childbirth or illness. This we accept as a matter of course but the joyous return to natural intimacy after such an interlude lends our embrace a heightened sense of pleasure.

Deprivation is a kind of abstinence. Few can afford to live as they please, whether their choice would be a jet set life style or simply living in a better house or a more peaceful environment. So when, perhaps on holiday, perhaps on a visit to friends, you are granted a few crumbs of a better life you may enjoy the moment while counting your blessings all the same.

In your case there was a time when you loved the theatre, wrote and directed (probably awful) amateur productions and went to the latest Pinter, Becket, Wesker, Osbourne or Anouilh productions in the main line theatre. Plays by these authors are often revived but the premiers now belong to Hare, Poliakoff and Stoppard. Ibsen, Shaw, Chekov and Shakespeare recur with great regularity, but it has become too expensive to travel to town and even if you did, you could never afford the fees and the tickets to watch a West End Production. You may indulge again in the theatre and music only when affordable touring companies and ensembles brave venues nearer to home.

Another kind of abstinence, the absence from friends and company generally, is perhaps peculiar to your earlier peripatetic life and present seclusion. Living and working in three year cycles in country after country, you made few permanent friends and lost touch with earlier ones. However there are those who remain true, some whom you try to see regularly, others more far flung whom you visit or who visit you at five or ten year intervals. It is frightening to count the number of meetings you have left, but every rendezvous is a pleasure renewed.

72

On Hearing a Familiar Song for the First Time

There are times when we are more receptive to outside stimuli than others. Often we are too busy, too rushed to hear a child's appeal for help, to notice a loved one's cry for affection. At such times we are blind, too, to poetry and music. For to enjoy either requires a little tranquillity and a measure of close attention. Such mental spaces circulate in the mind like bubbles of air in the bloodstream and their effect can be equally heart stopping.

That Saturday you felt very tired. You had been working under pressure for several weeks to meet a deadline, only important insofar as winning bread and promotion mattered. Though incomplete the project was on schedule. You had spent a disturbed Friday night worrying about all the things that could go wrong and in the morning woke unrefreshed.

Often you can squeeze your anxiety out with physical activity. So you went on a long bike ride, worked up a sweat on the slopes, washed it away in joyful downhill swoops. Afterwards you went for a swim. This frantic mind cleansing took all morning. In the afternoon, at last, you felt limp, relaxed and less troubled. You had an overwhelming desire to sleep but sleep would not come. You decided to listen to some music. Not simply to switch on the radio or play a recording but really to listen, to switch off the world and listen to some songs.

It was one of those limpid moments of receptivity. You had listened to the album dozens of times before; it had been in the background to one particularly tedious car journey and one memorable dinner party; you had written letters, done the washing up while this concert repeated itself. But for the last year at least you had not listened to it.

With the first few songs you were pleased you had chosen this recording, a jazz concert. Cleo Laine's subtle, skilful and gentle voice was soon engaging your full attention. Then you heard one particular offering, as it were, for the first time.

It begins with Cleo singing a rapid, expository introduction to a well known Mozart melody. The authenticity established, the band syncopates the rhythm, begins to improvise variations. Jazz breaks the classical mould. An extraordinary dialogue takes places, a duet between the singer with the unique instrument that is her voice, and her husband on the saxophone. The concert was recorded live and captures the reaction of the original audience. Appreciation first, as the saxophone teases the voice along, laughter as each tries to outwit the other, admiration at the versatility and sheer range of the singer and at the understanding between the two musicians, husband and wife.

Your own enjoyment rose to that pitch when it is manifest physically. Tingling hammers ran a quick scale down your spine's xylophone; a pricking made itself felt behind your eyes, your breath was checked. But the climax was still to come.

The saxophone is calling the tune. The singer follows. The saxophone sings another phrase. The voice imitates it. Then the saxophone flings out an impossibly high note, daring the singer to leap and catch it. The audience is about to titter; the challenge is too outrageous, unfair. However Cleo leaps, catches the note in full flight. The audience gasps, applauds. And that is not all, for through all the applause, through the roar of appreciation, she holds the high note, loud, strong and true. After that the piece races to a conclusion and the audience rises to its feet. And you are with that audience in distant New York. You are hearing that performance for the first time. You clap your hands and cry *bravo!*

You do not know whether Cleo Laine is considered 'great' or whether that song was particularly hard to perform, but you do know that at that moment when you heard it for the twentieth and for the first time, you were especially receptive. Such splashes of pure pleasure, of distilled experience, few and far between though they may be, made living worth the slog.

73

On Cuddling Up

There is nothing sexual about a cuddle: everything sensual and intimate. You may of course cuddle, snuggle up, nestle with a wife or a lover but in all likelihood this will be post coital, a prelude to sleep, the sharing of warmth, comfort, of love when the passion has been assuaged. A real cuddle has nothing either to do with the cuddle clubs of America where complete strangers roll around en masse with one another on the floor. You can only properly cuddle someone you know and the act is often unpremeditated even if predictable.

For years you lived in countries too hot for comfort. The very thought of another moist body next to yours was unappealing. Whenever you returned to a temperate climate after long abstinence, snuggling against one another again, two warm bodies between cold sheets was a pleasure renewed.

A cuddle is more elaborate than a hug and longer lasting. We may hug someone familiar in greeting, hug and hold a small child, give a grieving friend or an upset daughter a hug of comfort, give a hug of congratulation to a child who has gained a degree or won a race, or one of consolation if she has fared badly. A hug is an impulse of the moment, a wordless way of communicating reassurance or sympathy. Hugs have recently been devalued by overuse on reality television, in knockout dancing and singing competitions and popular youth culture where a hug is *de rigeur* for the slightest thing. A cuddle is more private and more personal.

An adult cuddles a child; a child, like a kitten or a chick, will cuddle against its mother for warmth and protection. In the human case better fathers cuddle their children, too, whereas tom cats will kill their kittens. Sometimes an adult craves the nearness of a child. It may be the same instinct as many a woman's wish to pick up and hold her baby, but it is different. The desire for bodily contact may be a basic human need of both sexes.

You did not understand this when you were a child yourself and your grandmother came to stay. She was a widow, thin, frail and lonely and she slept in the spare room next to the big bedroom you shared with your brother. She was devout and innocent but obviously missed the touch of another body, as now many years later you understand.

In the mornings when she heard you stirring her shrill, small voice would call your names. Obedient children you would go to her room and climb into her bed and she would talk or play 'I spy'. You remember the smell of soap and the softness of her nightdress but there was hardly any physical closeness. You did not cuddle up. You were wide awake now and fidgeting to get on with a new day. Reluctantly she would release you. If you were a disappointment, at least she had known love and still enjoyed being with her children and her grandchildren and all their dogs and cats and other pets.

How must it have been for the maiden aunt, though, who as far as you know at the age of eighty had never enjoyed close physical contact of any kind. Raised by a nanny, she had in all likelihood never been kissed or cuddled by her mother, known neither lover nor husband, kept no pets and had probably never experienced a human touch except for the handshake of a stranger, the attention of a hairdresser and the ministrations of the doctor or dentist. So inhibited, so deprived, it is little wonder she was such a dry old stick.

This is so different from your own life. When you go into your grandsons' rooms to read them a goodnight story they instinctively cuddle up, one on each side of you as you sit with the book in your lap and begin to repeat the tale. Arms around them you all enter another world.

Children also cuddle dolls and teddies and later and sometimes clumsily long suffering pets. Away from children, however, the connoisseur of cuddles is the dog. Dogs know how to make themselves comfortable and sprawl with abandon, but they are happy to share their space, be it on a sofa or your bed with them. A cat may be expert at finding the ideal spot to relax in, but it does not like to share. It might come to you on its own terms but does not invite you to encroach on its own space.

A dog will quite without inhibition push and kick against you, lay a cold nose on your neck or a paw across your leg until both of you settle into as comfortable a heap as possible. And when you are well and truly cuddled up it is not the dog who strokes you but you who might without thinking run your hand over the creatures back. In that moment you are reminded that it might only be a dumb animal but that there is much in you that is animal too. Many simple pleasures can be shared with the equally simple.

The greatest concession a cat may make, and purely for its own benefit once you are settled, is to sit on your back or chest and purring pummel you to sleep with its front paws. A feline cuddle of sorts.

74
Walking A Dog

You were about eight years old when you read in your *Observer's Book of Dogs* that even a small dog needed a minimum of four miles vigorous walking a day. That set you on a life style you have pursued in many lands and still pursue today.

There were other dogs before Meena, but this energetic dachshund bitch was the first for which you assumed responsibility.

On a normal morning walk the first stop was the playing field. To reach this you had to cross the busy road outside your house, then race, and it literally was a race, Meena yelping with excitement all the way along a hundred yards of pavement and through a hole in the hedge into the recreation ground. Having knocked the top off any fresh molehills, Meena charging them at full tilt with her snout, you kicking with your boot, you both circled the sports pitches and trotted off down the farm.

There were many routes. You had woods, ponds, dells and swamps urgently to explore. Your favourite trek in summer was to wade up the Kent ditch, the stream that divides Kent from Sussex, turning over the stones to catch eels. There were some in those days and you learnt firsthand, both hands, that they were slippery.

In your school holidays you were out from breakfast until lunch time with your dog. Through these walks you discovered in an unsentimental way the countryside and formed a deep attachment to it. Perhaps it is wrong to include those early expeditions as simple pleasures, but to walk a dog, any dog, carries echoes of all previous walks and perhaps of all the dogs with which we can measure our lives.

Walking a dog, without any Disneyesque anthropomorphism, you can vicariously share the animal's enjoyment. A dog adds purpose to the brisk constitutional as much as to the country ramble. In town or country the morning walk to relieve the bladder, to mark the territory, to sniff at which other dogs have passed this way or to scent for clues as to what else has transpired during the night is no doubt pleasurable routine for the dog.

It may have further expectations: a mutual barking frenzy with the Doberman lying in wait but safely imprisoned behind railings, except for the one occasion when the gate was left open, an omission both dogs prudently ignored, rushing past the gap as though it was not there; the meeting with a friendly dog, the circling and sniffing of bottoms, cocking of legs and perhaps a little other coquetry; startling or being startled by a hissing cat on a wall or under a hedge; the relish of something discarded and disgusting that can be eaten or rolled in. The town dog, though, is dreadfully deprived of the best of sensory satisfaction.

For a walk is not a walk if the dog is not released from its lead to run free, to follow scents, to leap fences, to stick its head down rabbit holes, to charge through bramble patches, to give tongue, to lose breath and pant, to sink its jaws into a rabbit or a stupid, gabbling pheasant, even to chase a fox or a badger, though usually careful enough not to catch it. If you return home with a clean, unbloodied dog, it has not been for a proper walk.

People who dutifully road-walk their dogs, without the poor creature breaking into a trot, let alone a tongue lolling sweat, and who return home to groom and feed it, are depriving the dog of its animal life.

Not that all walks have to be long and vigorous to be savoured. House sitting while your parents were away you stepped out of the house with their dog before turning in for the night. Under the light of the half moon the weatherboard looked paler than during the day when it could appear faded, in need perhaps of a fresh coat of white paint. The electric light glowed yellow within the house and from the uncurtained kitchen window spilled warmly out over the milk wash of the moonlit lawn.

The night was still. You could hear a sheep cough, Lady's claws clicking on the tarmac in the lane as each foot came down to touch that of her sharp shadow in a synchronised tap dance. So still you could hear the slapping of your trousers against your legs as you walked beside the dog. These and the soft footfall of your own rubber soles were the only sounds as night held its breath.

The next night was a contrast. As you left the house the security light clicked on and sent out feelers through the fog. When you had walked a little way down the lane, shafts of light as solid as staves poked through the hedge. Two sides of the house were discernible in the light, like the prow of a ship riding through the dark. The central heating boiler pumped dully like an engine, the lights winked and beckoned. You would have seen none of this had you not been walking the dog. Lady did her business, you both returned to board the ship of sleep.

75

A Sea Wall

Requirements: a flat, sandy beach and an incoming tide. Desirable extras: spades and children. Note: without the children you might appear somewhat eccentric; through the children's shrieks and sense of urgency you can enjoy the task more.

You go down to the beach while the tide is at its lowest ebb and you try to calculate how far it will have risen in one hour, two hours. Depending on your ambitions and the age and attention span of the children, you choose a dry piece of sand about an hour up the beach as the tide flows.

You draw a circle with a stick or a shell or with your finger. The back of the curve faces the sea. Later it will become a complete circle. If successful you and the children will stand inside it while the sea rushes on past, leaving you triumphant in your island fortress. If you are very clever and have chosen the right bit of beach, the children will have to be confident swimmers to regain the shore.

But this is a long way off.

The front wall is what matters now. If you have forgotten your plastic seaside buckets and spades, in the right kind of coarse sand you can form a scoop, a digging bucket with your hands. The best way to do this is to kneel down, put your hands together as though in prayer, open them at the thumbs so that you have a clam shell shape, then point all fingers down.

This provides you with a firm blade. Only beware! If the sand is gritty you may get painful pieces of shell or some sharp stone up your finger nail. In the right conditions, however, you can throw up mounds of sand in minutes, just like a mole.

Sand can also be bulldozed with your feet. Sit at a suitable distance from the wall, bend your knees so that your ankles are against your buttocks and push your heels hard into the sand, straightening your legs as you do so. By the time you have completed the circle you will have an impressive foundation for your fort.

If this is too tiring or if you wish to occupy the children you can comb the beach for driftwood, a large shell or some other appropriate bit of flotsam. You have in your enthusiasm in the past brought garden trowels and even once a garden spade to the scene, but this is sometimes regarded by the conservation minded as excessive. Only you know you are not planning to steal the sand or to divert the ocean.

When you have piled enough sand over your semicircle you will have a broad base for a wall. The children will not be interested yet: the sea is still far off and your castle is only just beginning to take shape.

You dig only from the outside of the walls. To remove sand from the inside creates a well below sea level, the salt water seeps in, the walls become soggy and collapse. No, you must maintain a hard base for later.

Your hard work is rewarded when the first waves lick at the wall and the children begin to understand or remember the purpose of the game. You all leap inside, watching the tantalising approach of the waves. Here comes a big one, surely this will reach us! – but no, it is repelled by the backwash from a previous wave.

Then to the left of you, or to the right, the sea makes a charge, as if dodging your defences altogether. Not for long. Three waves, one after the other in quick succession wash over your front wall. You jump out to repair the damage. There is still enough dry sand behind you to repair any breach.

The children are now excited, hopping about sprinkling and spanking the wall, getting splashed themselves, running in and out of the sea to wash off the sand, flying back into their sanctuary.

If your walls are broad and strong enough and the sea is not too choppy, they will stand some time after you are surrounded. As though in a boat you look back at the beach and watch people moving back their towels and picnic baskets and their deck chairs. They are pushed into a tighter and tighter space by the servants of the moon.

You and the children are deliciously marooned and happy, weary and warm with exertion. In a sudden chill flashback you see yourself their age in a school party on a sunless Camber Sands. You had been playing on a sandbank, broad like the back of a whale, when silent and unnoticed the tide had surrounded you all. The headmaster had been the first to notice that you were cut off from the beach by a fast flowing, swift filling channel of foam flecked sea water. He tested the flood. It was already up to his waist.

"Which of you cannot swim?" he barked. "Hold on to me." He waded off with three or four children, leaving the rest of you alone and stranded. You could swim, but not so far against this current.

Suddenly you spot the half-blind matron, dressed in her black, cotton summer frock dashing towards your group, half stumbling, half swimming, like an old porpoise. She had not taken off her glasses with one thick lense and one blanked out.

"Come on all of you. Link arms." She stood in the middle, two boys on either side. The water came up to your neck, you felt your feet bob off the surface. Then you were grabbed by a strong, masculine arm. Between them the matron and the headmaster rescued the lot of you, no drama was made of the incident and ten minutes later it was forgotten.

"How was your day at the seaside?" asked your mother.

"The sandwiches were horrible," you said.

But here the sun is out; the children are pretending to be at sea, which in a way they are.

"Come on then, you pirates," you say. "It's time to walk the plank."

76

On Watering The Garden

I n India you woke to the sound of sweeping. Barefoot, bent-over women in faded saris swept the drive and the paths with a bundle of twigs in one hand, the other limp in the small of their backs. In Africa you woke to the scrape of the rake on gravel or on coarse grass: tropical trees shed their leaves year round.

On both continents there was an even gentler sound: the soft sprinkle of water on leaves as the Indian mali or the African gardener saturated the borders from thick red, orange or yellow hoses stained with use. After a sultry tropical night this soft sound alone was as refreshing to you as it was to the hibiscus, the heliconia and the monkey tail plant, the roots of which soaked up the water like a sponge. But the satisfaction can only be fully achieved when you do it yourself, whether in hot or in temperate climes.

Whereas in a western city you might bash out the frustrations and tensions of the day on the squash court, in Sudan, in Ghana you would calm down, relax in the almost transcendent task of watering the plants. You would ease yourself from the sticky cage of your car, have a cool drink or a cup of tea perhaps, go into the garden, turn on the tap and pick up the large diameter hose pipe. You had to be careful. If it had been lying in the sun all day the first ten metres of water would be scalding.

You have watered many different plants and flowers in the borders around your verandahs in India and Africa, many of them now common to both continents. In India the delicate scents of jasmine, the cool fragrance of arum lilies and the overpoweringly sweet aroma of the temple flower mingle in your memory, but these blossoms were as likely also to be found in West Africa. The lush thick leaved and strident flowered scarlet and yellow cannas are ubiquitous; the crotons' modest patterned foliage akin to the variations in the plumage of a birds wing; bougainvillea, pink, white and rust now climbs whitewashed walls far from its native home.

You have usually lived in one place long enough to plant and harvest papayas and bananas. In hierarchical, socially ordered India it was difficult without causing offence to usurp the mali's job, but having a toddler to help gave you an excuse to play at watering. Children love exploring the possibilities of water; watering for an adult is in some way a return to that childlike satisfaction. The wonder of the flow of water, the discovery that you can direct it albeit inexpertly and the quick realisation that if you inadvertently give yourself a soaking, this, in a hot climate, is more pleasure than accident.

While the child plays and discovers these things, the man gets immense relief, almost a spiritual release, in watching the drooping plants gulp up the life-giving element as it disappears immediately and without trace into the thirsty ground. In the dry season when the remainder of the country was brown and dusty, your garden was always an oasis of green, restful on the eye and on the emotions.

Once, feeling guilty that you were wasting the city's precious water supply, a government official in Accra reassured you that on the contrary you were helping by paying for your consumption. "If more people paid their water bills, we should be able to repair the infrastructure. In fact, we rely on people like you."

In Africa the gardener might have been amused, even bemused to see you absorbed in manual work when you did not have to do it, but he never felt you were taking his job away from him when you indulged in your therapeutic watering. More often than not he would be asleep in the afternoon anyway.

Back home in England there is no one else to do any of the work. You have the garden and the watering all to yourself. And here you disregard the hose. Indeed, for several years its use was banned. You collect rainwater in butts and use watering cans to distribute it to the greenhouse, the pot plants and the vegetable plot; in periods of drought also to the borders.

Even in this temperate climate it is rewarding to observe how these plants slake their thirst with such relish. You can watch the wilting leaves of the hydrangea visibly stiffen

167

and green after good drenching and the flowers raise their pretty heads once more.

It takes about a week to drain all the water butts and a couple of nights' heavy rainfall to refill them. However the weather does not work like this. When it rains and the butts are full you do not need the water. When it is dry for a couple of weeks or more and you need to water the garden, the butts are empty. Only then, and if there is no ban, you use the hose. This is quick and efficient but wasteful. Better to fill the cans from the garden tap.

Wherever you are in the world, provided the sun is shining, there is this one constant small pleasure. It is a peaceful and relaxing activity, and as the soil soaks up the water it also sucks many of life's anxieties from your mind. Watering the garden nourishes the plants as it nourishes the parched soul. It is a form of active meditation.

77

On Taking A Bath

S ome activities that were common when you were young have now become unusual. For example writing letters, writing anything by hand; reading books; polishing shoes; indeed wearing shoes; tying a tie; indeed wearing a tie; never allowing a hot-blooded boy's hand to stray above his girl's stocking tops; wearing stockings and suspenders. Chief among these in your experience is taking a bath. You could not remember when you had last indulged and so last night you decided to revive the memory.

Growing up you had bath night once a week. You wore shorts during the day (jeans came in only when you were a teenager, along with the word 'teenager' and the drug that was Coca Cola) and your knees were usually caked in mud. Washing the sore flesh in the bath was painful. You also associate mud with baths after games of school rugby. Half a dozen of you would plunge into the warm brown soup of the communal bath together. If you came late you would be sitting on a cooling sludge that was rough on the buttocks.

When after graduating from university in England you arrived in Australia on a plane chartered for 'Ten Pound Poms' as you immigrants were called, a man came on board, sprayed you all with aerosol disinfectant and sneered, "Another load of the great unwashed."

Australians really did believe that the English kept coal in their baths and, of course, the shower hardly existed in English homes in the sixties. During your first week at work an Aussie colleague asked without a trace of irony how often you washed. "Well," you said, "I have a shower every morning. How about you?" He was astonished how quickly you were integrating.

You do not remember whether they even had baths in Australia. For much of your working life in India and in Africa, too, you only ever showered. In Madras, as Chenai was then called, there was no hot water at all and you did not need it. In Southern Sudan the water came direct and untreated from the Nile. You never needed hot baths. A cool swimming pool would have been nice, though, and it was a luxury you later enjoyed in West Africa. In Scandinavia you experienced saunas, quite a different kettle of cod.

On returning to England you found that bathrooms were still called bathrooms and they did, indeed, still have a bath in them. You used to bathe your children in them before bed. They liked to play in the warm water and this immersion calmed them down. You still use a bath for visiting grandchildren, but rarely use it yourself, not even for storage of coal. Anyway, what was coal?

A more painful recent bathtime memory is caring for ageing parents: hoisting them on an electrical device and lowering them into the water. An awkward procedure for all parties.

Even at swimming pools, squash courts and other public places, one finished the exercise with a shower. You do remember one Paris hotel with a bath so small it was not even possible to squat in it, and you are not referring to the bidet. Being tall you have rarely found a bath long enough to stretch out in.

Let's get to the point, then. Your present house boasts

a bath in the bathroom. Last night you decided to try it. You thought it might be a relaxing experience; you had not expected it to evoke the memories described above. You went over in your mind how to set about taking a bath, gathered the necessary towels, flannels, brushes and soaps (no bubble bath or candles, though), and turned on the taps.

With regular use you would have known how much hot and how much cold you needed. But this was a first. You knew that if the water was too scalding it would be difficult to put a foot in, let alone to lower your more sensitive parts below the water line. You feared, on the other hand, that if you allowed only a lukewarm mix there would not be enough hot water left in the tank to raise the temperature to a comfortable level once you got in.

As you stood there naked in the steam you were struck by how much water a bath uses. You remembered your mother-in-law saying that during the war they were allowed only six inches, and you understood why. You had both taps running faster and fuller and for a longer time than you would normally spend under the shower. A bath must equal ten or twenty showers.

With that thought you lowered yourself gingerly into the very hot water. The tap contained a lot more hot so you allowed yourself a further splash of cold before adjusting it back up. You were, you suddenly realised, having a bath.

What to do next? In bed, if you want to relax, you lie on your side or your front. In a bath on your own the only option is to lie on your back. It is impossible to straighten out. There are only three positions:

1. Feet under the taps, legs straight but the chest, arms and neck are well above water.

2. Feet raised on the wall above the taps. This allows you to sink your torso down into the warm water but leaves your thighs, legs and feet out of the water.

3. The hammock position where you lie on your back with your middle submerged but both ends of you high and dry. Think banana.

While the most comfortable and relaxing position is to have water around your upper body, you have to shift occasionally to dunk and warm your exposed limbs.

The most unexpected thing about this whole experiment was to be confronted at close quarters with your own body. In the shower you do not look at yourself. In a bath you cannot avoid it. You were shocked not to see the lean, taut body you remembered from your last bath probably twenty years ago. It had aged, wrinkled and plumped up considerably since then.

You duly soaped yourself, rinsed the suds off and lay back. Now what? you asked yourself. A bath is not relaxing at all. How much longer should you tolerate this semi-immersion in expensively heated water? At least you were wallowing only in your own dirt.

But your thoughts raced and you could not write them down in the bath. You had expected this piece to be another of your 'little pleasures'. Your wife, however, had opined that taking a bath was boring and she was, you now thought, quite right. Since there was hardly room or opportunity for the two of you to make it less boring together, you decided it was time to pull the plug.

78

Doors Of Perception

Since Aldous Huxley described his experiments with mescaline in *Doors of Perception* in 1954, mind altering drugs have become widely used. There are however other ways of opening those doors. One is to share the world of a toddler.

You have just spent three weeks in the company of your three-year-old grandson. Together you have explored your small garden and discovered wonders under the flower pots, made sorties into the jungle for raspberries and dug for worms; you have found a newt, toads, a frog and armies of slugs and snails; you have handled earwigs, woodlice, millipedes, centipedes and beetles; you have avoided touching red and black ants and bumble bees; you have observed spiders of every shape and size, and tested the strength and the fragility of their webs, some the size of a 5P coin in the space between bricks, others miracles the size of a pocket handkerchief hung between stems; you have watched creatures smaller than a grain of sand go about their business; you have dug potatoes, plucking each pink fir apple from the black soil for the treasure it is; you have picked and podded and tasted raw beans and peas; you have exalted in the early morning dew on a rose petal and later inhaled the flower's rich scent; you have visited the riches of the compost heap.

The much-frequented bird table and bird bath have been of less interest for the active three-year-old than for his one-year-old sister who could sit absorbed watching the constant coming and going of your garden residents and visitors.

Many busy parents perhaps take the intensity of their children's new minted discoveries for granted. For grandparents their quest contains both a memory of their own children's activity at the same age, and a rediscovery of their own discoveries long ago as children themselves.

What is unique is the invention of each child, his perception and his vocabulary. Your bilingual grandson has an efficient syntax. Instead of "I want to...", "please may I...", or "shall we..." he says "mebbe we'll...", as in "mebbe Grandpa will look under the flower pots for black beetles." This is of course an instruction.

His grandmother he calls 'Grandpa the Woman'. Presumably in these egalitarian times his sister, when she learns to talk, will redress the balance and call you 'Grandma the Man'.

79

High Tide

There is something profoundly satisfying about high tide. It is not just its reliability. After all, low tide is just as predictable, but low tide has quite a different feel. High tide is energetic, exciting, slightly threatening. If the rising tide contains all the world's possibilities and some of its dangers, high tide is its fulfilment, its completion; it is a twice daily demonstration of what can be achieved. High tide is a brief period of maturity and rest, before disappointment again; it precursors the few seconds perhaps that Sisyphus enjoyed before his rock rolled back down the mountain.

The spring tides, a few days after each full moon, are bolder still, creep further in. Twice a year, if the wind is right, you will find even higher water; you will find the sea in places it does not usually frequent, lapping over quays and promenades, filling dry rock pools, poking into creeks, racing up fresh rivers or pouring into brackish lagoons and flooding mangrove swamps.

As a child you spent one week every September in an English seaside town. The highlight of your holiday was when it coincided with equinoctial tides. If this exceptional high water was mid morning or early afternoon when the beach was most packed, it gently forced all the holiday makers to retreat to the promenade as it took over the entire sands. It filled the little harbour by the jetty setting all the boats bobbing, it entered the colourful huts at the top of the beach normally above the tide line; it climbed the steps and took glorious possession of the whole bay and a bit of the town.

The tide had a marvellous cleansing power, too, bubbling into the dry sand that had been trampled all summer long by so many dirty feet, and turning it into a smooth, hard surface. It removed cigarette butts and lollipop sticks and other discarded objects. Four hours after high tide a new and fresher beach emerged like new rolled pastry.

A high tide is like a snowfall that comes in the night, silently hiding eyesores, levelling the landscape, duplicitous, covering up what is best left unseen.

If the spring tide came at, say 6 am and 6:40 pm, you made sure to be up early or out late, to time it to the minute and linger while it lingered, hoping the wind or the currents would push it in that little bit more. For there is nothing more dispiriting than the ebb tide. As it runs out, not only does it empty the beach of glitter and pizzazz, it seems to drain the life force out of you, too. It is the death of optimism, the last breath of hope, the runaway rock of your endeavours. A high tide has no stamina. It does not last. Two hours is the most it can stretch to.

You try to compensate with the space offered by the low tide, with the rock pools to explore and the walks opened up beneath the cliffs, but your heart just isn't in it. You remain on the waterless beach, you play or you relax, but only because you know the tide will eventually cease its retreat, will turn and in about eight hours, its strength regained, the sea will be back. It may bound in on big waves, it may slink in like a cat on its belly, it may sparkle and foam, it may groan and grumble or remain dark and silent. The tide has many moods, but always it will come back. On that you may count.

Get the timing and the weather right and it is worth the suspense. There is nothing better on a hot day, on a shingle, steeply shelving beach, to dive straight from the shore into the waves at the very peak of the tide. Your happiness is brimful.

80

Low Tide

There is both an openness and a devilry about low tide. *I've nothing to hide,* she says, and shows you all. Sometimes she reveals secrets, especially at the spring tides when she recedes to uncover petrified forests, wrecks, unexploded bombs or rock pools unused to exposure.

Beneath this candour, this frankness, however, there lies cunning and seduction. *I'll show you a cave,* she hints, *just an hour along the beach beneath the cliffs past the headland.* And indeed there is a wonderful cave, moist and dripping, smelling of salt and seaweed. It becomes quite submerged as the tide rises as you would be if you lingered. *Come for a walk,* she says, *it's easy to get from Hastings to Pett Level beneath Fairlight and the Firehills...* and so it is if you get a move on, if you do not succumb to her wiles on the way, her attractions and distractions, as long as you do not stare too long into deep, fronded pools, turn up stones or old lobster pots, explore this ridge, or take a rest on that private patch of sand.

Equally you can walk beneath the skirts of the Seven Sisters at low tide, returning over the roller coaster downs, seven climbs up and seven down. But even along the beach the going is tough and slow. There are big boulders to work round, slippery rocks to negotiate, large irregular stepping stones to leap, barnacle encrusted rocks interspersed with treacherous green slime topped surfaces, hard flints in smooth chalk basins filled with butterfly blue water and tiny darting fish. One slip, one twisted ankle and you are bait for the crabs and the eels. And low tide would gurgle and chuckle next time round.

You may become intimate with low tide but you should never trust her. She will distract you, lead you into ambush, cut you off and abandon you. She will ground your boat, hole your hull. If you are on foot she will not do the dirty

175

work herself. She will appear safe and reassuring but when she turns she will send the sea to fetch you.

Low tide is a depressive, a down and out. Always wet and weepy, muddy and mournful, she grieves and hungers silently. But she always recovers her humour, gathers up her energy and her resolve and when the tide turns she leaps back with a vengeance to merge and become one with her other half, the high tide. They live at the extreme edges of the same truth.

81

Crab Island

You and your daughter, then aged seven, had swum side by side, aiming well up-tide of the island in the strong current, aiming to be swept sideways onto the shallow belly of the sandbank you came to know as Crab Island. You both lay for a moment or two in the warm water, digging toes and hands into the sand to anchor yourselves against the stream, against the force of the ocean pouring into the lagoon, rushing through the intricate arches of the mangrove roots.

Having regained your strength, you stood up to explore the island, which would be covered again in a few hours. Almost at once something strange happened. As you walked forward a shadow swept across the bare sand. You looked up. The sky was its usual hostile blue, burnished at the edges, empty of any cloud that might have cast the shadow.

Your little daughter had not noticed anything, so you put it down to your imagination or the effect of salt water in your eyes. Then it happened again. It was so fast it made only a fleeting impression, like a presence caught in the corner of your eye, like someone whispering behind your back in an empty house.

Birds, you wondered? The shadow of a flock of migrating

birds, or of a solitary fish eagle or circling pelican? But no, the sky contained only the heat that had dried the sea to salt on your bodies already.

Baffled, you were distracted by your daughter's cries. She had been following the water line, the perimeter of the shrinking island.

"Daddy! Daddy, just look at this crab!"

A purple crab the size of a large potato side-stepped her hesitant approach and retreated down a hole. A claw, as big as its body, remained on the surface, as though this clumsy, armoured trailer were too cumbersome to drag down to safety. You realised there were many more crabs foraging on the shore, trundling to their holes as you approached. They seemed in no hurry to escape, confident no doubt, in their massive defences. They wore many shades of armour, red and blue, mauve and pink, yellow and brown, but they all had one thing in common. One of their pincers was enormous, the other tiny and undeveloped, sprouting from under the carapace like a bit of weed floating on a current.

You picked up a piece of flotsam, a mangrove shoot, to test the strength of the claws, but all the crabs were reluctant wrestlers. It was as though the effort of carrying those swollen appendages about was more than enough; besides which, they wanted to get on with sifting the sand in advance of the rising waters.

You left them to it and decided to cross the island. Again you had the strange impression of just having missed seeing something: of a cloud, of a gust of shade that had disappeared as you blinked. As you strode inland, you saw that its floor was teeming, teeming with crabs. You were not looking at land at all, but at the backs and legs of millions and millions of crabs. As you approached, whole clouds of crabs disappeared, each creature scuttling silently into one of the countless holes that riddled the sand-flat, leaving a different, a lighter landscape. It was a complete vanishing act. It explained the shadows you thought you had glanced.

You both ran forward trying literally to catch the crabs out. All you achieved was to clear a path through the clouds, through the crowds. You might have been chasing your own shadows, for you never caught up with them *en masse*. You did manage, however, to isolate the odd individual, which for some reason decided not to join in this wild, illusionary game of grandmother's footsteps.

The island was not very big. Indeed it was getting smaller all the time; time which passed quickly, so absorbed were you both in your crab watch. By the time you swam back all the sand was covered and the tide had slackened, but now it seemed a frighteningly long way to swim. As you pushed off into deep water Emily remarked that you would be swimming over all those crabs.

"Don't worry," you said, "crabs stay on the bottom."

As if to prove you wrong, when you were about half way back to the spit of beach that divided the lagoon from the ocean, a plate-sized crab span up silently in front of you. It seemed to doff its hat before sinking like a turtle.

82

Bush Boys

You drove into the bush only a few miles north of the old and unfenced Juba airport and then cut off cross country. Your aim was to reach an unpopulated stretch of the Nile. However you came upon a marsh filled with water birds, on the other side of which at some distance was a cattle camp where a large crowd of people massed beside a pool. There was drumming and dancing, singing and shouting. Cattle were lowing and a cloud of dust hung over the scene.

You drew up at the water's edge. Here it was peaceful and secluded. Herons stood in the water, waders paddled about. The drumming thudded softly across the swamp. Two year old Emily had fallen asleep in the Land Rover. You left the doors open and enjoyed the evening breeze.

You were watching the birds through binoculars when four naked boys emerged from the bush. They were about twelve years old, their skins as dry as an old car tyre and black as charcoal except for a pink scar on one boy's buttock.

Their hair was shaved except for one small top knot each. Two of them seemed to have oil or cow's urine poured into their scalps. One boy carried a hollow metal pipe into which he blew occasionally, making a didgeree-do vibration.

Like all people who live intimately with animals these cattle-herding Bari boys were gentle. But they were so curious. You passed your binoculars round among them and they quickly got the hang of it, uttering sounds of amazement and delight as they looked across at their camp. One boy climbed inside the Land Rover and took the wheel, happily making driving sounds. Then they saw Emily sleeping on the passenger seat and they all wanted to stroke her hair. They also found a container of travel tissues impregnated with eau de cologne. You gave them a tissue each and imitating my action they rubbed their hands with them but remained mystified as to the point and purpose of it all. "Sabun", said one of them suddenly, this being the Arabic word for soap. Unnecessarily they went into the water and washed their hands with the now soggy tissue.

They would have climbed all over the vehicle, emptied all your pockets had you stayed long enough. One boy found Emily's T-shirt. Naked and barefoot he was fascinated by the soft, machine-made cotton garment. Another found a handkerchief. When they discovered the toolbox you decided it was time to leave. They made no protest. They waved goodbye as you drove back over the hill passing a line of men with long spears and bows and arrows who, contrary to their offspring, totally ignored you.

83

Poppy

The flowers of this poppy bloom and wither in the space of a day. The perfection of each flower remains unspoilt for less than an hour, less than a minute if the weather is not calm or the insects rise early. How to capture this perfection?

The promise of flowering is made weeks in advance as the heavy green and black bud swells on the end of its pale stalk which bristles with stiff white hairs.

The first opening is a miracle akin to a dragonfly emerging from its pupa to unfold and dry its wings, and as painfully, breath-holdingly slow. The uncreased tissue of the new poppy petal is thinner, more fragile than a dragon- or butterfly's wings, and larger. Moreover there are six of them, pale flesh pink like the inside of a mouth, and each corolla has a black square at its base. The whole flower is the size of a fist and pretty enough, but it is only at dawn and if the air is still that you can for a few moments wonder at the unblemished beauty of each petal and sense its vulnerability. As the flower opens fully the faintest movement of air, the draught from an insect's wings, crumples the petals. The smoothness, the purity is lost. The poppy is still delicate, beautiful, but now creased like a slept-in linen jacket, puckered like a deflated balloon.

This makes it no less attractive to the bees as the sun warms the air. They descend into the cup of soft petals landing on the black squares before touring anther and stamen and stigma, no doubt collecting and depositing pollen as nature intended. If, as so often in May, the weather turns wet or blustery, the delicate bloom will hardly last till noon, but collapse damp and bedraggled to dissolve like a discarded paper tissue; but if the day is hot the flower will flatten out, fully exposing in this languid abandon the symmetrical pink and black print of its immaculate design.

By evening, enjoyed by many bugs, the flower tries to pull

its silk skirt back around itself, but the fabric is rumpled and faded, the petals ready to droop and fall. As one flower withers so another bud prepares to splash its colour on another morning.

For a few short days this sequence is the plant's gift to the garden. It will not be long before the only record of the colourful dance is held in the deflowered, dark-capped seed pods that nod their blind heads to the summer's rhythm.

Some might be tempted to interpret these brief moments of perfection, the tarnishing and renewal of exquisite beauty, as metaphor. For most, watching in tranquillity, the wonder in the poppy is enough.

84

Bluebell Time

A shimmering blue flush beneath a translucent veil of sweet scent suffuses the woodland around your home in the spring. You find it difficult to imagine that for many who live in cities this annual bluebell spectacular is an unfamiliar experience. To attempt to describe the feeling of standing calf deep among the plants, your senses completely submerged in the dizzying miasma, is a task akin to explaining to a Nomad in the Sahara desert what it is like to swim in the sea.

One way of describing an object, a sight or an experience to someone for whom it is strange or new, is to liken it to something with which they are familiar. The very name blue bell is a giveaway. Most people will have seen a church or temple bell and will know the colour blue. Everyone knows what flowers are. But if you have never seen a bluebell before this is not very descriptive.

It does not help much to explain that each plant has one stem from which anything from six to a dozen bells hang; that the stem can grow to a foot in height and thrusts up from a cluster of dark, shiny green leaves, each straight and smooth and close to the ground, and the width of a wooden ice-cream stick; that the 'bells' themselves are small, each flower comprising six petals that are paler blue on the inside with white anthers delicately protruding; that the bell, or hood, is a steely blue, but darker than a forget-me-not. It means nothing to note that in the shade a blue-bell can appear almost purple and that sometimes there are white or pink variants.

For no one talks of a single bluebell any more than they do of one particular grain of sand on a beach. "Come and see the bluebells," we say, or "Have you seen the bluebells in Badger Wood this year?"

Writers and observers use familiar clichés, a carpet, a cloth, a sheet, but such metaphors are two dimensional. True, bluebells do in a sense carpet the woods, but a carpet, however deep its pile is inert, flat and motionless. The ground sheet of bluebells is organic, alive, and in motion. It dazzles, it hypnotises, it giddies the senses through sight and scent. Swathes, swatches, clouds of bluebells are better clichés, cloud capturing the shifting light and density, but the image is too ephemeral. Bluebells are a rooted presence though showing at their best only for three or four weeks. An ocean, then, a slow high tide. This is perhaps nearer the mark. A host, an army would do but that concept has famously been hi-jacked for flowers of a different hue altogether.

There is a stream not far from here that runs down a valley it has carved for itself over centuries. This is wooded with oak and chestnut and the stream lined with alder and willow. In May, as in all the woods, the ground is crowded with bluebells. A festival field of concert goers, perhaps, or land mushrooming with tents for a million refugees; the difference being that concert goers and eventually even refugees disperse, while the bulbs of the bluebells have been underground all along.

On one bend in the stream, though, no bluebells grow. Vigorous though they are, they have yielded to the wild garlic, itself giving a foaming display of cream and white that exudes a distinctive, culinary scent. The perfumes of bluebell and garlic mix, clean, piquant, heady and sweet all at the same time. In fact the garlic seems to be attracted by the bluebells and both flower together, a partnership repeated elsewhere in the woods. The varying shades of their greens, whites and blues create a tableau as dazzling as any staged at the Folies Bergères or in an American musical comedy. A truly live performance.

85

Tortoise

Yesterday you stopped the car to let a tortoise cross the road. It was one of the Hermann tortoises that live wild in the part of Corsica where you are writing this piece, but it put you in mind of all the tortoises that have given you pleasure throughout your life.

When you handle a Corsican tortoise it behaves in the same way as a pet tortoise. An initial hiss and retreat into its shell, then the scaly head reappears and the legs waggle frantically in space seeking a foothold. Set it down again and it will charge off in a jerky sprint heading for the cover of the *maquis* like an automaton.

You were five when you got your first tortoise and were staying with your grandparents in Windsor. Every day you accompanied your grandmother on her errands and on the way down a hill you walked past a pet shop. In the window, which you could just reach and look into, were all shapes and sizes of tortoises. For several days in a row you would stop for a brief look. You had your eye on one tortoise that was bigger and more active than the rest. Your grandmother was an impulsive woman and one day she took you into the shop and bought the magnificent creature for five shillings, a generous sum in those days.

This was the start of a lifelong learning curve, beginning with a fundamental mistake. You named your tortoise Mary. Later she was to be joined by Tess, Tim and Charlie. The difference between male and female was clear from the

shape of their tails and even at that age you could distinguish between dog and bitch, cock and hen, bull and cow,
but you were unable to tell which tortoise was which sex.
Forty years later you found you had got it wrong.

Mary was not pretty but she was impressive, being the
size of an upturned chamber pot. Her shell was a uniform,
caramel brown. When you got home to your grandmother's
house you put the tortoise in the back garden and watched
her until you grew bored.

When your grandfather returned from work you dragged
him into the garden to show him your new pet. But Mary
was nowhere to be seen. Grandma was as distraught as
you, mainly over her mis-spent five shillings. Fortunately
the garden was walled and you soon found Mary chomping
her way along a row of lettuces, a trick she was later to
repeat elsewhere. In the hot weather she would get through
four lettuces and several tomatoes a day, not to mention
dandelions and plantains.

Mary had character, which might seem a strange claim
to make of a tortoise, but she certainly possessed deter-
mination and intelligence. She broke out of the strongest
enclosures your father made, sometimes climbing over the
top. Living in a village, people who came across her very
often brought her back, but to be sure, you painted your
family name on her shell.

This sometimes worked against you, for when Mary got
into the allotments and destroyed another row of lettuces
the irate smallholder knew whom to blame. On other occasions she was found entering the Eight Bells Pub across the
village green and even once discovered marching down the
Hastings Road towards the seaside.

Mary lived until you went to university, and then died a
horrible death. Every autumn you would put the tortoises
down in straw in a wooden apple crate in the garage and
leave them to hibernate over winter. On one spring visit
home from university you asked your father whether the
tortoises were stirring. He said he had seen no signs yet. It
had been a hard winter and you wondered whether they had
succumbed. You brought the boxes out into the sunlight
and what you found was worse than you had imagined.
All that remained of Mary, that big, lusty, hungry reptile,
was an empty shell. It was surprisingly light to pick up and

quite dry and clean inside. During that bitter winter rats or mice had eaten all the tortoises in their sleep.

There were other tortoises in your life. A wild one discovered and left untouched in Kenya; Boring, another African tortoise given into your safe keeping in Ghana by a departing expatriate. Even to have named his pet Boring showed his complete lack of understanding of the species. Anyway the poor creature was not too boring to have been eaten, not this time by rats but most probably by the gardener.

Now history is repeating itself. Your grandchildren own small tortoises and Ralph has turned out to be girl and Olive a boy tortoise. They are the small, pretty tortoises bred in England since the import of exotic species is now prohibited. They still have the characteristics of the larger animals, but none compares with Mary.

When you watched the Hermann's tortoise cross the road just now you saw in her wake the ghosts of all the other tortoises you have known and which have given you pleasure.

86

A Blizzard Of Moths

At the hottest, dustiest, driest time of year many of the trees blossom in your garden in Accra. The sweet smelling frangipani, having lost all its leaves, sprouts pink and white or white and honey coloured flowers from its stubby fingers. A kind of magic trick, like drawing silk handkerchiefs from thin air. The flame trees give silent explanation of their name, their proud orange set off by a large tree decked out in mauve blossom, and another in yellow. Most delicate of all the row of bohemia trees, which each year so completely lose all sign of life that you think of cutting down their ugly skeletons, save themselves at the last moment by opening up, as you would open an umbrella or a sunshade, a canopy of pink flowers.

185

These generous but delicate fronds are the most beautiful blossoms you have ever seen. The leaves are light jade, each branch supporting many six-petalled flowers. Five of the petals are white with a pink blush on which deeper pink freckles appear to have been sprayed. The sixth and top petal is blood red. Each buoyant, springy sprig combines pale green and all the shades of the spectrum between white and red. The only tree that is out of phase with this celebration is a twisty, waxy leafed dome of a tree that opens a thousand tiny dark blue and white eyes after heavy rain. You seem to remember it rejoices in the name of *tabubia*...

Also at this time of the year, probably to join the fiesta, a plague of moths hatches out. It is a plague of biblical proportions. Walk alongside the garden hedge and the moths swarm and flitter in dense clouds; water the garden and they rise from leaf and stem like a stage mist; throw a stone into a bush and you have hurled a grenade that causes an explosion of moths. When the wind stirs the trees moths fall out like confetti from a bridal train. In the garden they seem to do little harm.

However, you have made the mistake of leaving the windows of the house open. By lunch time the house is full, every room, every half open cupboard. Walking across a room you have to close your eyes to avoid being blinded by the soft blows of a million wings. You have to grip your collar tight around your throat to stop them getting into your shirt. Women in skirts fare worse! It is like marching through a blizzard, blinking away the snowflakes.

All these wings beating against the windows and walls and lampshades fill the air with fine powder that makes you sneeze, sending the insects into further frenzy. Invisible in the air, the dust is grey when it settles, discolouring chairs and carpets, books and window ledges and staining the seat of your pants. Sinks and baths have a rim of grime.

In the night you have to wear a bush hat to battle through the dense blizzard and fetch a cool drink from the fridge. As you stand barefoot dozens of fallen, flailing moths try to burrow under the arches of your feet. A ticklish but unpleasant sensation. By morning it is not possible to walk on the floor without treading on dead or dying moths, husks of the souls that had earlier been so animated.

The moths are like snowflakes in another way. No two

are the same. Of the hundreds and thousands you sweep up, all dull brown and black, each has a different variation in the pattern on its delta shaped wings. Some have mock eyes, some broad stripes, some like clumsy potato prints made by small children, others fine, balanced designs. But they are all recognisably the same species. It is as if each moth has been cut from one huge piece of material, some getting wings from this part of the pattern and some that, and some getting wings from both. What a jigsaw puzzle it would be to put them back together.

87

A Silent Night

There is a sweet irony that to celebrate a certain silent night a carol is sung. There are good reasons for this, but in general it must be better to appreciate silence in silence. How? By quietly writing about it, perhaps.

You have touched upon real silence in your description of dark nights. Last night, early January, you woke and listened in awe to – nothing!

In summer nights you sometimes hear the snuffle of hedgehogs or the faint arousal of leaves under a passing breeze's caress. In the winter, as in the summer, you sleep with your bedroom window open and sometimes owls hoot and screech, a fox screams and cats may squabble. Last night, though, the stillness was complete, the very air held its breath. No distant aircraft complained to the sky, no car made the night swell to the thud of canned music or rattled and swished over the potholes, no festive fireworks tortured the countryside and neither did any wild life made itself heard.

Even the house was still, the central heating dormant until 06.30 and the fridges and freezers that in summer send up a constant hum were silent. You no longer have the grandfather clock that sent a clanky but reassuring pulse out into the night of your parents' cottage. You could not even hear your wife breathing though the warmth of her body beside you was a sure sign that she was alive.

There must be some sound, you thought, but apart from the peculiar ringing of true silence, the music of the spheres, all was at peace. You tried to find some metaphor for this quiet: a velvet cover? – but no, you could not touch it, feel it; an ocean, perhaps? – but however slowly you pass your hand through water you always feel some resistance. Silence is untouchable, yet so easily broken. A prayer then or a blessing?

At this point your observations must have ceased for you fell into that greater mystery, sleep.

88

Dark Nights

I don't know how you can live here without any street lighting," said a visitor.

"Well, it's not a street," you replied, "and I do not know how I could live here *with* lighting. Even a neighbour's security light makes me wince."

There are many pleasures of living in the countryside. Silence sometimes, fresh air, home-grown vegetables. One of the best is darkness, nights free of artificial light. Of course there will be lights on inside the house, cars will drive by with their headlights on, planes will drone blinking overhead. But late at night it is still possible to experience a few precious hours of darkness.

The darkness is not always complete. If there is a moon and the sky is cloudless your eyes adjust and you can follow the shining ribbon of the lane and even pick your way along the footpaths occasionally in summer decorated by glow-worms. You see the silhouette of the barn owl and if it flies towards you glimpse its pale and ghostly face.

On moonless nights to venture out after dark requires a torch. There may be stars, the sky may not be toe-cap black, but at ground level a deep flood of dark swamps all features. If you are indoors it may seem completely obscure but it is not: you can still tell where the windows are, where the sky should be.

But there are times when it is totally black. When you wake up in bed and open your eyes and your first fear is that you have lost your sight. There is no outline of curtain or wardrobe, you do not know if your bedroom door is open or closed. Your instinct is to fumble for the bedside lamp, but you resist, lie back and luxuriate, eyes wide open in the pure and silent caress of the liquid night.

This darkness can be thick or thin, warm or cold. Sometimes the night deadens sound, blanketing it over; sometimes it brings you a rustle or a screech from far away, the sounds swimming to your window like fish in a tank. On stormy nights there can be a whole symphony. The wind roars in the chimney, branches lash the house, climbing plants itch and rattle and there is a background of scurrying and crashing interspersed with lulls in which every creature holds it breath waiting for the next wave to break.

Should you need to get up in a dark night you seem at first to be wearing a blindfold. In your own house your fingers remember where the door handles and light switches are, your feet measure the rise and tread of the stairs. In a strange house you may grope and bump into things before you find a light. In a hotel it is never quite dark.

There is nothing to fear about darkness in the countryside. It feels right. It is part of the scenery. In a town, however, during a blackout or a power cut there is a real sense of unease.

You recall an incident during the Three Day Week when there was no power at night in the town where you were stranded. Walking home through the black canyons of identical suburban streets and past the cliff face of blacked out terraced houses there was a sinister silence, a darkness that seemed unnatural though for once raw nature was reclaiming its own. The disorientation was frightening, the presence of real people lurking, a distant unseen footfall, a muffled shout and the threat of blind anarchy more disquieting than the imaginary presences that haunt an English country night. You were more lost amongst these unseen bricks, this invisible concrete, than ever you have been in the wild.

No, in the city I do not know how it would be possible to live long without street lighting.

89

A Bean Row

There are many varieties of beans, from scarlet runners to dwarf French, that thrive in your garden, but earliest and perhaps most tasty are the broad beans. They are different from other beans in that, like peas you shell and eat only the seed, whereas haricots and runners, like *mange-touts* you consume entire. The broad bean, or *vicia faba,* you have read, was once a staple of the poor who ate them roasted.

A packet of beans bought from the farm shop costs about £1 and contains on average forty seeds. In your small garden this constitutes two rows. The yield from those forty dry and brittle seeds provides your accompaniment to scores of fresh meals and fills your freezer for as many winter helpings again.

Sometimes you plant your bean row in the late autumn for an early crop the following year. If it is mild they show before Christmas and can withstand the frosts and snows of January and February. However half of them rot in a wet spring and are eaten by slugs or garden mice.

When conditions are right the row will survive and flourish, literally having had a head start. Usually, though, you plant your broad beans in the early spring. They always do better, always catch up with the early beans, their growth depending you suspect more on the hours of daylight than on the time of germination.

The pleasure you derive from your bean row lies not so much in the clearing and the planting, the plucking and the podding, the cooking and the eating, though each of these activities is not without its own deep satisfaction. The real pleasure – and this applies to the sowing of any seed, from tiny carrot to single conker – lies in experiencing direct the miracle of life. How can a seed as small as a fleck of dandruff turn in a few months into a parsnip that will fill a casserole for a family of six; or over hundreds of years a single shiny conker grow into a tree many houses tall and bearing annually hundreds of new fruits? Why should a bean grow into a sturdy plant, each of its many ovaries forming a legume, each pod full of the seeds of the next generation, cushioned in soft vegetable tissue and attached to the placenta in orderly rows?

These seeds are what most of us think of as the actual broad bean. Is it any wonder that the stalk can reach up to the sky where the giants live? Every child should grow a beanstalk, shell the beans, cook and eat them, saving perhaps enough to replant the following year. Every child should grow and nurture something. The shelling of broad beans throws a light on the mystery of its growth. You strip the stalks of the most swollen and luscious legumes in early morning, sit in the garden with a bucket on your right for the discarded shells, a colander for the naked newborn beans on your left and the pile of picked pods in the middle.

You take each distinctive, sharp smelling pod in turn, insert a thumb in its side and slit it open. The inside will be mild and moist and once again you run your thumb nail down behind the seeds breaking their connection with the placenta and sending them, newborn, tumbling into the colander. Eaten young and raw they are delicious, too.

In some pods there will be one or two large beans and a couple of little ones, in others a row of six to eight as regular in size as American teeth, in yet others perhaps nothing has yet formed. If you leave the harvesting too late, however, instead of moist green beans, you will find hard, brown beans inside a dry casing. These can be planted but are too tough to be eaten.

The final pleasure is serving your broad beans to a guest at dinner. "By the way," you say modestly, "these are our own broad beans."

"Mmm, lovely!" they will reply, but unless they are gardeners themselves, they will not have understood, will never share your pleasure.

90

A Garden

A garden should be large enough for half a dozen children to play hide-and-seek in. It should have plenty of trees and shrubs, potting sheds, compost and bonfire heaps, walls, greenhouses, hedges and a pond. There must be nooks and crannies enough for a child to remain concealed and elemental earth and water enough for them to get thoroughly dirty.

More important even than a pond to dip in for newts and frogs and water beetles, more important than trees to climb and build in, is the lawn. The lawn does not have to be billiard table smooth. It does not even matter if it is not all close cropped turf like a bowling green. Neither does it matter if there are plantains and buttercups and dandelions in the grass. What matters is that it is big enough. Big enough for children to run around on, to ride bicycles over, to construct an obstacle course in. It must be wide enough and long enough to play British Bulldogs, for example, or for the smaller ones to play Grandmother's Footsteps, or the scarier What's-The-Time-Mr.-Wolf?

In British Bulldogs, in case you have forgotten, one brave volunteer stands in the centre of the lawn. The other players, a dozen is ideal, run from one end to the other. If they are caught by the one in the centre they join forces with him or her until the balance changes and only one child is left to run for his life. This is why a large lawn is a requirement. A more skilled and painful version of the same principle involves the throwing of a tennis ball. When a target is hit below the knee he joins up with the throwers until again one apprehensive child is left jumping and dodging.

The rest of the garden comes into its own for variations of hide-and-seek, such as tag and its visual equivalent Cocky Ollie and others, sometimes the same, sometimes masquerading under regional names.

Although a garden's first purpose must be as a playground and recreational space both for adults and for children, it should also have a horticultural content. Those trees should also bear cherries, plums and peaches, apples and pears and quinces; the bushes should produce gooseberries, raspberries, black and red currants. There should be a strawberry patch too, and tomatoes overpowering in their fragrance and as juicy to eat at their natural body temperature as a ripe peach.

Always there should be vegetables. Carrots to be pulled, lightly brushed clear of earth, and eaten raw there and then, peas to be squeezed straight from their pods or broad beans aborted from their soft, velvet wombs and popped still living straight into your mouth. What a delight to the palate, and difficult to get much closer to nature than by tasting it.

Then there should be chickens. At least a few hens scratching and crooning their quaint song of satisfaction to themselves, and a cat to hunt and to watch unseen over proceedings like a god or like a Douanier Rousseau panther. A dog, if there is one, will count as one of the children, with the odd canine moment taken out to retrieve or bury a bone.

Did someone mention flowers? There are people who watch TV programmes about gardening, who build decking and water features and who purchase garden furniture and patio heaters. These same people buy their gardens readymade at garden centres, bringing home plugs and pots of half grown plants and shrubs to imprison in their manicured space where it is not concreted over for a car port or a barbecue ground – and where children will never run free.

91

On Getting It Just Right

You clasp it gently like a breast and the pear falls from the branch into the palm of your hand. It is neither too hard nor too soft. It is just right. It is ripe. Ready to eat. Some pears, often smooth skinned, early plucked supermarket varieties can be eaten unpeeled. You pull out the stalk and eat your way down from the top consuming skin, core and all. There is usually more texture than taste. Many garden pears are too scaly and are better peeled and quartered. Freshly picked and ripe they are juicy and scented. They slide down your throat and you relish their flavour on your tongue and palate.

Unlike pears, apples rarely require peeling. Most of us eat and enjoy them in the conventional way, scrumping our way around the equator and discarding the core. But there are those who like to enjoy the skin and the meat separately. These people will make a ritual of peeling the fruit all in one go so that they have an unbroken red or green or russet spiral on their plate. Having sliced and eaten the apple they will set to work on the peel, very often the tastiest part if from your garden, perhaps full of pesticide residue if from a commercial orchard. Getting an apple just right, however, is not as crucial as with other fruits. It lasts longer. This is also to its detriment because it is more easily stored and eaten off season and off its natural peak

Take a peach. Like the pear it is incomparable when plucked direct from the tree, skinned and eaten still warm, still living. The flavour can be so fulsome that it seems to swell in the mouth, to fill your nasal cavities. The juice spills over your lips and fingers. Eating a ripe peach is a multi-sensual experience.

With plums it is more hit or miss. It is rare to buy a bag of entirely good plums. Even on the branch, though they may all taste delicious, that one meltingly perfect one may be inside or outside or alongside a whole cluster. Some are too soft, some still too hard. A clue is that if the wasps have started on a plum it is good. It is also then blemished.

Cherries are even more difficult. Coming earlier in the year they are the first taste of summer of the new fresh fruit. Sold at the roadside it is the luck of the draw when they were plucked and whether you hit upon a batch that is just right. The punnets usually contain very good cherries and whether driving or walking home you might absently be popping them into your mouth when all of a sudden one of them stops you in your tracks or, if you are driving, forces you to pull off the road to savour it. It is perfect. Firm yet juicy, rich in flavour, stroked by your tongue, crushed by your teeth it sings seduction to the taste buds.

And when you have swallowed this one and lingered with closed eyes to capture the aftertaste as you might try to remember a fading dream, you remember that there are more in the punnet. You open your eyes and search for another just like it but you have no idea what this exquisite ruby looked like, even with which other cherry it was paired or what marked it out from all the others except that it was just right.

It is only when you are fortunate enough to live in foreign countries that the true taste of the more exotic fruits is revealed in the same way. Picking your grapefruit for breakfast in Australia or, in all tropical lands the ubiquitous and prolific *papaya*. These pawpaws grow so quickly and abundantly that it is easy to take them for granted as we do blackberries in England. Choosing a papaya from the tree outside the kitchen window becomes as normal as pouring cereal from the packet back home, but what an aroma, what morning mouthfuls of refreshment.

But the most delicious, fragrant and evocative fruit in the world, if you get it right, must be a mango from the tree. Messier to eat than the peach, more fibrous than the pear, gorgeous in the original sense of the word, the fruit of the mango tree fills the throat with pleasure. No wonder so much Indian love poetry features the mango.

More difficult still to get into, but when just right the pineapple is almost as good and it will provide juice and flesh for several people. In taste it bears little resemblance to the insipid pineapples cut green for export and sold in European supermarkets.

All things have their best moments, but fruit, it seems, has such a short period of perfection that it is luck more than judgement (though the tappers and sniffers of melons might disagree) that once in a while, twice or thrice in a lifetime, that lands you with the perfect specimen.

92
On Doing One Thing At A Time

Y ou were driving along a good but twisty country road with limited opportunities for overtaking. Glancing in your rear view mirror you noticed with surprise a queue of cars behind you. Your speedometer showed you had slowed down to 35 miles per hour. You had become engrossed in a story on the radio. In giving it full concentration your brain had subconsciously decided that it did not have the resources to drive fast with adequate care and attention as well as to listen and react to a powerful piece of radio. While background music can be helpful to the driver on long journeys, you have often felt that a car radio was a dangerous distraction. You once drove into a lay-by to listen to a moving strand of music, rather than divide your attention.

Nevertheless, multi-tasking seems to have become the norm. Women are said to do it better than men. As a man you think the practice is to be deplored, doubtful that anything can be fully enjoyed if you do not bend your mind exclusively to it. TV channels exhort us to tweet our thoughts while watching their programmes. While possibly there is a role for this interaction during a chat show or a discussion programme such as Any Questions, when it comes to a drama or a documentary you fail to see why instant comment is more important than a considered critique in the fullness of time.

There is nothing new about doing several things at once,

however. For years people have read the daily newspaper with their breakfast. So did you until one day when pointedly asked whether you had enjoyed the home-baked rolls and the fresh quince jelly, you could not remember having eaten them. Your mind had been elsewhere, your taste buds numbed.

Nowadays you eat and savour all your meals, however routine, without the distraction of newsprint, the Today Programme or, God forbid, anything on a TV or monitor screen. You can daily enjoy the few minutes it takes to break your fast with relish before catching up on the news and other horrors later.

You once had a job bringing influential statesmen and officials together over lunch. You booked them at the best London restaurants and ordered the finest food and wines. Few of them noticed what they were eating and drinking. The meal, delicious though it was, was only the pretext for their meeting. You might just as well have fed them in Macdonald's and saved the taxpayer a small fortune. Yet if those same important people were to return privately to the same restaurant with their lover or their partner they would surely appreciate the food.

To enjoy something fully, whether it is communing with your cat or writing an opera, you ought to do so single-mindedly. Give yourself up to it unreservedly. Turn off the phone and shut down the tablet, the TV and the radio. Start to write that story or the next chapter in your novel. For the next two hours or so you become lost, absorbed. True, some people find background music a help. In your case you would not even notice what had been playing. If you did you would have to decide between the two pleasures – listen, or work.

Studying (as opposed to tweeting), critical thought (as opposed to instant reaction), also demand complete concentration – and let us not even venture into the field of sex. Music, candles, food, mood setting apart, it seems that if there is one activity that rewards full concentration by both parties... but no doubt even there someone has tweeted, "coming, coming, aaahh!!"

93

On Doing Nothing

There are different ways of doing nothing and different circumstances. For some people doing nothing means no working, for others it might mean lack of entertainment.

To do nothing you must make an effort. Because of course you cannot really do nothing. Even if you are asleep your brain and body are working hard to replenish themselves. If you are in a prison cell the lack of space and activity is possibly as close as you might get to doing nothing. In a monastic cell on the other hand you might be meditating or praying.

There are less extreme cases of forced inactivity. Many people find it hard to cope with routine travel. A few decades ago commuters would happily read a newspaper or a book or listen to music on their Walkman. Nowadays a smart phone enables passengers to kill time. Others, usually the plumpest, kill time and themselves by eating. But why kill time? Why not enjoy it and do nothing?

You, too, were guilty as a commuter of thinking of the journey as a waste of time if you were not doing something. Over five years you read the whole of Thomas Hardy and Charles Dickens. You did not realize that it was and it still is equally rewarding to do nothing. Here is how it is done.

Go back to that journey. Yes, you have done it many times before. You have an hour to fill and kill. Now put down that book or Kindle or cell phone, sit back and look around. The seasons change, the landscape changes and even the other passengers sometimes change.

You can eavesdrop or simply observe. As a writer you still find it hard to do absolutely nothing. You feel like recording a pithy remark, a colourful turn of phrase, to record an incident or share a story that you hear or witness on the train. Regrettably you have observed and forgotten many more moving, tragic, heroic, amusing or frightening events than you have written down. Why? Because you did nothing about them. You listened and time slipped by unharmed. You learned simply to enjoy what was going on around you.

You may also take pleasure in people-watching from a park bench or in a packed art gallery. In the former you might be eating a sandwich, in the latter taking a rest, so strictly speaking you are hardly doing nothing. Similarly strolling about the city, perhaps sightseeing, you are occupied. Doing nothing is not easy.

The worst scenario is an airport lounge when your plane is cancelled or delayed. You are so busy having to queue for information, watching the monitor boards or waiting for an announcement, that you are neither doing nothing nor doing something. You are in the limbo of uncertainty and anxiety and the problem is that you do not know how long it will last. It is stressful. Some resort to drink and will become objectionable passengers.

The best place to attempt to do nothing is at home. There are always jobs to do. Drop them. Turn off music, TV, radio and telephone. Close that book. Sit in silence. Silence is important. You may daydream, let your thoughts roam. Have communion with yourself.

If you live in the country, leave the housework and the gardening and all the other chores. Just go and sit. By all means look around, enjoy the birdsong, the buzzing of bees and other insects, the scent. Feel the sun or the breeze on your skin. Let your thoughts run free. This is the closest you can get to doing nothing while conscious, even though all your senses are registering the activity.

There have always been such fads and fashions as yoga, meditation, mindfulness. All require an element of concentration. Doing nothing is a step beyond. Release your thoughts. Sit, or lie and do... nothing. It is no contradiction to say that this will recharge your batteries, allow your energy to surge back and cope with all the busy-ness of the rest of your life.

For if you literally did nothing you would be dead. And even then you are decomposing.

94

On Leaving The Dentist

There are many kinds of relief: relief at the safe return of a loved one, relief at making landfall where you had hoped, relief at finally emerging from a motorway jam – and relief from pain.

The reason that still today you feel huge relief walking out of the dentist's door, even if you only went in for a check-up, goes back to your childhood. For your terror of the dentist springs from real ordeals.

When your mother took you to the dentist she could not bear to go in with you. Not that Mr. Campbell would have allowed it. Mr. Campbell was a thin Scot who had fought in the war. He had no sympathy for whingers. Boys should withstand pain without flinching.

These were the days, remember, before high speed drills and numbing injections, and when for extractions dentists sometimes used gas. This had to be administered by a doctor, usually the patient's GP.

The slow grinding drill which sent vibrations to the very caverns of the skull was menacing enough with its faint smell of burning bone. These drills were not water-cooled. When Mr. Campbell hit a nerve with his blunt instrument you jerked in pain but he did not pause. His only concession was to coat the tooth with essence of cloves. To this day you cannot suck a boiled sweet or swallow a dessert that contains this Pavlovian association with agony.

There was one occasion when you broke down completely and your hysteria allowed a small concession from the impatient Scot. If you were such a wimp, he conceded, he could do the work under gas. You no longer remember what the procedure was but you do not think it was an extraction.

Called 'laughing gas', you found the operation no laughing matter. There you were, pinned in your chair and confronted by two men in tweed jackets, the gaunt dentist and the florid doctor. White jackets, rubber gloves and the idea of hygiene must have come in much later. The doctor placed a mask over your nose and mouth; you heard a hissing sound and began to drift away. Instead of a pleasant relaxation, however, you felt a sudden, sharp panic. In your fight to retain your senses you rose up from the chair, tore off the mask and you pushed the doctor aside. You ran out of the room.

To this day you have no memory of what happened next or whether the dental work was completed. Nevertheless that fear of letting go, of losing consciousness and control, has remained with you. For this reason you have hardly ever taken drugs and rarely even excessive alcohol. You were scared off all intoxicating substances by a doctor and a dentist at an early age.

Actually, apart from the occasional filling there was never much wrong with your teeth and even now you are only missing two of them. But even though present day dentists' tools are faster and more refined, the chairs recline and pain relief is available, by the time you reach the surgery you are already in a damp, clammy condition of fear. The dread begins the day before; your night's sleep is broken by dreams of anxiety and panic sweats.

You force yourself to the dentist's and sit in the waiting room in a fraught state of mind. You try and read the newspaper, fighting the impulse to go home, pleading nausea or headache. You steel yourself for the encounter. Part of the torture is being kept waiting, because no doctor or dentist is ever on time.

Finally when the tannoy calls, "Mr. Wood, please," you hardly have the strength in your legs to climb the stairs up to the consulting room. On the landing half way up you invariably call in at the toilet.

Your present dentist, a pleasant, relaxed man, is used to this. He knows you are 'a nervous patient.' Accordingly he tries to make conversation, to put you at your ease when all you want to do is scream, 'get on with it!'

Often it is just as inspection but sometimes there is a filling. For these you do not mind the injection itself though you fear it will numb all areas except the tooth to be worked upon. Sometimes he will say, "You might feel this," a euphemism if ever you heard one. "If you do, just raise your hand," he adds. This makes you flex your whole arm in readiness, to the point of getting cramp and chest pain.

This misery goes back, not just to childhood, but to an inexperienced interim dentist who struggled to give you root canal treatment more recently. She was a slight young woman with long hair that she was incapable of keeping pinned up. Worse, she was very nervous and kept up a commentary on how difficult she found the job. She even told you to relax because your evident distress made her too nervous. Particularly stressed out one day, she said that you were a difficult patient. She struggled not only to drill through the tooth, but then to insert the dental files into the root to extract the putrid pulp.

The first session lasted an hour. In addition to the barely anaesthetised pain was the worry of choking to death. The water circulated by the drill was supposed to be sucked out by a pump in your mouth. Instead it pooled in the back of your throat. You felt you were being water-boarded and would have confessed to anything. And this was before she even attempted to lunge those fine spikes down to the root.

The frenzied woman's hair had by now all fallen down and was dangling across your face like a collapsed spider's web, or more like fronds of seaweed. How she could see what she was doing you do not to this day comprehend. Perhaps she could not see anything. After an hour you were both limp and defeated and she announced that she did not have the strength to continue. She was too tired and the strenuous task was made worse by the allegedly unusual configuration of your jaw. She collapsed into a chair while the dental nurse looked on aghast.

You went back twice more before this dentist managed to complete the treatment. Then she had the nerve to charge for all three appointments. Fortunately she was soon replaced by your present, more competent and understanding dentist. But the damage had been done. The childhood nightmare, the trauma, had been re-awakened.

This is why even today you need to summon up all your courage to visit the dentist for your annual check-up. Usually there is nothing much to do. However, you suffer just as much even if he only gives you a light scaling to earn his living.

So that is why it is such a great relief when you have paid the bill, tucked the card for the next appointment in your breast pocket, opened the front door and walked out onto the High Street, a free man again. A real relief, another small pleasure.

95

Honesty

H onesty, *this* honesty, is a wildflower now. In America, where it came from, it is called silver dollar or silver shilling, and it is because of its silver disc that you pick it, for the translucent interior wall of the seed pod. Peel away the outer scales and you are left with the beautiful, opaque partition, the silver coin that in reality is more the size and shape of a communion wafer and just as thin.

Even the botanical name *Lunaria* must refer to this inner moon that is invisible beneath the outer case. Each moon has the wisp of a tail at the bottom like that of a tortoise or a turtle though less stubby. With a little imagination the disc itself can be seen, too, as a fragile shell, or more accurately perhaps, as the flat underside shell of that tortoise.

The small pinkish purple flower that blooms in May and June is unremarkable except to a bee or a butterfly, and yet it was for the flowers that this plant was originally imported. When more exotic plants were introduced it became over-looked and escaped to the hedgerows and roadsides where it now flourishes.

You pick it for its everlasting qualities when the seeds have set in July or August; you will use it for the shimmer of its silver lanterns to light up winter vases. To expose these papery lights you need patience and a steady hand. It is a time consuming task so you tend to take one branch of the many branched stem at a time, sometimes with days in between. You have the whole of the late unhurried summer to work on it.

At first the flower pods are grey green, turning brown as they dry out. You can already see the seeds through the parchment like membrane, four on each side. Each seed has a black root or tail that links it to the delicate brown ring, thin as fuse wire, running round the circumference of the disc. The seeds look like tadpoles encapsulated in the pod. Once released the dark lines that were their tails remain embedded in the silver, almost mother of pearl surface of the silver shell. It is these decorative slashes that give the one dimensional disc the appearance of a Chinese lantern.

It is no simple task to skin the pods. You do not want to tear the fabric. You run a thumb back and forth across the edge until the two sides separate slightly from the central partition. If your finger nails are long and sharp enough it is possible to prise the side walls out, grip and pull them gently down. As you do so the four seeds, small as the head of a drawing pin, brown and light, drop out from either side.

Bit by bit your dry stalk with its dull brown flower pods is transformed into a glittering wand of organic light. You may snap off one twig with a score of discs to stand on its own as a minimalist display, or you may go to town and prepare the whole frond of discs, a painstaking task for a hard-earned reward, as blatant a display of honesty as you will find at any synod.

96

A Goat Named Sally

One Sunday breakfast Sally comes to the kitchen door to greet you as usual, but instead of demanding a biscuit she seems only to want your company. She stands with her hindquarters held high, and when she rolls briefly on one side, kicking at her belly, you know she is having contractions. She stands up at once but spasms ripple the length of her body. Instinctively she makes for a sheltered space among the air-conditioning units outside below the study window.

The birth is quick and easy, the kid shooting out like a child on a mat emerging from a helter skelter. Sally immediately licks its mouth and nostrils clear and begins to clean up the rest of its body. Within ten minutes the baby is on its feet, nosing under its mother for a place to find its first drink.

Sally stands still and patient. It is the first time you have seen her at a loss for words! It takes an hour before the kid really gets the hang of suckling, and just as it is taking its first real gulps Sally's tummy rumbles again. A mixture of a groan and a burp, and to your surprise – you had been told the first pregnancy produced only one kid – a second pre-packaged baby shoots out at the speed of a clay pigeon from its launcher.

Sally cannot quite believe it, either, and continues to tend her first-born. The slimy bundle on the ground struggles to breathe, still enveloped in its membrane. As soon as you point out to Sally that she is now the mother of twins, she sets to work to release number two from its sack. The first, a male, tramples all over his new sister, still sniffing for milk. Within no time a rather dazed Sally and the damp twins are standing nuzzling one another in the drive.

The bleating of the kids, not unlike the amplified mewing of kittens, even attracts Oscar, the cat, from his day-long nap in the armchair on the veranda. He comes cautiously down the steps and out into the day-lit garden, peering round the corner to see what the commotion is all about. The sight of two more goats about his own size is too much for your sensitive puss. In panic and horror he bellies it back into the house.

You are so enthralled by the event that you ignore even the monkeys in the trees above, back for a Sunday browse after a long absence.

There are more visitors. Looking out of the window you see vultures in the drive, and thinking they are after the kids, you rush out to shoo them off. But these gentle birds have only come to clear away the two neat piles of afterbirth that Sally by now had deposited.

Charity, your cook, returns from church, and amid loud oohs and aahs of jubilation says to your goat in English – a language she uses for all your animals – "Congratulations,

Sally!" ... adding, "Thanks be to God!"

Being male and female, and born on Sunday, the kids are aptly named Kwesi and Kussa. Sally is more amazed at her achievement than any of us.

97

On Gaining The Trust Of Animals

Y ou have come to mind a remote house and its animals while the family is on holiday. Very quickly you fall into a routine and are made welcome by the animals. You are under no illusions that the chief reason for their friendliness and their early morning greetings is that you feed, exercise and shelter them. All the animals, that is, except for the cats that assume you are merely a paid servant here to wait on them.

With most of the other creatures a real rapport gradually grows, though if you are late with their breakfast they will let you know. If Wilbur the donkey has not had his morning hay by 8 a.m. he will bray across the farmyard, for your first task is to go into the stable, fill the manger and top up the drinking water. Once fed Wilbur is a placid beast. Very furry for a donkey, and with a huge head and larger-than-life ears straight out of *A Midsummer Night's Dream*. His companion, Honey, is a pony – smaller and slighter, but she is the boss. Wilbur will not approach the hay until Honey has had her fill and if you feed them titbits by hand she will try to snatch both shares. But by day and released into the paddock they will graze happily together side by side.

While you spread the hay the dogs, who sleep in each their cage inside the front door, will charge around the barns sniffing for rats and other delights. When you are ready they will come to the bin, from which you give them a helping each of biscuits. Aloof, the cats sit above the commotion, ignoring you as best they can while secretly watching for the moment you put out their biscuits on their feeding station. After a few days of the new regime, the cats might now give you a little burp-like purr of acknowledgement, rather as you might leave a tip for the waiter.

Next the chickens flock to the edge of their run under the apple trees on your approach. While you scatter scraps for them or mix their porridge they cluck and chortle around your feet. They are relaxed, happy birds, always talking gently to themselves as they scratch about in the grass. They will brush against your legs and peck at your toes. They are quite unafraid and seemingly content in your company. Many people play whale or dolphin sounds to chill to. The singing of hens, the quiet chorus of chickens, is more musically serene and even more relaxing.

You must admit that you receive less response from the guinea pig, and even less from the fish, whether you are feeding the indoor tropical ones or the goldfish outside. They float gently up to their food but have little idea where it comes from. Perhaps fish are in a permanent state of dementia.

So far so routine. But as the week progresses you begin to experience moments of growing trust, indeed of real communion, with some of the animals. The dogs, like all dogs, love to accompany you on walks, but also when you are just sitting reading or resting they will often spot you and come and sit with you. They are companionable beings and it is not only cupboard love or the expectation that you will leap up and entertain them that makes them so. And if you do drive away in the car, leaving them behind, they do not bear you any grudge on your return. Indeed all is immediately forgiven. They are simply delighted to have you back.

Honey and Wilbur, too, are prepared at times to share your company. They will stand calmly while you stroke, brush or simply lean on them. When you offer an apple core or a carrot in the palm of your hand they take it so gently in their soft lips that it is like a light kiss on the cheek. And their breath is sweet.

After a week one of the cats comes to be stroked, but even then she expects food in payment for the privilege. However you can confidently say that you are now accepted. And who does not want that?

98

The Wealden Advertiser

Were you to be sent to a desert island and permitted only one publication it would have to be the *Wealden Advertiser*. Many communities have free sheets advertising local services and events, but few can be as varied and comprehensive as the *Wealden Ad*.

Quite apart from its usefulness (despite the internet it is still the first place you look to find a plumber or an electrician, a ferret kit or a point of lay pullet, to check what is on at the cinema, the WI or in the open air) it is a fascinating microcosm of your semi rural society.

The unedited entries in the for sale section display an embarrassing collection of grocers' apostrophes, misspellings and unintentional humour – eg *large dog kennel*. *Sleeps 2*: unintentional ambiguity, at least. Browsing through this section is like strolling around a large boot sale. From exotic pets to jars of old screws, a preponderance of wood burning stoves, logs and kindling, but also tractors and trailers, computer accessories, and whole kitchens – everything is up for grabs. There are always wooden railway sleepers that you hope, unlike the copper signal wire, are not stolen from the track, and enough furniture and fittings to set up a second home.

Cars have a clutch of pages all to themselves, though many traders still talk of motors. You have not, however, seen mention of charabancs for some years now. Mercifully estate agents have a separate pull-out section for their homes and jargon.

In contrast to items for sale another section lists things people want: bowler hats, pre-decimal coin collections, pre-war sweet wrappers and of course 'unwanted' gold and silver and broken cutlery. Some collectors will buy failed watches, dead lawn mowers, vinyl records. Others are very precise in what they are seeking. *Olympia manual typewriter required made in Germany in 1959*. Or *theatre programmes from November and December 1948.*

Between *For Sale* and *Wanted* are occasional announcements of objects lost and found. You wonder what story lies behind *lady's watch found on the top floor of Cranbrook windmill.* What was she doing there and why did she take it off? Who found it and what was he doing on the top floor? You wonder whether one week someone will have found and will advertise a murder weapon. *Kitchen knife with bloody blade,* or *revolver, one round fired.* Similarly the lost *very friendly female polecat* makes you question whether the lass was not a bit too trusting.

Perhaps what more than anything else, however, define the richness and inventiveness of this small community, are the services on offer. *Dog stressing you out? Dan will sort it.* You imagine him coming round with his stun gun. The services provided run to pages of healers and therapists of every persuasion, though the masseuses and prostitutes of its more sleazy rival the Friday Ad are excluded from the wholesome Wealden Advertiser. Nevertheless there are charlatans of every ilk as well as the ubiquitous and dubious Reiki healers and homeopaths. There are so many cures and treatments available that it makes you puzzle how you have managed to survive so long without the help of practitioners and counsellors and life style advisers. You wonder whether perhaps your posture does need improving, your lymph nodes draining, or your colon irrigated; do your deep tissues need relief and should your unsightly blemishes be removed? Does your smile need improving? Well, some of the entries do at least raise one.

There are services other than those relating to hypochondria and vanity. People will iron your shirts, tidy your garden, valet your car or as in the case of *poo-pickers* happily come and remove the horse droppings from your paddock. Taking a leaf from this book *Doggy Poops* will clear your house and garden of dog mess, that is if Dan has not already shot your dog. A simpler solution would surely to be to walk the dog, and there are scores of people who will do this for you, too.

Some services you did not know you needed. Stump removal refers not to teeth, as you had first imagined, or limbs but to tree stumps, for example. One offer you did fall for, partly because it seemed useful and partly because of the picture it created in your mind was the oven fairy who would clean your oven for only £60. You were disappointed when answering the fairy's tap on the door you were confronted not with a dainty female in a white dress waving a magic wand, but by a bearded man in overalls carrying a toolbox.

"Are you the fairy?" you asked.

"Yes," he replied good-naturedly, "and I've heard all the jokes."

There are many other sections all of which repay close reading. *What's On* must encompass all human activity, from the currently fashionable *zumba* through line dancing, tango, Pilates, and wind surf tuition at Bewl Water, to talks on Kipling and compost, local history and astronomy. There are boot sales and jumble sales and exhibitions, places to visit, numerous farmers' markets; there are the Red Barrows, men dressed in red who perform with red wheelbarrows in the street what the slightly better known Red Arrows team do in the skies, complete with coloured smoke. There are seasonal fairs, and even 'fayres', and late openings of this and that, not to mention the standard tourist fare of the area.

Even the obituary column of the *Wealden Ad* contains if not all life, all death, though people tend to pass away, pass over, or are taken. Few die. Here you will find bad verse, mawkish and sentimental but sincere beyond mockery.

Though we live in difficult times it is hard to imagine that a motivated person could not find some kind of work in the situations vacant pages. It may not be quite the occupation they had in mind. Carers are always in demand as for some reason are dental nurses. Cleaners and caterers are forever wanted as are delivery drivers, tutors and receptionists. Every so often something more specific crops up such as a cat care assistant for a cat sanctuary or an industrial machinist in the wire factory. Fruit pickers are in demand seasonally to pick hops, cherries, plums and apples; egg collectors are often wanted by free range chicken farms and at Christmas turkey and goose pluckers are sought. Or as one ad had it, *goo'se plucker's*.

When you have browsed the weekly events, scoured the small ads and checked the obituaries, you skim through the larger, more commercial advertisements, visiting restaurants, studying menus, planning changes to your garden or your home. Within the pages of the *Wealden Advertiser* you can enjoy a day out, a night out, a weekend break at a health spa – and it does not cost you a penny.

99

Poetic Exchange

In the mid-eighties you were called upon by the British Council to mind their shop in Dakar, Senegal, where you made the acquaintance of a teacher of English called Mike Kelly. He was also a poet and photographer with several publications to his name. You would meet sometimes for a coffee and a croissant (Senegal is a francophone country) and decided one day to drive down to Casamance, the southern part of Senegal, to work on an English project. All part of your duties, of course, but also an opportunity to visit this lush part of the country.

There was one obstacle: Gambia.

Gambia sits in the middle between the two halves of Senegal, and you had to drive right through this tiny country. But to get into Banjul in the first place you had to cross the River Gambia. The queues for the car ferry could last as long as four hours and even then you fight to get on.

Imagine then your bearded poet friend and you sweltering in your Land Rover under the white sun's grill in a stationary queue of vehicles big and small. No cafés, no shade, no water other than the river. You decided to get out of the Land Rover and go for a walk while Mike dozed behind the wheel. It was cooler out in the breeze and you took some photographs of the scene.

When you returned to the vehicle you described the varied pictures to Mike and challenged him to put all the objects you had captured in one of your photos into a single poem.

He laughed, the queue moved fitfully forward as the ferry

took on a fresh load, and you thought nothing more of it.

Your night in Gambia and your week or so in Casamance might give rise to other stories, but it was some time after your safe return to Dakar that you received the following poem from your colleague:

Gambian Scape

The British Council Acting Rep said to me:
How much content can you get in a photograph?
I've just shot a Muslim praying on the beach,
A pig walking past him on the beach, a canoe
Marked 'Concorde' and the row of cars
Waiting for the ferry all in one photo. I
Challenge you to get that all in one poem.
But it's natural for a local poem. It is the sort
Of thing we all recognise and enjoy as soon
As any stranger points out what he sees as
Our oddity. Our lives are made up of these
Mixtures of things which outsiders see
As paradoxical or incompatible. We pass
The local wife of a retired Scottish Forestry
Officer learning to drive near the tourist
Hotel complex. She kisses us. She has
An open-sided local cotton blouse and magnificent
Breasts. We drive on to lunch. The cows
Trail through the lagoon on their way to eat
The grass on the golf course. A military aeroplane
Flies overhead and the palmwine tappers trudge
To their groves. The beer is poured by the girl
Who might be the lover of a diplomat whose tour is ending.
We're not a bit short of content, surface or deep, our
Focus can be all right as well.

You do not remember how much later it was but in due course you sent the following reply:

Gambian Scape 2

The poet did better
Than the amateur
Photographer
But neither of their pictures
Captured the discomfort
Of uncertainty, sweat
Wet shirts, the thirst
For shade, immersion
In cold water.
Missing are the smells
Of diesel and ozone,
Black bodies massed
And white ones in their shells.
No concord on the ferry, but
Survival of the pushiest.
I don't think the pig smelled
Particularly
Or the Scottish wife's nipples
Spread any discernible rings
Of perspiration in her blouse
But further down the beach
Where men squatted discretely
For their low tide crap
The sand contained
Its richer litter, all
Good biodegradable stuff.
And surely the best
At long journey's end
In night's aquarium
Those first two throatfuls
Of lover's beer.

Mike had translated Greek erotic poetry, and one of his books contained his photos of nude young women juxtaposed with a poem about them, all his own work. It had occurred to you when writing this reply that you had never read a poem of his that did not contain a mention or a description of breasts.

You thought him somewhat obsessive and issued another challenge – to write a poem with the following title: *A Poem Without Breasts.*

It was not long before you received a hand-delivered reply headed:

A Poem Without Breasts
(commissioned by W. Wood Esq.)

A poem without breasts
Is like swimmers in vests.

Without a tit
The apple unbit.

Minus boobs
Blown cathode ray tubes.

Missing mammary
Erogenous zones
Depriving famished dogs
Of favourite boneless bones.

A poem with nary a nipple
Is a poem as makes no ripple.

This is not his best work, merely a light-hearted piece of nonsense that you are sure he tossed off in a jiffy, but you both loved playing with words. Words you would have forgotten had you not, decades later, turned up the correspondence while clearing out some old files.

Mike had a stroke and died after frustrating years of blindness some years back. But his spirit lives on in his photos and in his verse. And you remember now, holding up his faded manuscripts, how once he made a routine tour over endless red, African roads into something of a literary game.

100

A Reprieve

W hen an acute infection laid you low for several weeks you thought nothing of it. A course of antibiotics relieved the symptoms. When a few more weeks later you still felt listless, you went to the doctor again. You probably had a virus, he told you, the usual ploy of medical folk when they do not know what is wrong. In another era it would have been a 'miasma' or possibly a 'humour'. You, too, felt a bit of a fraud. It was not as though you were ill. As a precaution, though, the doctor arranged for a blood test.

By the time the startling result came through and you faced the doctor again at his behest, not yours, you were feeling as fit as a fiddle. Until, that is, he interpreted the results and made an appointment with a consultant.

There is nothing worse than the internet when it comes to medical problems. You consulted it at once, of course, and discovered that with appropriate treatment you might have at most only another eight years to live.

Eight years is a long time, but how many of them, you wondered would be active and free of the punishment of pain. This death sentence put the rest of your life into context. Long term projects had to be cancelled, plans to move house put on hold. Even holidays, for how many more visits would you be able to make to children and grand children now? And was there adequate provision for your wife? Was it even worth it now to complete that unfinished novel?

You have no fear of death, but as Woody Allen once remarked, you would rather not be there when it happened. The prospect did, however, turn your priorities upside down. Any remaining ambition dissolved as you realised that your achievements, if any, now lay in the past. There would be no more prizes and surprises. Your life, for what it was worth was nearly wrapped up.

The consultant, although he did not openly laugh at

you or criticise your GP, said that your blood results were probably caused by your recent infection. You had to admit that you felt perfectly healthy physically, if not psychologically, and he suggested that you wait six months and have another test.

During those six months you gradually forgot the death sentence. You were, slightly to mix metaphors, only out on bail. You felt well. Life was as normal as it could be, but after the next blood test the wait for results reawakened all the anxieties and tension. When there was no phone call from the doctor after a week, instead of inferring this was a good sign you imagined he could not bring himself to break the bad news. In fact he had not passed the results on to you because now there was nothing wrong with your blood or with you. The whole thing had been a false alarm.

Twice before you have been in life threatening situations, a shipwreck and a car accident and in both cases, after the emotion, nay commotion, had subsided you were immensely thankful to be alive. Both these incidents had been rapid and over in a short time. Nevertheless for days, for weeks afterwards you felt you had been gifted a new life, another chance.

This time the soul searching had lasted nearly a year, your outlook on life had shifted considerably. The probability of many active years still ahead of you was and still is a calming pleasure.

101

Home At Last

There are few other languages that have a word for the concept of home that we have in English. Other cultures speak of homeland, birthplace, house, but when in a novel you were writing in French you wanted a character to say that he had never had a home, you were at a loss. For you were not talking bricks and mortar. You meant a nest, a place of one's own, a single vessel of private experience and memory. Your character was rootless and *dépaysé*. He might have lived in several different places but he could not remember ever having had a place to call *home*.

In your own life there are several houses you have called home. As a child, home was where you were brought up, the house where your parents lived, a true family home. It remained so for a while after you left it and before you established an independent life of your own. There were many subsequent homes, for home to you has usually been where you were living at the time. Since most of your working life was abroad, away from home some might say, you have nevertheless made your home, *felt* at home in Australia, India, Norway, Belgium, Sudan and Ghana. In each of these countries you have lived from three to five years. When there you were content to be there, and it was home.

Nevertheless throughout this peripatetic career you also had a small cottage in the UK, a home base, though you never thought of it as home. You returned to it sometimes during your home leave. It was an address the tax man and other authorities regarded formally as your principal residence, but staying in it felt more like visiting a holiday home and when you went back to work again you were able to dismiss it from your mind.

There was, come to think of it, a home posting of five years when you did live in it – when it did become home, not only to you but to your children. Over a career this was a brief interlude. Only on your return for good to the UK did this house and village truly revert to your true home, though by then your children had grown and left for homes and children of their own.

When recently you sold this house in Sussex to buy one in Cumbria, you in effect moved home as well. You left the memories, the friends, the habits of a lifetime behind, taking only your worldly goods with you. When people now ask where your home is, despite sixty years based in Sussex, you tell them that home is now physically your riverside cottage in Cumbria, where you are writing this.

You are making a fresh start: there are fresh faces to recognize, new routines to form and places to discover.

But you still have your same books and your music, your pictures and your clothes, your tools. Yes, there is a new garden to establish, new rooms to furnish, but as before, already it is home.

Nevertheless *home* is not synonymous with *house*. I might be *chez moi* but in an abstract sense. Home is where you are, where you settle. Not where you have been. Creating a new home is an act of self expression, a creative deed. The physical home might also be a refuge. Home for some remains the place where they grew up; it is a memorial, a nostalgic swamp. For you, on the other hand, you make yourself at home wherever you are, in your working life where you were sent, in your retirement where you have chosen to be.

Unless you end up in an old people's home, not a home at all in the true sense of the word, you fervently hope that this Cumbrian village will be your final home, a place of calm, a place to write. A small pleasure indeed. And you hope to share it for as long as possible with your loved ones.

102

Waiting

S ome pleasures have a dark side to them. One such is waiting: waiting might contain happy anticipation or dreadful anxiety. It depends what you are waiting for.

When, for example, you accepted an offer on the house you had lived in for 40 years the subsequent wait was fraught with uncertainty. Until contracts were exchanged there was no sense in packing and making arrangements for the move. Much could go wrong. But you had a house to go to and you were raring to start afresh. All you needed were the proceeds of the sale. You waited in limbo.

The uncertainty made the wait more painful. We could make no firm plans. You hung on, fingers crossed, well aware that if the sale fell through you would have to begin all over again and put the house back on the market.

This made you think: we spend almost as much of our lives waiting as we do sleeping. You do not mean the every-day waiting for trains and buses, waiting at traffic lights, waiting for a wife or daughter to get ready.

Waiting starts early in life. As a child you longed for the school term to end. You loved the school holidays and being home, free to roam the woods and fields. Waiting for Christmas and birthdays when young was pleasurable anticipation. Waiting for the dentist was terrifying. The appointment in those days was always an appointment with pain. Childhood illnesses sometimes required quarantine and then you had to wait weeks before playing with your friends again.

In my teens, waiting for exam results was nerve wracking, too, and waiting for the postman to bring an offer from a university a mixture of hope and dread.

Your working life passed in a flash all over the world. Like school holidays your home leave was eagerly awaited. Every three years you returned, often from a developing country, to enjoy the freedom and comforts of real home. During this time there was the waiting for childbirth, too. Nervously, the first time. On one occasion the mind-numbing vigil beside twin babies in an incubator, waiting for them to die, one after the other. Weeks of hopelessness. Days of hope both would die soon and find rest and give you and your wife respite.

Much later in life as a carer you did not hope for your parents' death for your own release, but for their repose and an end to their anguish. The four year wait, your retirement plans on hold, became more and more difficult. You could barely conceal your impatience as you struggled with them and with yourself. You also felt such deep, sad sympathy which is why you waited so badly for the end to come. When finally they were admitted into a care home you knew, despite their dementia, that they knew too that this was the waiting room of death. They would never see their beloved home and garden again. You had sold it to have them cared for professionally.

In an age of the internet where everything is instant, it is easy to forget how often you waited in the past for news, any news. Working in India and Africa you had no contact with family at home during the three years between leaves. You never served in a country with external phone connections. Your news came by letter, usually in the form of an aerogramme. You looked forward to the weekly arrival of your private mail and newspapers in the diplomatic bag. In South Sudan a small plane brought your office and personal mail once a month. A mixed blessing. You waited apprehensively for office mail from Khartoum, Nairobi and London. You waited pleasurably for personal mail.

The same thing happened when your children went travelling. The term 'Gap Year' had not yet been coined or commercialised. They did their own thing. There was no email or Facebook, and you received only the odd postcard or letter weeks after the event or the country it described. By then they had moved on. Sometimes you waited months for news and became anxious. Often you had no idea which country they were in. When letters did arrive from Africa, India, Asia, not always in chronological order, sometimes indeed in batches, you treasured them. And they all happily survived this rite of passage, nowadays little more than a holiday for most students.

As you grew older there were other, anxious waits: Waits for medical results; longer waits for operations to cure the condition; waits to convalesce. Before you knew where you were you had been waiting two or three years to return to normal.

Compared with these life-changing events some waiting is simply irritating. A good meal out with excellent food, and service can be spoiled by the interminable wait for the bill. Why all waiters disappear at this juncture you do not know. Waiting home for a plumber who does not turn up or for a delivery that requires your signature but that is delayed is equally annoying, especially when you, too, have other appointments to go to.

Sometimes, not too often, you cannot wait for a film, a lecture or a party to end or for visitors to go away. Cannot wait means you have to see it out, of course. Cannot wait is wishful thinking. So wait you do, and it plunges you into a black mood.

You have spent a lifetime saying goodbye – at railway stations, sea- and airports. On the other side of the coin, an equal time must be spent waiting to say hello and to greet. One long winter you waited every fortnight in growing excitement in the cold dark night of Oslo's former East Station. You were just married, but you worked in Oslo and your new wife was seeing out her contract in Bergen. You still remember that freezing, snowy Platform 3 where you fervently hoped the train would make it over the mountains on its three-hour journey from Bergen, up through the snow, through Hell (a railway station) and down again to Oslo. You still see your wife's broad smile in the night, her glinting eyes and the drive back to your house for hot drinks and passion. We had both waited for this.

Now, 40 years on, you are still excited waiting for her at the airport or railway station after she has been visiting family, but the journey home is longer.

And now, quite suddenly, there is a longer wait, a wait more uncertain than any before, for that same wife has been diagnosed with cancer. Hospital waits for treatment and consultations have become the norm, but you are both still holding your breath for a happy outcome.

Epilogue

S ince the first edition of this book in 2011 in which you tried to portray the small pleasures that make life worth living, the English speaking world has discovered "hygge", familiar to you from Norway but hijacked recently by the Danes. There is no English translation, though the Germans call it Gemütlichkeit and the concept was already to be found in many of your own essays.

It means recognizing the special moment or insight, alone or together with friends, that has its own peculiar resonance. It involves a gentle feeling of well-being and contentment that the English word cosiness does not quite capture. It has become something of a cliché in the popular mind concerning candles, slippers and firelight. Your book showed, and still shows, there is more to it than that.

Even more recently the Norwegian writer, Karl Ove Knausgård, acclaimed for his detailed and addictive books about his intimate life, has in his latest publication *Autumn* begun to see the world anew and has written some delightful vignettes of the simpler pleasures. What a pity he could not have read your 2011 edition of *A Little Book of Pleasures!*

For your book, too, has been about the small pleasures of your life. You may have experienced the grander passions and have occasionally been swept off course, but what you have reported here are less the crueller emotions and more the sweeter, life-sustaining delights of daily life. They are there for most of us to seize. This might be fond familiarity with a place or an object, a fleeting feeling or observation, an action or a favourite taste. It might be the tingle of delight you get when even the most ordinary Cabbage White butterfly lands on the page of a book you are reading in the garden, or the fascination when you look up from your keyboard to watch a spider in the corner of your study window jump on, paralyze and wrap a fly in its web for a future feast.

So what has it been all about, this book? Does it have to be about anything? Does life have to have a meaning? The pleasures depicted here may be enduring or short-lived. Let us say, whether you are inclined to take it in the literal or in the figurative sense, that these moments are God given

$\mathcal{G}lossary$

À la rigeur	At a pinch
Amour fou (Fr.)	No English translation of this illness possible because the English are perhaps incapable of being completely and blindly head over heels in love
Aperçu (Fr.)	Insight
Appellation Contrôlée (Fr.)	A name, title or definition under which a wine or food product can be marketed exclusively
Bakelite	A type of resin or plastic
Bol (Fr.)	Bowl
BTF (Fr.)	*Vraie baguette de tradition française,* or: real baguette in the French tradition
Baguette (Fr.)	French stick (bread)
Bic	A disposable razor, sometimes a pen
Bungalow (Ind.)	Originally a Bengali-style single-storey house with a large veranda
Cache-sexe (Fr.)	Small garment that covers the genitals. Worn by men or women
Carpe diem (Lat.)	Seize the day
C'est le bonheur complet (Fr.)	It is complete happiness
Chappals (Ind.)	Type of footwear
Clientèle (Fr.)	Customers
Coup de foudre (Fr.)	Lit. thunderbolt. Fig. love at first sight
De rigeur	A must

Dhoti (Ind.)	Traditional Indian male garment. Can be worn in many ways
Flymo	A hover mower
Folies Bergères (Fr.)	Theatre / entertainment for tourists in Paris
Gaustatoppen (Norw.)	Name of a mountain
Geitost (Norw.)	Goat cheese
Gitanes (Fr.)	Lit. gypsies. Once a popular brand of cigarettes
Hoola hoop	Large ring for exercise or play
Hytte (Norw.)	Traditionally a log cabin but now often a comfortably equipped second home by the sea or in the mountains
Hyttebok (Norw.)	Visitors' book in said cabin
Ile de beauté (Fr.)	Lit. Isle of Beauty. Corsica
Isère (Fr.)	A department named after its river in S.E. France
Jibba (Ind.)	Long coat worn mainly by Muslim men
Jotunheim (Norw.)	Mountain range in central Norway
La Pinéade (Fr.)	Mountain in French Alps
Les Deux Magots (Fr.)	A café frequented by writers and intellectuals and named after two figurines
Mali (Ind.)	Gardener
Maquis (Fr.)	Scrubby undergrowth in Corsica that gave its name to the French resistance in World War II
Médecins sans Frontières (Fr.)	Lit. Doctors without borders. An international medical charity
Mofussil (Ind.)	Rural areas
Musak	Background music in supermarkets, airports etc
Le mot juste (Fr.)	Exactly the right word
Objets trouvés (Fr.)	'Found objects'. An artistic term
Ostehøvel (Norw.)	Cheese slicer: see article 26

Pari (Fr.)	Bet
Pendolino (Fr.)	French designed railway carriages used by Virgin West Coast line
Poste restante (Fr.)	Post office box where travellers can collect mail
Pulk (Norw.)	A sledge pulled by a skier and attached to waist. Often containing a baby
Que sais-je? (Fr.)	What do I know?
Quinze Contes (Fr.)	Fifteen Stories (An A level set book)
Rawlplug	Insert to secure a screw in a loose hole
Schneeberg (Austria)	Lit. Snow Mountain. A mountain outside Vienna
Soufflé	Light, airy egg concoction
Stade	Area in Hastings where fishing boats come in and nets used to be hung or stored
Tagore (Ind.)	Bengali Nobel prize winning writer
Vin rouge (Fr.)	Red wine
Vidda (Norw.)	High plateau

About The Author

Brought up on the Kent/Sussex border, William knew continental Europe better than the U.K. To remedy this he chose to study at Nottingham University, associating it with Robin Hood. He then emigrated to Australia as a 'ten pound Pom' and took a further degree at the then new University of Monash in Melbourne. Subsequently he spent his working life as a nomad moving between Africa, India and Europe. William now lives in Cumbria.

He has written plays, stories and poetry for as long as he can remember and he likes to explore language and languages. He prefers the wilderness to the city but requires a fix of theatre and gallery from time to time. Many of his short stories and poems have been published in the small press. An anthology, *Stories for Sale* (Circaidy Gregory Press), is available as a paperback. He has published several novels. His first, *No Time For Poetry,* is out of print but still available as an e-book. Another book, *Some of Them Were Human,* is a fond satire of life in Brussels. More recently, dismayed by the folly of Brexit, he has written his latest novel in French and it is due out shortly.

William still likes to travel, visiting children and grandchildren in France and Spain and in-laws in Norway, not to mention those in England and now a little bit nearer.

http://williamwoodswords.wordpress.com

9 781907 984181